ROLF HICHERT   JÜRGE

ROLF HICHERT   JÜRGEN FAISST

SOLID
OUTLINED
HATCHED

HOW VISUAL CONSISTENCY HELPS
BETTER UNDERSTAND
REPORTS, PRESENTATIONS
AND DASHBOARDS

IBCS MEDIA

TABLE OF CONTENTS

PREFACE

I had the good fortune to be introduced to the world and concept of the International Business Communications Standards (IBCS) in early 2015. I was working on preparing the content for a global Financial Planning and Analysis (FP&A) conference and one of the submitted proposals came from Andrej Lapajne in Ljubljana, Slovenia who laid out in great detail how organizations like Royal Phillips, Coca-Cola Icecek, and Lufthansa utilized IBCS to create more efficient and effective reports and dashboards and greatly improved their business communications through standardization.

For me, it was an epiphany. And I do mean that in the truest sense of the word – an experience of sudden and striking realization that allowed a problem or situation to be understood from a new and deeper perspective.

For over twenty years in the corporate world I have focused mainly on FP&A, Treasury, and Investor Relations for mostly very large (up to $1.3 trillion) financial services organizations. This is the environment where I went from being an apprentice to a certified expert in financial and analytical sciences. I was then given the opportunity to create a global FP&A practice for a professional society. My mandate was to travel the world to meet and connect with as many FP&A professionals, service providers and vendors as possible.

I was able to meet and discuss best practices with regard to technology, people, processes, culture, and especially communications with hundreds, if not thousands of FP&A and Finance professionals. There was and continues to be a great need to better standardize and define the work FP&A and Finance teams produce.

Now in my current role as a consultant and educator, I assist organizations all over the globe in their Analytics journey to increase their finance maturity, value creation and analytical intelligence.

I had always struggled with how poorly and inconsistently dashboards and reports were constructed, and here before me with this report from Ljubljana was a business case that explained in a very direct and easy to comprehend manner the "right" way to design the communications businesses need in order to make better, faster, smarter decisions that help their organizations thrive.

Utilizing IBCS is a way for FP&A teams to increase their value to their organizations. By leveraging the efficiency and effectiveness of IBCS-designed analysis, teams would be able to spend more time providing descriptive, diagnostic, predictive and ultimately proscriptive analytics rather than designing and beautifying reports and dashboards. This is a tool to help assist FP&A in its journey from being the trusted scorekeeper to becoming a strategic partner.

I greatly appreciate the opportunity to share a few of my thoughts on why I believe the publication of SOLID|OUTLINED|HATCHED is so important and will be so valuable to those focused on analytics, finance and/or business.

Focusing on the work of IBCS, I really like the idea of simple visual standards, e.g., "solid is actual, outlined is plan, hatched is forecast" and "time is horizontal, structure is vertical". But I truly believe there are so many more components that need to be addressed, including captions and labels, time periods and their abbreviations, absolute and relative variances, highlighting, and so many more.

Will there ever be a uniform concept for measures and scales? I certainly hope so, and truly believe it will be developed. Organizations that adopt these standards first, will be the entities that will reap the benefits of increased efficiencies and effectiveness sooner.

To be completely honest, I was a bit skeptical when I heard about the concept of dimensioning standards based on font size, but now that I have taken some time to reflect, I do agree it is a very useful idea when it comes to visual standards: Everything really looks very similar.

My understanding of the power and utility of IBCS was only enhanced when I had the opportunity to attend Jurgen Faisst's presentation of "What Data Analysts and Report Designers Can Learn from Musicians" in New York City in the summer of 2017. When listening to that presentation, same as when reading the first chapter of this book where semantic notations in other disciplines were presented, I became convinced by the analogies with sheet music that both demonstrated the potential of standards and showed us that we in the business world still have a long way to go. I personally love sharing the sheet music analogy when I am introducing the IBCS philosophy to audiences around the world. It is just so clear and impactful. You can almost literally see the lightbulbs illuminate over the participants' heads.

Today it is inconceivable that someone would create an alternative method for writing music and that endeavor being be successful. The same could be said for how electrical engineers express their designs, the universe of traffic signs and signals, architectural designs, and geographic maps. Sure, someone could produce a map that shows water as red, land blue and North at the bottom of the page, but most people would find that map too confusing and disorienting. They would have to spend additional time just to understand how the information is being presented, and lose time interpreting the information in order to make better informed decisions.

The same could be said about reporting and dashboards. Authors are proud to constantly find new and different visualization concepts, new layout ideas – not only in lavish annual reports but also in day-to-day spreadsheet charts. Visuals should be striking, should capture your attention and make an indelible impression in your mind.

We should aspire to reach the state of enlightenment that musicians and engineers have reached. Musicians play music - we do not evaluate the beauty of the written sheet music; engineers present new product ideas - we do not evaluate the attractiveness of their drawings; designers of reports and dashboards should be judged on their ability to convey information - not on the loveliness of the charts being used.

I like the suggestions presented here, but I do concede it will probably be a significant period of time for the development of a well-accepted international standard. But then again, when we consider the development of sheet music, didn't this take a few hundred years?

In closing, I would like to wish this book, this concept and these ideas the success they all richly deserve. As Rolf and Jurgen ruminate about standards, they become standards because they are widely accepted/adopted. And you, the reader, will hopefully be a part of this wonderful journey.

Brian Kalish

SCOPE OF DESIGN

SEARCHING FOR RULES

This book should have been written earlier. Perhaps at the end of the 1960s when Jacques Bertin[1] was occupied with signs and their meaning in connection with the visualization of data. Or ten years later when engineer Rolf Hichert joined McKinsey as a consultant and created his first business presentations. This would have come just before the first companies started to develop software designed to help people present information clearly in written form (notation). In other disciplines like music, engineering and architecture, the designers of notation software knew exactly what the visual output should look like. Established notation standards ensured that the same melody always looked the same regardless of the software program used. The same for circuit diagrams and construction plans.

It was different for the business profession. Since there are still no binding specifications for the notation of reports, each tool provider designed their charts and tables as they saw fit. Even worse, while providers of notation software from other disciplines are competing for the most user-friendly way to achieve the same result, providers of reporting software are deliberately trying to differentiate themselves from their competitors through distinct visualizations. The end result is easy to spot: Every report looks different. The beginnings of a uniform language have not even begun to emerge.

Business professionals lag behind other fields. So now we want to propose a uniform language using our years of experience in teaching, consulting, software development and business management. The great amount of positive feedback we have received, gives us the confidence that we are on the right track.

In a moment, we will take a deeper look at other fields, in particular engineering and music, as these are our original backgrounds. Firstly let's introduce ourselves and share our early experiences with business presentations and management reports before uncovering the real challenge we are facing with this book.

BUSINESS PRESENTATIONS BY THE ENGINEER

My name is Rolf Hichert. Actually, I didn't want to be an engineer. My passion was art, drawing more than painting. But in the 1960s, fathers still had an influence on what their sons studied—especially when it was entrepreneurial fathers thinking of their successors. So, I studied mechanical engineering, then worked at an institute of the Fraunhofer-Gesellschaft, before graduating with a doctorate in engineering. I never became a full-blooded engineer with bending moments, pressure curves and flow properties, but I learned how to think like an engineer. It all started here and continued with a consulting job at McKinsey: in-depth analysis and results presentation, using charts. My time at McKinsey strongly influenced me. There were role models like Dietmar Meyersiek and Peter Kraljic, Barbara Minto and Gene Zelazny—to name just a few. It was the time before PowerPoint and, of course, there was a strictly policed Corporate Design: everything black-and-white, a lot of physical pasting, Letraset and

1   Bertin, Jacques: Sémiologie graphique, Editions Gauthier-Villars, Paris 1967.

output clearly produced using IBM's "Composer" typewriter. Close attention was paid to typeface and typography—a single glance told you an exhibit came from McKinsey. What I missed, however, were uniform guidelines for the visualization of concrete business topics—despite the positive influence of Gene Zelazny and the many examples from earlier studies.

A short stint at university, after McKinsey, propelled me into my next role as an entrepreneur: We developed so-called management information systems (MIS), which, for the first time, started to include visual representations. This work coincided with the beginnings of Visicalc, Multiplan and Lotus 1-2-3. Because Apple did not yet have its own charts, they used *our* charts for a 1985 Macintosh advertisement. After another short period at a technical college—now as a professor for management accounting—Jürgen Faisst, whom I had hired ten years earlier, brought me back into the software industry.

In a 2004 lecture at the International Controller Association e.V. (ICV) conference and through my seminars, I outed myself as an opponent of the omnipresent PowerPoint culture. This received a tremendous response and once again led to independence—now with a focus on the design of presentations and reports. I still find myself just as exasperated, as in those early days, by the masses of inadequate, inconsistent, manipulative and often difficult to understand charts that confront us every day—not only in annual reports but also in daily newspapers and text books. My goal is clear: I want to make sure that business professionals can use international standards to present their findings with the same naturalness that mechanical engineers have had for decades whilst drafting gear designs or that electrical engineers have when laying out circuit diagrams.

MANAGEMENT REPORTS FROM THE MUSICIAN

My name is Jürgen Faisst. Actually, I didn't want to become a business professional. My passion has always been music. But why not do both? So, I studied business administration with a focus on operations research and business informatics followed by a doctorate on corporate planning with neural networks. And at the same time as much music as possible: trombone in various jazz and soul bands, my own big band, but most of all writing sheet music—from horn parts for Elvis Presley tribute shows to Bert Kämpfert arrangements for the WDR Radio Orchestra in Cologne.

And that's when it happened: As an arranger and musician, I was used to not having to worry about how to put my musical ideas on paper. Everything is regulated: from the arrangement of the black dots on five lines within bars and the structure of the piece with a time signature, bars and repetitions, through to the notation of individual parts for orchestra instruments in the correct clef and with the correct transposition. Labels like title, composer, instrument, speed, volume and much more—all controlled. At the time I didn't realize how great this was, I just took it for granted... until I had to write my first management report.

It could have been worse but I got lucky. After completing my doctorate, I joined Rolf Hichert's company, whose MIS software already offered much more support in the visual design of management reports than many of today's Business Intelligence software packages. And yet: There was no consistent concept of how to get from the analytic task to a clear-cut presentation on paper or on screen. And with the other software providers even less so. To this day, it is up to the developers and users of the respective reporting software to decide what a report looks like. A pie chart or rather a table? Today maybe pastel shades and maybe 3D? The latest software can do this now. Let's truncate the axes. Actually the software does this automatically now if nothing happens in the lower part of the chart. Isn't that great?

Enough with cynicism. It's time for change.

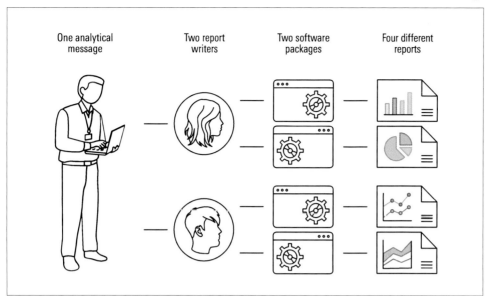

One analytical message   Two report writers   Two software packages   Four different reports

FIGURE 0-1

Different reports.
In business management the written result depends both on the report writer and the software used.

THINGS THAT MEAN THE SAME SHOULD LOOK THE SAME

If a management accountant were to communicate the same message via two different report writers using different software tools, the reports would look completely different FIGURE 0-1. We, however, want them to look as similar as possible. Impossible? We don't think so. In the end, the blueprints for two identical designs by an architect, created by two different draftsmen with different drawing programs, also look the same FIGURE 0-2. The same applies to technical drawings by engineers and scores by composers. Architects, engineers and musicians have standardized the way they record their ideas. Over many years, they have developed a kind of visual language that makes building plans and technical drawings always look similar. The same applies to music notes, too.

It's easy to prove this visually. If we search the internet for sheet music, the result is FIGURE 0-3. We can clearly see a uniform visual language, even though the results span music from different epochs, styles

and regions. Even in Asia, they now use the standard notation, as we see from the sheet of music on the right of FIGURE 0-3.

Here is our challenge: If we search the Internet for management dashboards, as we often call management information systems today, we get a sobering result FIGURE 0-4 (PAGE 12): no similarities, not in the least. Everyone is doing their own thing—and is surprised when nobody understands it. Changing this is the reason for this book.

In Chapter 1 we build the need for notation standards by looking at other disciplines where things that mean the same also look the same. We explain how this semantic notation allows for pattern recognition in visual perception and the benefits this brings. We then look at how we can establish a standard notation for management reports, as other disciplines have done successfully.

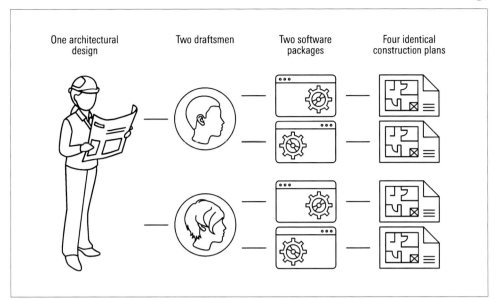

FIGURE 0-2
Identical construction plans. In the case of architects, musicians and engineers, the written result does not depend on the writer or the software used.

FIGURE 0-3
Visual language for music notes. Musical notes always look similar, regardless of style, composer, region or software used.
Source: Result of an image search for "Sheet music" on the internet.

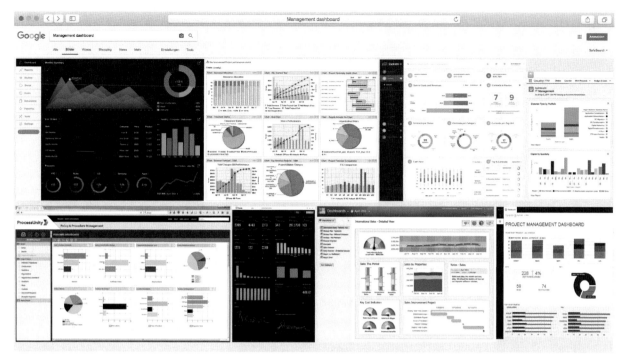

FIGURE 0-4

Lack of a visual language in dashboards. Dashboards have no similarities. Their appearance depends on the report writer and the software used.

Source: Result of an image search for "Management dashboard" on the Internet

In Chapter 2 we identify those aspects of business communication that could be semantically notated to increase the speed and quality of their comprehension. For example, we develop concepts for the visualization of scenarios, variances and highlights, just to name a few. First, we focus on visualization concepts already widely accepted and in common use. In an excursus, we then share some concepts for visualizing further aspects, such as measures and scales, whose standardized notation we consider necessary, but whose concrete form is still under discussion.

In Chapter 3 we apply the concepts: We start with simple charts and tables, then move on to the comparisons, time series and variance analyses based on them, and finally cover specific business topics such as balance sheet analysis. The end result is a set of templates we can use in a wide range of situations and thus support pattern recognition at a higher level.

Chapter 4 deals with practical application. We explain how to transfer these concepts and templates into a corporate notation manual for reports, presentations and dashboards—similar to a corporate design manual. We also share practical examples already created using this approach: Genuine reports and dashboards from different companies created with a variety of software packages.

To wrap up, we review how we are progressing towards our goal of a reporting notation standard and give a brief outlook for the coming years.

Rolf Hichert and Jürgen Faisst

CHAPTER 1

COMPREHENSION
THROUGH PATTERN RECOGNITION

WHAT WE CAN LEARN
FROM MUSICIANS AND ENGINEERS

COMPREHENSION THROUGH PATTERN RECOGNITION

WHAT WE CAN LEARN FROM MUSICIANS AND ENGINEERS

Something is wrong with business communication. Executives find themselves tortured with overloaded reports and bored by confusing presentations. Some feel downright harassed. Be honest: Have you found just one of the many recent business presentations so exciting that you wanted to see it again? Most of the time we are happy when it is over and we can finally get back to real work.

The authors of reports and presentations, on the other hand, frequently complain that their managers do not take the trouble to study and understand their explanations. Not to mention the receivers failing to interrogate the dashboards the senders design, even though "self-service" is one of the latest trends in Business Intelligence. If the sender is not being understood and the receiver is not feeling well served, something is wrong with business communication.

We think we've found the reason: Business communication in written reports, live presentations and interactive dashboards is not effective. It can be slow and painful to extract the information. Why is that?

Drawing on the authors' engineering and music backgrounds described earlier, we are convinced that a lack of standards in visual communication is the primary cause of this problem. The lack of notation standards means that every chart and every table looks different. Discerning no patterns, the readers must re-orient themselves each time. We suspect—and this is great news—that we can make business communication much more effective by introducing easy to recognize patterns.

In the following sections of this chapter, we will explain how we arrived at this view. We will derive the best approach to harness the potential of pattern recognition.

STANDARD NOTATIONS IN OTHER DISCIPLINES

As our start point, we take a look at written communication in other disciplines. Lo and behold: music notes, traffic signs, circuit charts, construction drawings and maps—to name just a few—all have standardized notations. What degree of freedom exists in writing down an idea? Almost zero. Pattern recognition? Up to 100 percent, depending on experience. But when it comes to the visualization of business data? Nothing in sight.

HISTORY OF DATA VISUALIZATION

People have been wrestling with visualizing data for over 200 years. We will point out where improvement has been attempted and where things have been left untouched. Historical records are littered with complaints of varied design, visual overload and inadequacy of certain forms of visual representation. The preferred way to remedy this challenge has been to focus on education—so far with modest success. Solving this problem with a standardized notation has not yet been put forward.

CAUSES OF MISSING STANDARDS

Given the use of standard notation in other disciplines and the long history of data visualization, it is surprising that there are still no comprehensive notation standards for reporting. A commonly given reason is that no one wants to restrict the creativity of report writers. We will show that this is a misunderstanding based upon a confusion between form and content.

PATTERN RECOGNITION THROUGH SEMANTIC NOTATION

The next step is to demonstrate the potential that springs from adopting semantic notation. Looking at the way that our brains work shows we perceive intuitively much faster than we make rational decisions. When "things that mean the same look the same" and "things that do not mean the same do not look the same", we can take advantage of our brains' vast capabilities in intuitive pattern recognition. This use of pattern recognition dramatically speeds up the understanding of reports.

DE FACTO STANDARDS WITH CREATIVE COMMONS

Having made the case for standardized notation in reporting, we then look at what makes a set of rules the standard and what needs to happen for its successful adoption. We rely on collaborative development and free availability under the Creative Commons license terms for acceptance and distribution.

The design of a standard notation for business communication is then the subject of Chapter 2.

Music notes. Centuries ago, musicians agreed on a standardized notation. Here is an excerpt from the Bach Suite BWV 1067.
Source: Manuscript by Jürgen Faisst

1.1
STANDARD NOTATIONS IN OTHER DISCIPLINES

NORTH IS UP

To assess the current status of standardized notation in business reporting, we look at corresponding developments in other disciplines. First sheet music, then traffic signs, circuit diagrams, construction plans and maps.

SHEET MUSIC

"Musicians of the Middle Ages found out how to make marks on parchment to capture sound in space, an achievement that required extraordinary conceptual leaps and technological advances. What began as a method to represent the general shape of a song evolved over several centuries to become not only a recording but a playback device, allowing musicians to transport music and learn songs they had never heard before. Translating something invisible that takes place in time into something visible and fixed in space is a remarkable transformation."[1]

Today, we take musical notes, and their high degree of standardization, for granted. Musicians from different regions, eras and styles use more or less the same notation: black and white dots with (and without) stems and flags on five lines, framed by standardized inscriptions on the sheet of music such as the title of the piece, the composer and the intended instrument.

The consequences of this standardization are remarkable: Would a professional pianist be able to play the piano part shown in FIGURE 1.1-1 for the accompaniment of a flute, flawlessly, without ever having seen it before? The answer to this question is clearly yes. Surely it is impossible for pianists to read all those black dots at the same speed at which they have to play? How can they reproduce the music without mistakes? There must be other mechanisms at work here.

Let's compare reading music notes to reading text. Children learn to read by first learning letters and then assembling the individual letters into a word whose meaning they understand. As they advance, they no longer read individual letters, but whole syllables, and later whole words. Understanding music notation follows a similar development path: Pianists don't read note by note but recognize whole chords and lines. Not only are they much faster, but they also understand the musical text on a completely different level.

---

1   Kelly, Thomas Forrest: Capturing Music: The Story of Notation,
    page XIII, W.W. Norton & Company, New York 2015.

FIGURE 1.1-2

Traffic signs. Traffic signs in Kuwait (on the left) correspond largely to those in Europe. On the right are country-specific variants of the stop sign used worldwide.

Sources: Wikimedia "Road signs in Kuwait" and Wikipedia "Stop signs"

ROAD SIGNS

Road signs are a much more recent standard. We recognized the need for standardized traffic signs in the first half of the 20th century because of the rapidly growing road traffic. Initially standardization took place at a national level then, later, at an international level (an example being the Vienna Convention on Traffic Signs and Signals framework in 1968[1]). At the instigation of the United Nations Economic Commission for Europe (UNECE), 63 states had signed up to this Convention[2] by 2014. In FIGURE 1.1-2, you can see familiar looking traffic signs from Kuwait and to the right you will see almost identical looking stop signs from 30 different countries.

Standardized notation aims to improve the safety of road traffic across national borders. The effect is similar to that of musical notes: Here, too, the speed of reading counts. Recognizing the traffic sign conveys the rule in an instant as you drive past them, a much faster process than the slow and inefficient process of *reading* the sign text.

Global standardization of traffic signs also has a second thing in common with musical notation: It is extremely helpful to be able to rent a car at any airport in the world and drive off without first having to learn the local traffic signs. We see a similar practical advantage for musicians: George Gershwin using the same notation as Johann Sebastian Bach.

CIRCUIT DIAGRAMS
AND CONSTRUCTION DRAWINGS

Electrical engineers also appreciate the unmistakable language of standardized visualization: Standardized symbols in circuit diagrams increase not only

---

1   United Nations Treaty Collection: Chapter XI: Transport and Communications, B. Road Traffic, 20. Convention on Road Signs and Signals.

2   Source: www.unece.org.

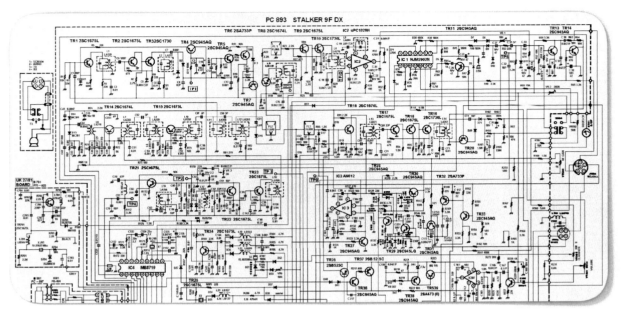

FIGURE 1.1-3

Circuit diagrams. Electrical engineers understand each other because they standardized the way they draw circuit diagrams for electrical systems. The figure shows the circuit diagram of a CB radio.
Source: Teaberry Stalker IX Service Manual

the speed of communication between designers and engineers but also the quality of the machines built. With this in mind, the Institute of Electrical and Electronics Engineers (IEEE) Coordinating Committee for Letter and Graphic Symbols formalized standardization of graphic symbols for electrical and electronic circuits.[3]

For lay people the most fascinating thing about these electric circuits is the high density of information. FIGURE 1.1-3 shows the circuit diagram of a CB radio from the 1980s. It is fair to compare it to an orchestral score. Conductors and electrical engineers don't complain about the many black lines and dots on one page because they know they need them. This is the only way to get an overview of an electronic system or an orchestral work.

The mechanism electrical engineers use for quickly understanding such complex drawings is similar to that of book readers and musicians. They don't read every single symbol for a resistor or capacitor, but they grasp larger correlations at a glance.

The situation is similar for architects and civil engineers. Construction drawings are concerned with the dimensioning of components and the specification of materials. Therefore, the notation of dimensions and materials was standardized. The drawing uses a scale related to the size of the object such as 1:10 or 1:100. As with musical notes, the title of the architectural drawing in the plan header is standardized to a large extent. In addition to the name of the construction project, there is also the drawing number, scale and version history. Through this use of drawing standards, experienced readers of architectural drawings can quickly find their way around.

3   IEEE Std 315-1975, confirmed 1993.

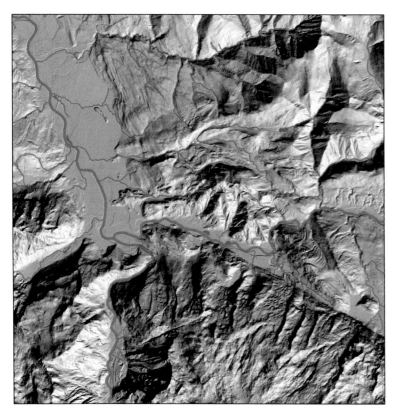

FIGURE 1.1-4
Topographic map with incorrect illumination.
We are used to the fact that in topographic maps the illumination comes from the northwest although this does not correspond to the actual conditions in the northern hemisphere. But if we, as shown here, illuminate it as it really is from the southeast, we are left with the impression that the rivers flow on the mountain ridges.
Source: Land Salzburg, OGD Austria – Creative Commons. Robert Kalasek, TU Vienna

MAPS

Cartographers have developed one of the best-known standard notations: maps. In addition to the well-known visualizations such as contour lines and symbols for conifers and deciduous trees, there are also standards we don't know explicitly but we are still familiar with. For example, the lighting and shading of topographic maps: The terrain profile is reproduced as vividly as possible by hatching and shading, where the map standard has the light coming from the northwest. Although not explicitly known, this convention is adopted across the globe even though it does not reflect the actual direction of sunlight in the northern hemisphere. FIGURE 1.1-4 shows a topographic map with lighting from the southeast—which is the reality in the Alps, but not the standard. As this change in lighting direction alters our perception of highs and lows on the map, it can turn a hike along a river into a summit tour.

The best-known rule for maps: North is up. It wasn't always like that. In earlier cultures, they often drew maps in such a way that they pointed in the direction of the most important place of that culture, e.g. Jerusalem or Mecca. There have been different attempts to explain the increasing orientation of maps to the north, for example orientation based on the northern polar star or the statement that at the time when the first detailed world maps were created, most of the locations were on the northern hemisphere. Whatever the reason, North-pointing maps really established themselves with the use of magnetic compasses in seafaring from the 15th century. FIGURE 1.1-5 shows just how much we have grown accustomed to north-pointing maps: Many of us would have problems orienting ourselves with the map of Europe shown on the left side (with South up), whereas most of us feel comfortable with the map shown on the right.

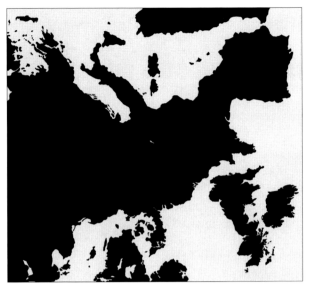 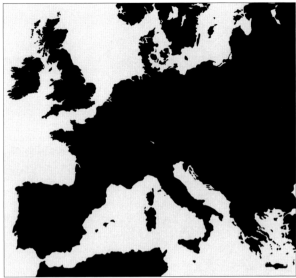

FIGURE 1.1-5

North is up. Every kid knows that on maps, north is up. Those viewing the picture on the left only find their way around after some time. The representation of Europe on the right is familiar to us. Here it is easy to see how our pattern recognition reacts to standards.

What is interesting is the way the north-facing approach has been implemented, as initially there was no definition by a professional association or standardization body. The northern orientation was originally used by Europeans purely as a convention in the course of colonization but has now established itself as de facto standard with worldwide adoption. Probably because it's convenient to align all maps the same way.

"The practical thing with maps is that north is always up and rivers are always blue. Similar rules would also improve understanding of business charts."

RECAP

Musicians, engineers, architects and cartographers are just a few of the many professions who employ specific professional notation standards. Standardized notations make it easier for the senders of content to record their thoughts in writing. This also enables the receivers to quickly capture and accurately reproduce these thoughts. From an abstract point of view, the areas covered by the standardized notations are similar across the disciplines: It is mainly a matter of titling and labeling the recordings, of content identification through symbolism and of representing different scales.

These three areas are also important in business reports and dashboards: labeling, content identification, and scaling. In the next sections we look at the current situation of business communication and what we can learn from musicians and other professions.

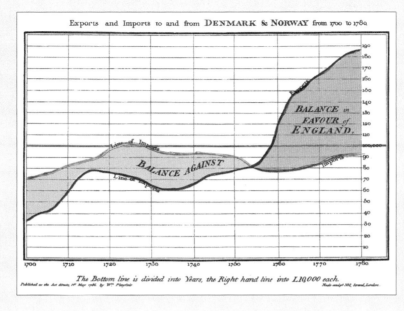

FIGURE 1.2-1

Line chart in the 18th century. At the end of the 18th century, William Playfair was the first to use business charts to visualize economic data. Here he uses lines and areas to show the export surplus over 80 years. Source: William Playfair, The Commercial and Political Atlas, 1786

1.2
HISTORY OF DATA VISUALIZATION

PIES ARE THERE TO EAT

Economists and statisticians have been involved in the visual communication of their messages for over 200 years. In this section we will take you on a whistle-stop tour of the key thought-leaders and their ideas: William Playfair, Willard C. Brinton, Jacques Bertin and Edward R. Tufte.

WILLIAM PLAYFAIR

The Scottish engineer and economist William Playfair (1759–1823) is seen by many as the founding father of data visualization. It is thanks to his work that since the late 18th century charts have been used in business and politics "to give a more simple and permanent idea of the gradual progress and comparative amounts, at different periods, by presenting to the eye a figure, the proportions of which correspond with the amount of the sums intended to be expressed[1]". Our visual example FIGURE 1.2-1 comes from his "Commercial and Political Atlas", in which Playfair visualizes the development of England's export surpluses in relation to individual countries through the use of lines and areas.

Unfortunately, William Playfair's ideas for visualization spread very slowly, perhaps due to technical problems with the implementation and publication of charts: While the book typesetter could set texts and tables, charts still had to be engraved like images in printing plates.

---

1 Playfair, William: The Commercial and Political Atlas, London 1786.

> *"This type of chart [radar chart] should be banished to the scrap heap. Charts on rectangular ruling are easier to draw and easier to understand."*
>
> WILLARD C. BRINTON

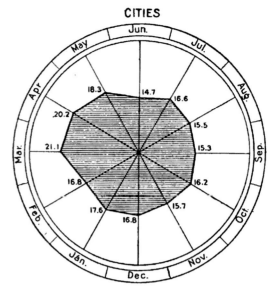

United States Statistical Atlas of the 1900 Census

FIGURE 1.2-2

Radar chart. Willard C. Brinton examined which chart types are particularly suitable for which form of analysis, or—as in this case—not so suitable. Source: Brinton, Willard. C.: Graphic Methods For Presenting Facts, The Engineering Magazine Company, New York 1914, page 80

WILLARD C. BRINTON

It was more than a hundred years before Willard C. Brinton (1880–1957), another engineer, became deeply involved with the visualization of economic and business figures. His book, "Graphic Methods for Presenting Facts"[1], published in 1914, categorizes the various analytical purposes (component parts, simple comparisons, comparisons involving time, time charts, etc.) and discusses the advantages and disadvantages of certain chart types using practical examples.

We don't know why Brinton's proposals did not catch on. Despite his assessment of the disadvantages of pie charts and his justified criticism of radar charts, FIGURE 1.2-2, both chart types remain highly popular to this day. Despite this lack of popular recognition,

Brinton's chart typing system remains the theoretical basis for more recent publications by authors such as Gene Zelazny[2] and Stephen Few[3].

JACQUES BERTIN

In 1967, the French cartographer Jacques Bertin[4] (1918–2010) wrote about the concept of content identification. In his "Sémiologie graphique", he designs a comprehensive theory for the use of the visual variables position, size, opacity, texture, color, orientation and shape, FIGURE 1.2-3. He wants to use these visual variables to transfer thoughts (contents) into corresponding sign systems (charts and maps) to record and communicate them. He discusses the

1   Brinton, Willard. C.: Graphic Methods for Presenting Facts, The Engineering Magazine Company, New York 1914.

2   Zelazny, Gene: Say It With Charts. McGraw-Hill Education, 4th edition, New York 2001.

3   Few, Stephen: Show Me the Numbers, Analytics Press, Oakland 2004.

4   Bertin, Jacques: Sémiologie graphique, Editions Gauthier-Villars, Paris 1967.

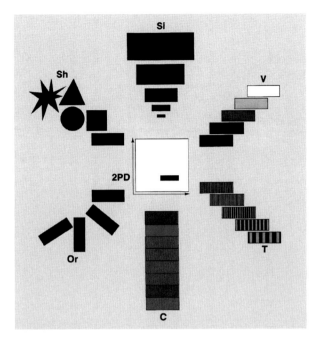

FIGURE 1.2-3
Visual variables. Jacques Bertin discusses the suitability of so-called "visual variables" such as color and texture for the communication of quantitative facts (2DP = position, Si = size, V = opacity, T = texture, C = color, OR = orientation, Sh = shape).
Source: Jacques Bertin: Semiology of Graphics, 1967, page 43

"Graphic representation is the transcription of information known through the intermediary of any given sign-system."

JACQUES BERTIN

suitability of individual visual variables for mapping content-related facts against the background of their properties:

SELECTIVITY
Is a change in this variable sufficient to differentiate elements from each other? This applies, to a greater or lesser extent, for all variables.

ASSOCIATION
Can similar elements be identified as such by similarities in this variable? This is also applicable, to a greater or lesser extent, to all variables.

QUANTIFICATION
Can numerical changes be derived from changes in this variable? This is hardly possible with colors, shapes, textures and opacity, for example.

ORDER
Do the different states of this variable have an order? This is especially true for the variables' position and size, but also for their opacity.

Now the question remains: How many distinguishable states can this visual variable assume? Here the properties range from "practically infinite" in position, size and opacity to "theoretically infinite", but in practical application they are limited to "maximum 8" in colors and orientations.

Bertin's goal was a clearly defined transcription of content to its graphical representation.

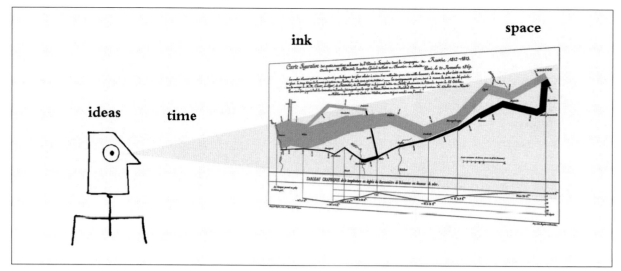

FIGURE 1.2-4

Graphical excellence. For Edward Tufte, "graphical excellence is that which gives to the viewer the greatest number of ideas in the shortest time with the least ink in the smallest space".
Source: Edward Tufte, The Visual Display of Quantitative Information, page 51

EDWARD R. TUFTE

The statistician and political scientist Edward Tufte (born in 1942 in the USA) attracted a broad audience with his two appealingly designed books "Envisioning Information"[1] and "The Visual Display of Quantitative Information,"[2] as well as with his lectures and seminars, helping the topic of data visualization gain enormous popularity.

Tufte vividly explains the function of receiving information by visual perception and sets up rules like the following:

AVOID CLUTTER

Purely decorative elements and redundancy disturb the visual perception of the information to be conveyed. The aim must be to maximize the data-ink ratio.

INCREASE INFORMATION DENSITY

Tufte notes that most charts are still easy to read even if they are significantly reduced in size ("shrink principle"). This way more information fits on one page.

SCALE CORRECTLY

Incorrect scaling leads to misinterpretation. To assess misinterpretation, Tufte calculates the "lie factor" by measuring the relationship between the size of an effect as perceived visually and the size of the effect as derived from the data.

Tufte's aim is to convey as many thoughts as possible to the observer as quickly as possible with as little ink as possible on as small an area as possible, FIGURE 1.2-4.

1 Tufte, Edward R.: Envisioning Information, Graphics Press, Cheshire 1990.

2 Tufte, Edward R.: The Visual Display of Quantitative Information, Graphics Press, Cheshire 2001.

RECAP

For more than 200 years, research and education have addressed many problem areas in visual perception, mostly under the banner of "data visualization". This work has shown which visualizations work best in particular situations through practical examples. This mainly involved the choice of chart types, but there were also initial approaches to content identification (Bertin) and detailed discussions about scaling issues (Tufte).

These works aimed to make report writers aware of common problems and to produce better reports through a deeper understanding. This approach is quite different from the notation for other disciplines, where, through the application of the standard, users automatically avoid a number of potential issues they are not even aware of.

"... it is first necessary
to strictly separate the content
(the Information to be transmitted)
from the container
(the Properties of the graphic system)."

JACQUES BERTIN

1.3
CAUSES OF MISSING STANDARDS
CONFUSION OF FORM AND CONTENT

As discussed earlier, musicians, engineers, cartographers and many other professionals use standardized notations to put their ideas on paper or on screen. In the field of economics, only isolated problem areas of visual perception were addressed so far, and only limited discussions of the pros and cons of the potential solutions were conducted. Binding notation standards still seem a long way off. There are two main reasons for this: Firstly, confusing form and content and, secondly, underestimating the problem-solving potential that standards provide.

FIGURE 1.3-1
Beautiful or understandable? The picture on the left may be nicer, but on the right the traffic light stands out more.

FORM AND CONTENT

Jacques Bertin pointed out in 1967 that when drawing charts and maps the content is sometimes confused with its written representation[1]. When writing texts, no one would make the mistake of confusing what is written (the form) with what is said (the content). The same applies to musicians: The sheet of music and the music recorded on it cannot be confused. You read the notes and you hear the sound.

Business economists, on the other hand, often mix the content of a report with its written manifestation. Here are three frequently heard reservations about standardized report notation that illustrate this problem:

"I WANT OUR REPORTS
AND DASHBOARDS TO LOOK NICE"

The confusion between form and content cannot be expressed more clearly than with the demand for visual attractiveness. This would be like Beethoven saying: "My score should look beautiful". His hasty scribbling ensured that this was never the case. His music, however, is beautiful, and this is all that matters. Are the beautifully designed management reports possibly intended to conceal declining market shares, increasing losses and dissatisfied customers? The primary aim of a report's visual design should not be beauty, but simple comprehension—at least if we assume an interest in transparent reporting. Many will find the richly colored picture on the left of FIGURE 1.3-1 more beautiful than the one on the right. But, if our message concerns the traffic light, it is much easier to see it in the picture on the right. In the end, that's what matters.

Some will claim that in times of *information overload* our objective should be "winning the competition to capture the attention of the viewer". To this end, a good looking report is particularly important. This argument is both wrong and dangerous: From a business perspective, it is not the most attractive reports that should be read, but those with the most important content. At best, we might want to make important reports more visually appealing than less important ones to draw the reader's attention to the right content. However, this approach would require an editorial decision by the creator as to which reports are most important and this would involve a full review of all reports the reader will be looking at any given time.

1   Bertin, Jacques: Sémiologie graphique, Editions Gauthier-Villars, Paris 1967.

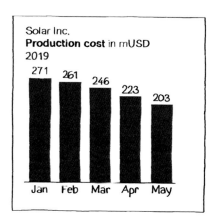

FIGURE 1.3-2
Few chart types. The four basic types of column, line, bar and XY charts and their variations (stacked, grouped, standardized, indexed, etc.) cover most business analysis and visual messaging.

"WE DO NOT WANT TO RESTRICT THE CREATIVITY OF THE DESIGNERS"

Confusion between form and content crops up again when reference is made to the creativity of the designers. Some argue that they do not want to restrict the report writer's choice of chart types, colors and forms. After all, we love "freedom of choice".

We also want to encourage creativity of report writers and dashboard designers, but only when it comes to *content*. When it comes to the visual implementation of their ideas, the introduction of creativity is harmful, because it forces readers to think their way into the creator's head, i.e. to learn the visual language developed by the creator himself. Imagine every composer transcribing his or her musical ideas using a specially created musical notation—a catastrophe for the musicians, who would have to learn new notations every time. It would also be bad news for composers, who would have to concentrate on the development of a suitable musical notation rather than on the creative process of composing. In reality, composers do not feel restricted in their creativity by the existing musical notation. Quite the opposite: They are pleased that they don't have to worry about the method of recording their ideas. And if, in the future, musical notation reaches its limits, the standard would simply be extended as needed.

The misguided desire for creativity in visual report design can also be seen in selection lists for chart types. It is easy to get the impression that creativity is expressed by using as many chart types as possible. It would be simpler, for both report creators and readers, if the assignment of analysis purpose to chart type were as clear as possible—and limited to as *small* a selection as possible. The four basic types of columns, lines, bars and XY charts shown in FIGURE 1.3-2, as well as their variations (stacked, grouped, standardized, indexed, etc.), will successfully serve most business analyses and message visualizations.

The increasing importance of Corporate Design has led to an absurd situation, not only in external reporting, but often also in company-internal reports: Coloring and other design elements are subject to a set of rules that does not relate to the business meaning of what is being presented, instead the aim is to achieve as uniform an appearance as possible. In extreme cases, all columns, bars and lines—regardless of their meaning—are drawn in red, blue or magenta, because this is supposed to communicate the Corporate Identity.

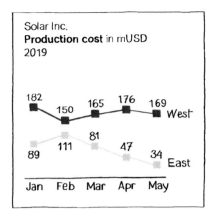

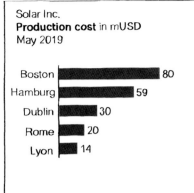

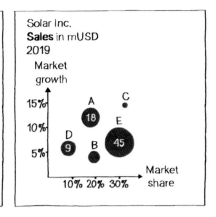

"OUR REPORTS AND DASHBOARDS SHOULD NOT BE TOO COMPLEX"

Unfortunately this demand for a simpler design often isn't focused on the removal of decorative elements—which would be welcome—but the reduction of information density. People incorrectly apply a concept to the content that should be applied to the form. When they plead "Please don't show so much on one page", they are often asking for a reduction in content, rather than form. It's like a conductor complaining about too many black dots on a score page.

In fact, it is the opposite: Conductors need the complete overview of the notes of all instruments playing simultaneously to lead the orchestra. FIGURE 1.3-3 (PAGE 32), for example, shows the first few bars from the final movement of an arrangement for symphonic wind orchestra with about 40 different parts. We have to ask ourselves: Is the control of a company less complex than the control of an orchestra playing a piece of music? Using this reasoning, Edward Tufte rightly demands maximum information density constrained only by relevant technical boundaries, such as screen resolution[1].

If we don't understand reports with a high information density, then we shouldn't wish for less information, but rather ask ourselves what we could do to improve the comprehension of it. Again, it helps to look at other professions. There are two main reasons why musicians, electrical engineers or cartographers can cope with a much higher density of information in graphic presentations than business economists: One, these professions have a standardized notation and two, the practitioners have learned to read it. Depending on the level of learning, the information density can also be varied: Whilst practitioners of different professions such as conductors have learned over the years to read high-density notations, sheet music for recorder lessons in kindergarten are, of course, simplified.

"We never hear conductors complain about too many black dots in their score."

1   Tufte, Edward R.: The Visual Display of Quantitative Information, Graphics Press, Cheshire 2001.

FIG. 1.3-3

Information density of conductor scores. Scores have a high information density.
Here are a few bars from an arrangement for a symphonic wind orchestra.
Source: Udo Jürgens, The Man with the Bassoon, manuscript by Jürgen Faisst

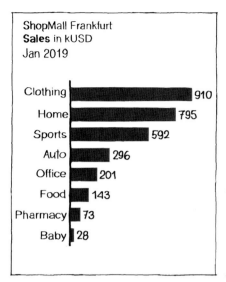

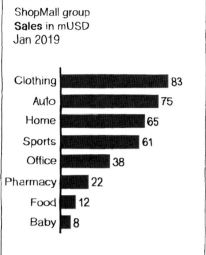

FIGURE 1.3-4
Store sales. The two bar charts show January sales by department—left for the Frankfurt branch, right for the entire group. Both look exactly the same although the left shows sales in kUSD and the right in mUSD. The difference in the unit of measurement is not visual and is only noticed after reading the label.

THE PROBLEM-SOLVING POTENTIAL OF STANDARDS

While musicians, engineers and many other professions see norms and de facto standards as a positive achievement simplifying their work, in business life such things still suffer the stigma of restricting civil liberties. This is a pity, because the problem-solving potential of standards is enormous.

QUICK RECOGNITION OF MEANING

Standards can be used to assign meaning to visual elements and their properties (semantics). Let's look at the scaling problem that musicians, cartographers and business economists all struggle with. Musicians have introduced clefs to visually distinguish high and low ranges.

Maps with different scales are drawn in different forms so that you can immediately see when you switch from the surrounding map of a city to the detailed map of the city center. Each map has a scale bar on which the scale is recorded and labeled with the distances represented. Scale bars and clefs are good examples of semantic notation standards. With their help, it is possible to deduce clearly and quickly the precise meaning of the content from the appearance.

This type of semantic notation standards does not yet exist for the design of reports. A bar chart showing the sales revenue of a small store looks exactly like the corresponding chart for the entire company even if these two charts are displayed on the same page, despite one showing sales in thousands of US dollars (kUSD) and the other in millions of dollars (mUSD), FIGURE 1.3-4. Without visual cues to tell the reader there is a difference, the report creator must add labels to explain this and the recipient must read them.

FIGURE 1.3-5

Clefs solve scaling problems. Musicians solve their scaling problems implicitly through a standardized notation: The high flute notes are notated in treble clef, the low bass notes in bass clef.

Source: Bert Kämpfert, A Swinging Safari, manuscript by Jürgen Faisst

DO IT RIGHT WITHOUT THINKING ABOUT IT

For those who use notation to put their ideas down on paper, standards have another huge benefit: Just using them solves problems, without the creator having to consider the problem or the solution.

Let us consider the scaling problem of composers who want to write high tones—say for a flute—and low tones—say for a double bass. Obviously, these tones do not fit on a uniform staff with 5 regular and some auxiliary lines. Without a standard notation they would become aware of the problem of scaling, look for a visual solution, probably not find one and perhaps add some text to both parts to explain how the notes are to be interpreted.

Composers are spared this pain. They apply—without thinking long and hard—the norm that flutes are notated in the treble clef and double basses in the bass clef and that the staves are marked accordingly, FIGURE 1.3-5. This is an excellent and practical solution, which is applied by musicians without any consideration of the difficult scaling problem that has just been solved.

Such implicit solutions through the application of standards do not yet exist in report notation. Report standards would increase the speed of creation and significantly improve the quality of reports. Report writers wouldn't be constantly thinking about the "how" and "why" of the notation, but simply apply a known standard.

RECAP

Commonly given advice for beautifying report appearance, advocating freedom of choice in design and limiting the amount of information displayed, has held back the development of notation standards for reporting. They reveal the confusion between the content of a report and its written manifestation (form)—something Jacques Bertin identified as early as 1967.

There is still work to be done to change that mindset and we can look to other disciplines with successful standards for guidance. Looking at other fields, we can clearly see the problem-solving potential of standards: Using a standardized notation not only accelerates comprehension but also means we sometimes do not even notice there are problems to solve. These problems are solved automatically by applying the standards.

This potential remains largely untapped in the visualization of business reporting.

1.4
PATTERN RECOGNITION
THROUGH SEMANTIC NOTATION

UNDERSTANDING WITHOUT THINKING

When we reviewed the standard notations from other disciplines at the beginning of this chapter, we found that concert pianists would probably be able to play the sheet music in FIGURE 1.1-1 (PAGE 16) correctly, even if they had never seen it before, even though it is impossible to read every single note at the speed at which the music is to be played. We speculated that in these situations other mechanisms must come into play rather than reading note by note—just as with the standard notations of other disciplines. In this section we want to explore these mechanisms in more depth. First, we explain the functioning of the so-called System 1 and System 2 procedures in our brain. We then explore the interaction of visual perception and visual memory in the context of pattern recognition and explain the effects of semantic notation on pattern recognition. Finally, we discuss what all this means for the density of the information to be consumed.

THINKING, FAST AND SLOW

We all know the situation: Someone is introduced to us and we intuitively put him or her in a, supposedly, suitable box. The more reasonable alternative would be to get to know this person properly before we reach any conclusions. Obviously, there are two procedures in our brain for assessing situations. But what is the difference? In his book "Thinking, Fast and Slow", Nobel Prize winner Daniel Kahneman[1] describes the two procedures called "System 1" and "System 2".

INTUITIVE SYSTEM 1

System 1 reacts spontaneously, quickly, intuitively and often unconsciously. In contrast to System 2, it does not evaluate the specific situation but limits itself to association with similar situations in the past and decides based on the experiences made then. We use System 1 when speed and efficiency are more important than logic and accuracy. This speed is an advantage which can save lives and that is probably the reason why the course of evolution has equipped us with this system.

Imagine we are hunting, and suddenly we see something brown-haired looking out from behind a tree, FIGURE 1.4-1. We could investigate the situation more closely, discuss it with our hunting colleagues, determine that it might be a bear and then decide to run. Alternatively, we could trust our intuition and run away immediately, which might increase our chances of survival.

There are also situations in business life where speed and intuition are important. Let's think, for example, of a broker on the stock exchange: Well-founded analysis might in principle lead to better buying and selling decisions, but is useless if the share price has already reacted in the meantime.

---

[1] Kahneman, Daniel: Thinking, Fast and Slow. Farrar, Straus and Giroux, New York 2011. Kahneman adopted the terms "System 1" and "System 2" from the psychologists Keith Stanovich and Richard West.

FIGURE 1.4-1

Thinking, fast (System 1) and slow (System 2). Sometimes it is necessary to react quickly and spontaneously. To protect us from wild animals, for example, evolution has equipped us with the intuitive System 1. Our System 2 would evaluate the situation too slowly. Illustration: Rachele Mascarin

> *"This is your System 1 talking.*
> *Slow down and*
> *let your System 2 take control."*
>
> DANIEL KAHNEMAN

RATIONAL SYSTEM 2

Unlike System 1, System 2 deliberates. It analyzes, evaluates and finally makes a decision that is as rational as possible. Compared to System 1, System 2 probably makes the better decisions most of the time, just sometimes too late or with too much effort.

Long-term investment decisions, for example, should be left to System 2. In this case, the weighing of advantages and disadvantages and the exact financial calculation are more important than the speed of the decision-making. The greater effort spent in making the decision would seem worthwhile here.

INTERACTION OF SYSTEM 1 AND SYSTEM 2

The two systems are not separate from each other and are not individually controllable. In fact, the interaction between both systems determines our behavior. Because our brain is lazy, it tries to solve tasks with as little effort as possible, as thinking consumes a relatively large amount of energy. In fact, our brain underestimates the complexity of tasks and tends to delegate them to System 1. In the worst-case scenario, we make a mistake, but sometimes we are a little suspicious during the decision-making process and activate System 2 as a precaution. Then a small fight takes place in our heads. System 2 usually wins.

So what does the interaction of the intuitive System 1 and the rational System 2 have to do with sight reading musical notes and the intelligibility of reports?

PERCEPTION, STORAGE AND PATTERN RECOGNITION

If System 1 is the faster and more resource-efficient decision-making process in our brain, then we should consider how we can harness this system for our own purposes. This is exactly what we are doing when we use any kind of visualization in a report, instead of restricting ourselves (as we did until the late 18th century) to texts and tables.

What happens in System 1 when we look at a business chart?

VISUAL PERCEPTION AND VISUAL MEMORY

Initially, we perceive a chart, with the help of our eyes, as a kind of "picture". Visual perception is the fastest and most powerful instrument of information recording that humans and most animals possess. But it's not only about perception, we also have an excellent visual memory. Due to the highly parallel processing of information and a pattern-based associative memory, our brain is much better suited for images than for speech.

PATTERN RECOGNITION

Looking at a bar chart activates experiences with previously seen and stored bar charts. Our System 1 reports: "Experience shows that the length of a bar is proportional to the number it represents."

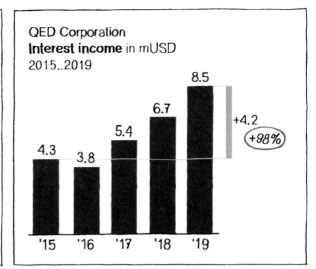

Development of interest income

Interest income of QED corporation amounted to 4.3 mUSD in 2015 but rose to 8.5 mUSD by 2019. This corresponds to an increase of 4.2 mUSD or 98% within five years.

QED Corporation
Interest income in mUSD
2015..2019

FIGURE 1.4-2

Fast visual acquisition versus slow reading. In the chart on the right we can see the doubling of net interest income within a fraction of a second. The green color of the difference marker even helps our System 1 assess this change.

Getting the same information in written form like on the left takes much longer. It first occupies our System 2 with reading and arithmetic and then we still have to figure out if the higher interest income is an advantage.

This comparison between the visually perceived information and our visual memory is called pattern recognition. System 1 largely relies on pattern recognition. It works quickly and efficiently because our brain is particularly good at recognizing patterns.

EXAMPLE: INTEREST INCOME

Let's try this out: A glance at the bar chart on the right in FIGURE 1.4-2 reveals within a fraction of a second that the interest income of the company in question has roughly doubled in the past 5 years. The green color of the deviation indicator also tells us that this is good news.

Now we turn to the text on the left in FIGURE 1.4-2. Reading alone takes three seconds. Then we have to remember the figures and do a five-second calculation to conclude that the interest income of the company in question has almost doubled in the past 5 years. After that we still have to consider whether higher interest rates are good news or bad news. System 2 takes much longer.

SPEED VERSUS ACCURACY

Pattern recognition is the principle that allows us to compare the length of columns at a glance and that also helps the concert pianist to read the notes quickly enough.

However, we have also alluded to the fact that System 1 can be somewhat inaccurate. If we want to improve the quality of the knowledge gained through System 1, we must ensure that pattern recognition leads to more accurate results. Musicians had to come up with a system to visually package—i.e. write—their music in such a way that pattern recognition automatically led to the correct movements of the fingers on the keyboard. Since System 1 works relatively flawlessly with practiced musicians, the musicians seem to have developed a notation where the recognition of the patterns accurately leads to the desired reactions.

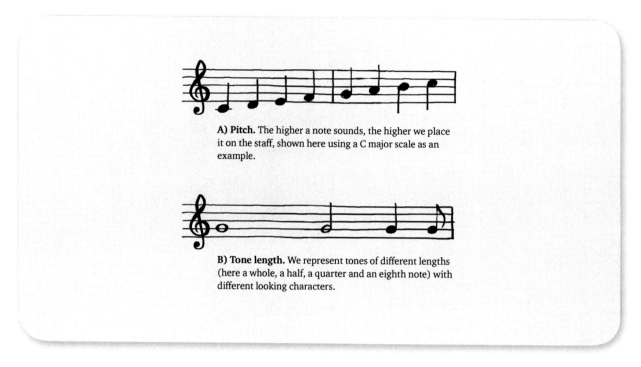

A) **Pitch.** The higher a note sounds, the higher we place it on the staff, shown here using a C major scale as an example.

B) **Tone length.** We represent tones of different lengths (here a whole, a half, a quarter and an eighth note) with different looking characters.

FIGURE 1.4-3
Notation of music. Pitch and length of tones.

SEMANTIC NOTATION

The procedure for improving the accuracy of pattern recognition is the same in the notation systems of all disciplines: Things that mean the same look the same. Things that don't mean the same don't look the same. We call this principle *semantic notation*—a standardized notation where the meaning is expressed by the appearance of the item. The simple design rule "Same-same and different-different" increases the selectivity of the recognized patterns and results in unambiguous reactions. With sufficient training, these reactions will also be the right ones.

ACCURACY

Now the question arises of which aspects are of particular importance for an accurate reaction to the recognition of a pattern.

Let's look at music notation again: The pitch of a tone is critically important to the performing musician. It makes sense to arrange a higher note higher up and a lower note lower down on a staff as can be seen in the illustration of a C major scale, FIGURE 1.4-3(A). The closer the association is, the easier we find pattern recognition. Equally important to musicians are the length of tones, but the signs used do not offer visual cues for this. Although not immediately intuitive, music notation uses distinct symbols for notes of different lengths: A hollow dot for a whole note, a hollow dot with a stem for a half note, a solid dot with a stem for a quarter note and a dot with a stem and a flag for an eighth note (B).

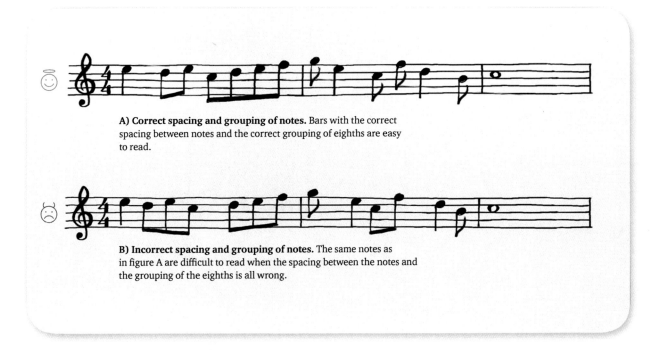

A) **Correct spacing and grouping of notes.** Bars with the correct spacing between notes and the correct grouping of eighths are easy to read.

B) **Incorrect spacing and grouping of notes.** The same notes as in figure A are difficult to read when the spacing between the notes and the grouping of the eighths is all wrong.

ABB 1.4-4
Notation of music. Spacing and grouping.

However, a closer look reveals that the length of a tone is also visualized by the width of the horizontal gap after a note, and the breakdown of a bar is also supported by rules for grouping eighth notes with flags, FIGURE 1.4.-4 (A). Every musician will confirm that without these two visual characteristics, pattern recognition is almost impossible (B).

In Chapter 2 we deal with the question of which aspects like, the pitch and length of tones in music, are of particular importance in reporting, and how to visualize them.

INFORMATION DENSITY

Semantic proximity of similar patterns ("the same looks the same") along with the semantic distinctiveness of different patterns ("different looks different") not only increases the accuracy of the reaction triggered but also allows for higher information density. We still recognize single music notes and capacitors, even if many, many of them are displayed on one page. The information density of conductor scores, electrical circuit diagrams and maps shows that this works. Our next example will show that this also works in reporting.

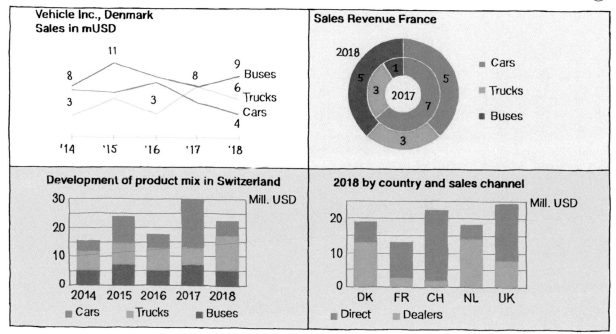

Before: Charts without standardization. Four charts with no recognizable visual pattern—unfortunately quite often the case with dashboards. The two upper charts and the lower left show similar data in different forms, the two lower diagrams show different data in the same form.

EXAMPLE

We want to communicate the regional sales of Vehicle Inc. We are interested in both the development over time and the contributions of the individual sales channels.

The report layout of FIGURE 1.4-5 is shows four relatively randomly selected chart types placed together. We only understand this report page after closely studying it. It also looks as though adding further information may overload the report.

Although the two upper charts and the lower left one look different, they show similar measures for Denmark, France and Switzerland. If we had chosen the same chart type (e.g. columns), the same labels, the same formatting (fonts, colors etc.) and the same scaling for these three charts, the reader would have had to deal with one instead of three representations.

For the lower two charts it is the other way around. They look the same, which is why we assume they represent something similar, but they do not. While the columns in the left chart represent years and thus a development over time, the columns on the right represent a revenue comparison by country.

Vehicle Inc.
Sales in mUSD

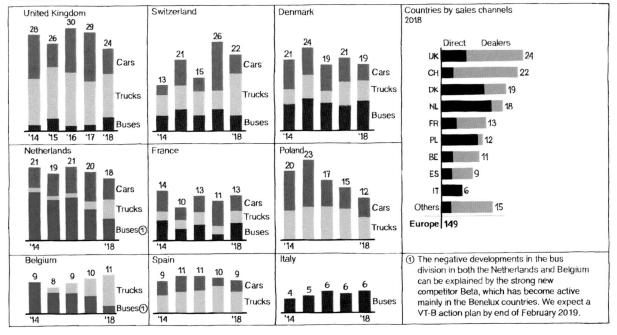

FIGURE 1.4-6

After: Better understanding through standardization. 10 charts
using similar patterns show sales developments in 9 countries and
a different pattern is used for regional comparison by sales channel.
Although more information is presented here compared to figure
1.4-5 our understanding is actually improved.

In contrast, the report layout in FIGURE 1.4-6 tries to
make things that mean the same look the same. Each
country uses the same chart type (stacked columns),
the same labels, the same formatting, and the same
scaling to represent sales development. Once you
understand one chart, you understand them all.
Although the number of charts that show an evolution over time increases from three to nine, it doesn't
feel overloaded. The additional charts actually provide a better overview, making the reader feel more
comfortable.

We also deliberately chose a different chart type for
the only chart that does not represent a time series.
That chart compares the sales of the countries. The
stacked horizontal bars (instead of columns) signal
that this is a different type of analysis. To make it easier to compare countries' sales we have also sorted
the bars of the chart in descending order. We even
managed to use the same scale for columns and bars.

RECAP

Evolution has equipped our brain with the intuitive System 1 for the rapid acquisition of large amounts of information subconsciously. This system compares perceived patterns against familiar, previously stored, patterns. In the case of a match (pattern recognition), we compare past experiences with this new pattern and a spontaneous reaction follows without using the "conscious" brain. If we want to use System 1 for business communication, we must first define patterns that are recognizable. That is why things that mean the same should look the same. Conversely, things that mean something different should also look different. This semantic notation promotes better and faster understanding while allowing for increased information density. This approach is a powerful tool when it comes to representing the complexities of corporate management.

1.5
DE FACTO STANDARDS WITH CREATIVE COMMONS

DEVELOPED TOGETHER, SHARED WITH ALL

Given that the benefits of notation standards seem obvious, it appears sensible to develop such a standard for reporting. What needs to be done? A standard does not spring solely from the results of scientific research and empirical studies; we will also need agreement on certain conventions. Who should determine these conventions? Standardization committees, market leaders or public initiatives? And when is the time right?

SCIENCE AND EMPIRICISM

A standardized notation should be based on scientific findings from the field of visual perception, particularly the functioning of the eye during the conversion of light into electrical signals (sensory *physiology*). Scientific research also shows that how we comprehend this physical signal is strongly affected by perception *psychology*. These findings are known and well documented.[1]

We also need to take into account the findings of empirical studies. These empirical studies often involve the use of eye tracking systems[2], which record and evaluate the eye movements of the reader when viewing a report. From these studies, it can be shown that our eye can compare track lengths better than areas or volumes. So, the length of bars best represents numerical comparisons—only in exceptional cases should the area of rectangles or the volume of spheres be used FIGURE 1.5-1 (PAGE 46).

[2] The book "Eye Tracking: A Comprehensive Guide to Methods and Measures" by Holmqvist, Nystrom et al. offers a good introduction to the topic. Falschlunger et al. are especially concerned with the use of eye tracking for the visualization of data for decision making: Falschlunger et al.: Deriving a holistic cognitive fit model for an optimal visualization of data for management decisions, Conference paper of the 2nd International Symposium on Partial Least Squares Path Modeling, Seville (Spain), 2015.

[1] Colin Ware: Information Visualization: Perception for Design. Elsevier, Oxford, 3. edition 2012, offers a comprehensive compilation of scientific findings for visual perception.

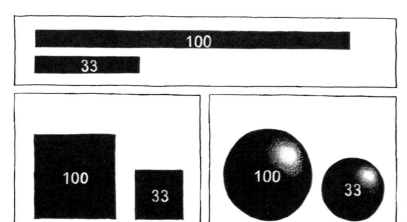

FIGURE 1.5-1
Linear comparison vs. comparison of areas or volumes. Our eyes find it easier to compare linear lengths than areas or volumes.

SEMANTIC NOTATION AS A CONVENTION

There is no scientific basis for the semantic notation presented in the previous section. We can only prove the benefit of a standardized semantic notation compared to an individually created one empirically, through methods like eye-tracking.[1] However, eye-tracking does not help define the design details of semantic notation.

Let's say we want to visually express the different meanings of actual and plan figures. We need to guarantee two things:
1. Actual data must always look the same, as should plan data.
2. Actual data must look different from plan data.

But what exactly should they look like? Should we use the color blue for actual data and show the future in pink? Or do we show actual data with a solid fill and use outlined columns and bars for planned figures that still have to fill up?

Neither science, nor the laws of nature are going to help us with these decisions. Does it even matter which specific representation we choose? No. The only thing that matters is that all report writers do it the same way and that the notation is as intuitive as possible. They just have to agree on a joint convention.

This creates a new problem: If it's hard to define a suitable notation for a certain meaning, it's even harder to get all report writers within a company, an industry—or even all over the world—to apply that notation consistently.

ESTABLISHMENT OF A STANDARD

The only reason nuts fit screws is that they are standardized, FIGURE 1.5-2. The same applies to plugs and sockets and to paper and envelope sizes.

This kind of harmonization is usually started by industrial companies looking to reduce costs, and is often formalized by standardization bodies such as the International Organization for Standardization (ISO) further down the road. All participants follow these standards out of self-interest.

1   Freyer, J. et al.: Mehr als nur ein Standard — wie die IBCS die Wahrnehmung von Geschäftsdaten erleichtern. Creative Space Publishing, Charleston, USA, 2019.

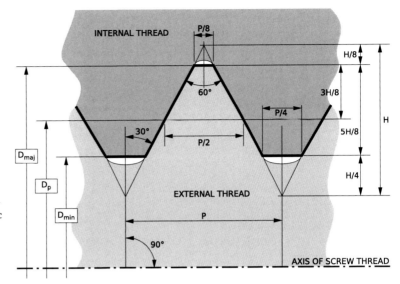

FIGURE 1.5-2
Standard for screw threads. Schematic representation of the profile of all ISO 68-1 standardized metric threads. It is thanks to this standard that the nuts of one (also standardized) size fit on the corresponding screws. Source: ISO and UTS Thread Dimensions, Inductiveload, Public Domain via Wikimedia Commons

There are also cases in which industrial companies have been able to turn innovative solutions into international standards simply by virtue of their market power. Examples include Philips' and Sony's Compact Disc, Adobe's PDF file format and Gardena's water plug system. These are industry standards—or de facto standards.

If a market-leading provider of reporting software had developed a concept for the semantic notation of business communication, consistently implemented

it and made it available to all customers, then perhaps this would have become the de facto standard. But this didn't happen.

There remains a third, and probably most modern, way to develop and disseminate a standard: Creative Commons.

"If a plug fits into a socket, it is not a matter of over-standardization, it's simply practical."

CREATIVE COMMONS

The idea is simple: If everyone has the chance to take part in the design, the result of the joint design is open to everyone and is available free of charge. Then the developed product will probably establish itself as the de facto standard.

This is the approach used with *Open Source Software*: The source code is accessible to everyone and usable free of charge. Any software developer can contribute to the next version—a "sharing economy" for intellectual property.

If the copyright of intellectual property such as texts or music is freely made available to the public, this is usually done under one of the various license terms of Creative Commons. The best-known application here is Wikipedia with the CC BY-SA provisions, FIGURE 1.5-3. Business analysts also need a similar platform to jointly develop notation standards and make the results freely and publicly available.

INTERNATIONAL BUSINESS COMMUNICATION STANDARDS (IBCS®)

Together with several like-minded members we founded in 2013 the IBCS Association, a non-profit organization with the purpose of developing and disseminating notation standards in reporting. Members of the association include executives, accountants, consultants and software developers. With www.ibcs.com/standards FIGURE 1.5-4, the IBCS Association has a platform for the publication, discussion and further development of International Business Communication Standards (IBCS). Using the contents is regulated by a Creative Commons license. This provides the practical basis for the creation of de facto notation standard by the global reporting community.

However, IBCS will not become the real standard through the existence of a non-profit association or the free provision of its rules and regulations. IBCS will only become the de facto standard when the set of rules are widely accepted and adopted globally.

ibcs ® INTERNATIONAL BUSINESS COMMUNICATION STANDARDS

IBCS® VERSION 1.1

CONCEPTUAL RULES

SAY CONVEY A MESSAGE
- SA 1 **Know objectives**
- SA 2 **Introduce message**
- SA 3 **Deliver message**
- SA 4 **Support message**
- SA 5 **Summarize message**

STRUCTURE ORGANIZE CONTENT
- ST 1 **Use consistent elements**
- ST 2 **Build non-overlapping elements**
- ST 3 **Build collectively exhaustive elements**
- ST 4 **Build hierarchical structures**
- ST 5 **Visualize structure**

PERCEPTUAL RULES

EXPRESS CHOOSE PROPER VISUALIZATION
- EX 1 **Use appropriate object types**
- EX 2 **Replace inappropriate chart types**
- EX 3 **Replace inappropriate representations**
- EX 4 **Add comparisons**
- EX 5 **Explain causes**

SIMPLIFY AVOID CLUTTER
- SI 1 **Avoid unnecessary components**
- SI 2 **Avoid decorative styles**
- SI 3 **Replace with cleaner layout**
- SI 4 **Avoid redundancies**
- SI 5 **Avoid distracting details**

CONDENSE INCREASE INFORMATION DENSITY
- CO 1 **Use small components**
- CO 2 **Maximize use of space**
- CO 3 **Add data**
- CO 4 **Add elements**
- CO 5 **Add objects**

CHECK ENSURE VISUAL INTEGRITY
- CH 1 **Avoid manipulated axes**
- CH 2 **Avoid manipulated visualization elements**
- CH 3 **Avoid misleading representations**
- CH 4 **Use the same scales**
- CH 5 **Show data adjustments**

SEMANTIC RULES

UNIFY APPLY SEMANTIC NOTATION
- UN 1 **Unify terminology**
- UN 2 **Unify descriptions**
- UN 3 **Unify dimensions**
  - UN 3.1 **Unify measures**
  - UN 3.2 **Unify scenarios**
    - Actual scenarios: measured data
    - Planned scenarios: fictitious data
    - Forecasted scenarios: expected data
  - UN 3.3 **Unify time periods and points of time**
  - UN 3.4 **Unify structure dimensions**
- UN 4 **Unify analyses**
- UN 5 **Unify indicators**

UN 3.2 Unify scenarios

Scenarios (also called data categories, data types, or versions) represent different layers of a business model. Typical scenarios are "Actual", "Previous year", "Plan", "Budget", and "Forecast". In special cases benchmarks such as competitor data or market averages are also called scenarios.

Often comparisons and variances between different scenarios are presented to provide business insights.

There are two basic types of scenarios:

Actual scenarios refer to measured data about things that already happened in present or past time periods. These data might not be perfectly correct because of difficulties with systems, unclear definitions, and false data acquisition – but they are as correct as possible. The terms we use most often for scenarios of this type are 'Actual' and 'Previous year'.

Planned scenarios refer to fictitious (not materialized) data. The terms we use most often for scenarios of this type are 'Plan' and 'Budget'.

In-between those two basic scenario types there is a third one:

Forecasted scenarios refer to expected data which are strictly speaking fictitious but already taking into account measured data. A typical example forexpected data is the sales forecast based on the measured order entry. Forecasted scenarios represent a higher level of certainty than scenarios with planned data but are not completely materialized yet. The term we use most often for scenarios of this type is 'Forecast'.

COMMENTS [13]

Actual scenarios: measured data

Scenarios with measured data are identified by a solid dark (e.g. black or dark grey) fill for the areas of the respective visualization elements.

If measured data of recent periods ("Actual") are compared with measured data from earlier periods (e.g. "Previous year", "Previous month", "Month YoY") the areas representing the earlier periods are identified by a lighter solid fill.

The suggested two-letter codes for the most important measured data scenarios are "AC" for "Actual" and "PY" for "Previous Year".

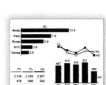

Planned scenarios: fictitious data

Scenarios with fictitious data are identified by bordered (outlined, framed) areas of the respective visualization elements. The areas within these borders literally "fill up when materializing", e.g. when changing from fictitious data to measured data.
The suggested two-letter codes for the two most important fictitious data scenarios are "PL" for "Plan" and "BU" for "Budget".

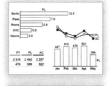

Forecasted scenarios: expected data

Expected data is strictly speaking fictitious, so they are also identified by bordered (outlined, framed) areas. However, as it is based on measured data, the area fill of the respective visualization elements becomes hatched. The color of the dark stripes correspond to the color of measured data (e.g. dark gray).
The suggested two-letter code for the most important expected data scenario is "FC" for "Forecast".

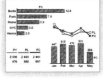

ADD A COMMENT

POST COMMENT

FIGURE 1.5-4

International Business Communication Standards (IBCS). On the platform www.ibcs.com/standards the IBCS Association publishes and discusses proposals for standardized report notation. The free use under the Creative Commons license CC BY-SA enables fast distribution and further joint development, two basic requirements for the creation of de facto standards.

RECAP

Notation standards are mainly based on conventions that can neither be scientifically nor empirically derived. These conventions do not become standards through the definition of a standardization body such as the ISO, but through wide acceptance and adoption.

Today, modern methods using web technology and Creative Commons, like those used by Wikipedia, are available for defining and distributing standards. This is why the non-profit IBCS Association was founded, where executives, accountants, consultants and software developers jointly develop International Business Communication Standards (IBCS) and make them available free of charge under a Creative Commons license at www.ibcs.com/standards.

CHAPTER 2

SIGNS AND THEIR MEANING

WE DEVELOP A VISUAL REPORTING LANGUAGE

SIGNS AND THEIR MEANING

WE DEVELOP
A VISUAL REPORTING LANGUAGE

Clearly, notation standards for reports, presentations and dashboards are needed. A common visual language in which things that are the same look the same and things that are different look different. A standardized notation that helps both report writers and recipients do their jobs better, faster and more cost-effectively.

In developing this visual language, our goal is to understand reports faster through pattern recognition. For this purpose we want—just like with music notes, building plans and maps—to design report objects such as charts and tables so that they simply and quickly reflect the *meaning of* what they present (semantic notation).

In the following sections of this chapter, we work out the relevant aspects of business notation: What is important for quick understanding? What is suitable for standardization at all? Then we make suggestions as to how such a semantic notation might look. First, we discuss those aspects we are sure of—both their relevance and their semantic notation. Most of these have already found their way into the *International Business Communication Standards* and hundreds of companies have already implemented them. Afterwards, we look at some missing aspects and discuss the advantages and disadvantages of possible semantic notations.

CAPTIONS AND LABELS

In the excursus that follows, we want to make the captions and labels within reports more understandable. This includes headings, legends, value descriptions, comments and footnotes, etc. Besides the clear definition and spelling of the terms used, their uniform notation and arrangement help orientate the reader.

TIME

There are hardly any business analyses that don't reference either a point or a period in time. This makes it even more important to make any time reference quickly understood. Clear rules for the design and use of timelines can have a significant benefit here.

SCENARIOS

Business management is frequently about comparing different types of data such as actual and plan figures—we call them scenarios. In this section, we pattern these scenarios to make actual data look different from plan.

VARIANCES

When comparing scenarios we also want to identify variances. We underline the importance of variances with color: Red is bad.

HIGHLIGHTING

Especially in charts and sometimes also in tables we want to see the message of a report confirmed. We achieve this with uniformly designed color highlighting.

TABLES AND THEIR STRUCTURE

So far, we have hardly mentioned tables. But tables also need semantic notation rules that give them a similar appearance. The bold font for totals, already widely used, is one such rule. More to come!

FONT SIZE-BASED LAYOUT

We recognize similar things by their similar appearance: The size may be different, but the proportions must be the same. The chapter on concepts for semantic notation concludes with our recommendation to scale all lengths, widths, areas and distances relative to the selected font size. Only then does the same thing really look the same.

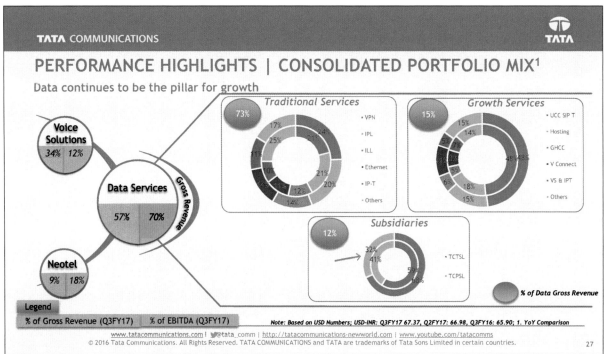

FIGURE 2.1-1

Unintelligible labels. It is difficult to find out what the figures in this report mean. For example, we fail to compare the green 32% with the green 41% in the Subsidiaries block. The measure *Gross Revenue* can be found after a long search in the "Boomerang", and the time periods (Q3FY17 versus Q3FY16) are very small in the footnote. But whether the outer or the inner ring of the chart represents the previous year cannot be determined. Standardized lettering would help. Source: Tata Communications Investor Presentation, January 2017

2.1
CAPTIONS AND LABELS

UNIFORM DESCRIPTION AND COMPREHENSION

We start with a topic that may seem surprising at first glance: It is not graphic elements like line or bar charts and their business significance, but captions and labels, i.e. text elements, because a visual language also includes text elements such as headings, legends, value labels, comments and footnotes. Along with the uniform definition of terms and their abbreviations, the uniform notation of captions and labels also eases orientation.

The practical example in FIGURE 2.1-1 shows it done badly. We will not discuss the unfortunate choice of ring charts here, but focus on the poor captions and labels. As we are missing uniformly structured and exhaustive titles, no one knows what it is all about: Which organizational unit, which measure, which time period and which reference scenario? Let's look at the two ring charts in the subsidiaries block: It's impossible to figure out which of the two ring diagrams represents the current year and which the previous. And as far as legends are concerned, we suggest integrating the data series labels directly into the chart, removing the need for external legends that need color for proper allocation.

Let's discuss these and other topics in further detail.

DEFINITION AND SPELLING OF TERMS

To manage expectations: We consider a globally uniform standard for the definition of terms to be unenforceable in the near future—however desirable it might be. For example, the ISO standards for the notation of currencies (ISO 4217), dates (ISO 8601) and numerical values (ISO 80000-1) are not understood as binding rules but, at best, as well-intentioned proposals. If we limit ourselves to financial accounting terms, IFRS[1] provides us with a comprehensive set of terms, especially regarding the standardization required for XBRL[2]. However, we are not aware of any further internationally accepted glossaries for business metrics in areas such as logistics, sales and production.

Since we cannot fall back on a comprehensive and internationally-accepted catalogue of terms and abbreviations, the only choice remaining is to eliminate this shortcoming within a given organization. It doesn't matter too much how we define the terms and their spelling. It is only important that they are technically correct and their regulated use is both uniform and mandatory throughout the company. With this background in mind, we don't intend to make binding proposals here, but confine ourselves to addressing the issues that need unification.

1 The International Financial Reporting Standards (IFRS) are international accounting standards for companies.

2 The eXtensible Business Reporting Language (XBRL) is an XML-based markup language used to create electronic financial reporting documents.

FIGURE 2.1-2
Designation of business measures.
The variety of terms for what is actually the same thing both creates uncertainty and runs the risk of misunderstandings.

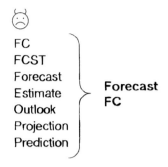

FIGURE 2.1-3
Standardized descriptions of scenarios. Uniform names for terms such as actual, plan and forecast, along with fixed abbreviations are very useful.

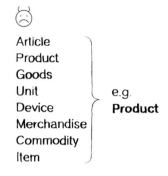

FIGURE 2.1-4
Standardized designations for products. It probably does not make sense to demand that the same terms are used across the different industries.
But we should, at least, speak the same language within an organization.

TECHNICAL TERMS AND THEIR ABBREVIATIONS

The technical terms and abbreviations used in the company belong in a glossary. It's so easy to say, but really hard to do. We are touching on the management of master data and metadata used throughout the entire company. Those responsible for reporting often have limited influence on its design. However, this doesn't change the fact that we must standardize the following terms and their abbreviations in the interest of comprehensible reports:

MEASURES Visualizing a business measure (as we will do in section 2.8) assumes that its definition, spelling (incl. abbreviation) and consistent application is already set in stone. But it's not. Today, for example, a single report can use the abbreviation HR for both Human Resources and Croatia (Hrvatska). The surprising variety of designations, especially for measures, becomes clear in FIGURE 2.1-2. We can easily imagine the chaos of terms that arises when it comes to translation into foreign languages.

SCENARIOS Not only should we strive for a uniform visualization of scenarios such as actual and plan (see section 2.3) but we should also describe them consistently ("FC means forecast"). Consistently used abbreviations are also important because we often cannot use the full word in charts and tables due to space constraints. FIGURE 2.1-3 shows a practical proposal.

Facilicom Group 2017 turnover by country

Netherlands	€ 1,003,236,000
Belgium	€ 188,590,000
United Kingdom	€ 51,130,000
	€ 1,242,956,000

Facilicom Group
Turnover in mEUR
2017

Netherlands	1 003
Belgium	189
United Kingdom	51
	1 243

FIGURE 2.1-5

Number of digits. An overly large number of digits in tables and charts is not only difficult to read, but also gives the illusion of accuracy when none exists. Source: Facilicom Group, Annual Report 2017, page 6

STRUCTURAL HIERARCHIES We also want to standardize the concepts in all other dimensions of analytical interest, such as products, regions, customer groups and corporate divisions. At the lowest hierarchical level of such a dimension, uniformity is inevitable: Imagine a customer has ordered spare part ABC-12a. He or she would be annoyed receiving the spare part ABC-12b instead! It is also helpful to assign unique names and a similar design to higher levels like product groups, customer groups, and distribution channels. Shouldn't it be possible to work with uniformly defined structural terms within our own organization, FIGURE 2.1-4?

NUMBERS, UNITS AND TIME

All aspects concerning numbers, units and time are relatively easy to define. If in doubt, look at the ISO standards 8000-1, 4217 and 8601. There are several parameters that require definition. Here is a non-exhaustive selection:

NUMBER OF DIGITS In which reporting products (e.g. management dashboards), in which objects (e.g. column charts) and in which measure units (e.g. monetary figures) do we use how many digits? For which measure units is it useful to specify the number of decimal places? As an example, we try to limit ourselves to 3 to 4 digits in charts. In tables, 4 to 5 digits are usually sufficient, FIGURE 2.1-5.

FIGURE 2.1-6

Thousand delimiter. Different coutries use different characters to separate the decimal and the thousand. Here is a comparison of entry forms of a German and an American bank. The bank customer is the same in both cases so he has to be very careful.

NUMBER SEPARATORS Which character is the decimal separator and which the thousands separator? For example, do we write 1,234.56 as in the U.S. or 1.234,56 as in Germany? FIGURE 2.1-6 shows the comparison of two e-banking forms where the period and comma are swapped. Incidentally, ISO 80 000 excludes any character other than the small space in between as a thousand delimiter to avoid misunderstandings. Here, we have to make the decision whether to allow regional differences (but then clearly define them) or whether to insist on a company-wide standard. We recommend the latter. Whilst on the subject: We notice how much we have become accustomed to the triple grouping of large numbers when we want to calculate with the Indian numerals Lakh (1.00.000) and Crore (1.00.00.000).

NEGATIVE NUMBERS Does it make sense for us to use not only the minus sign "−89" but also the parenthesis "(89)", as is sometimes the case in financial reports? We recommend using the usual and more space-saving algebraic notation with minus signs. This also makes it easier to align numbers in tables. In the context of the negative numbers, we should also look at the addition and subtraction of measures in a calculation scheme, which we will discuss in more detail in the section on tables (2.6).

MEASURE UNITS How do we abbreviate measure units? For physical units such as kg, km and kWh, we mainly use the International System of Units (SI). But the situation is different for currency units. In practice, different systems exist side by side: Should we write out Euro and Dollar, abbreviate them with three letters (EUR and USD) as ISO 4217 says or represent them as symbols (€ and $)? The currency symbol saves space, but is unsuitable when we are dealing with many and unknown currencies. We can write the currency designation before or after the corresponding number but a company should settle on one way.

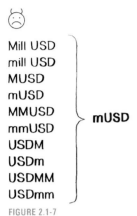

FIGURE 2.1-7

Multipliers. The diverse range of terms found in practice is incomprehensible and often leads to misunderstandings. For example, the abbreviation m or M is used for both thousands and millions (!).

FIGURE 2.1-8

Time specifications. When looking at different countries we also find a great variety in designating time periods.

MULTIPLIERS Values are often given with multipliers such as "thousands" or "millions" to keep the number of digits manageable. Two different scales divide the world: Europe (except for Great Britain) uses the so-called "long scale" with thousands, millions, milliards, billions, while the USA and other countries use the so-called "short scale" with thousands, millions, billions, trillions. However, in predominantly English-speaking international financial circles, the short scale has been established for quite some time. Fortunately, the multipliers in full form are hardly relevant for us, but we have to think about how to abbreviate them—mostly in connection with currency units—in as uniform a way as possible. FIGURE 2.1-7 shows the almost absurd variety of abbreviations used in real life and makes a proposal for standardization.

TIME ASPECTS We write dates in identical looking formats but with different meanings—for example 05/06/18 can mean June 5th 2018 or May 6th 2018. Different notations for the same date do not exactly facilitate a quick understanding—for example "5.6.", "05/06", "05.06" and "06/05" can appear right next to each other for "June 5". The same with months: Isn't it confusing to see different labels for the same period, such as "04/2018", "Apr 2018" or "2018–04"? Binding internal standards are urgently required here, FIGURE 2.1-8.

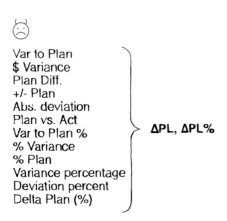

Var to Plan
$ Variance
Plan Diff.
+/- Plan
Abs. deviation
Plan vs. Act
Var to Plan %
% Variance
% Plan
Variance percentage
Deviation percent
Delta Plan (%)

ΔPL, ΔPL%

FIGURE 2.1-9

Variances. The most important variances are the absolute and the percentage variances of the actual values from the planned values. How easy would it be to agree on the abbreviations ΔPL and ΔPL%?

PL	AC	ΔPL
345	601	256
- 6	- 9	-3
123	132	9
145	155	10
- 7	- 9	-2
56	86	30
- 11	- 4	7
178	545	367
823	**1 497**	**674**

PL	AC	ΔPL
345	601	+256
- 6	- 9	-3
123	132	+9
145	155	+10
- 7	- 9	-2
56	86	+30
- 11	- 4	+7
178	545	+367
823	**1 497**	**+674**

FIGURE 2.1-10

Plus sign for positive variances. If it's not just the negative variances receiving a minus sign, but also the positive variances a plus sign, then variances in tables, charts and texts can be distinguished more quickly from the base values.

COMBINATIONS

We often combine scenarios, periods and figures in variance and time series analyses. Designating these combinations uniformly avoids ambiguities and misinterpretations.

VARIANCES Variances are usually calculated between scenarios and we discuss this in further detail in section 2.4. Plan variance, for example, usually refers to the difference between actual values ("AC") and plan values ("PL") and could be uniformly labelled "ΔPL", FIGURE 2.1-9. The variance in percent from the plan, i.e. ΔPL/PL x 100, would then be "ΔPL%". If, however, it is not clear whether actual values or forecast values

are compared with the plan, then it is better to write out the difference: "AC-PL" or "FC-PL".

We also recommend a uniform notation for the numbers representing variances: Just as negative variances are preceded by a "–" sign, positive variances get a "+" before the number to make them immediately recognizable as variances, FIGURE 2.1-10.

Jan..Apr	4 individual months from January through April
.Jan	Begin of January
Jan.	End of January
Ø2019	Average of the periods of 2019 (generally months)

_Apr	Accumulation of the 4 months January through April (Year to date, YTD)
Apr_	Accumulation of the 9 months April through December (Year to go, YTG)
Apr_Jun	Accumulation of the 3 months April through June (E.g. when fiscal year is not calendar year)
~Apr	Accumulation of the 12 months May previous year through April actual year (Moving annual total, MAT)

FIGURE 2.1-11

Time relationships. The abbreviations proposed here are already being used successfully by some companies, but not yet widely. Fairly popular is the proposal to use the simple "_Apr" instead of "Jan to Apr cumulated" or "Apr YTD".

TIME RELATIONSHIPS If the four months from January to April are shown, our recommendation for labelling is "Jan..Apr" (with two points, as three points implies an omission) and not "Jan-Apr", possibly misunderstood as a difference or variance. For the addition of period values (accumulation, "Year To Date" YTD) we recommend "_Apr". It's shorter than "Apr YTD" and it also lets us define "Apr_" as "Year To Go" (YTG). A point before or after the name of a period labels the start and end values (".Apr" or "Apr."). FIGURE 2.1-11 suggests some abbreviations for such time relationships useful for practical work. Find details on the presentation of temporal developments in Section 2.2.

CONSISTENT APPLICATION

To state the obvious: Establishing a uniform definition and spelling of all business measures, scenarios, structural hierarchies, numbers, units and time data in a glossary is a mammoth task. But as is often the case, enforcing the consistent use of an existing glossary is even more difficult.

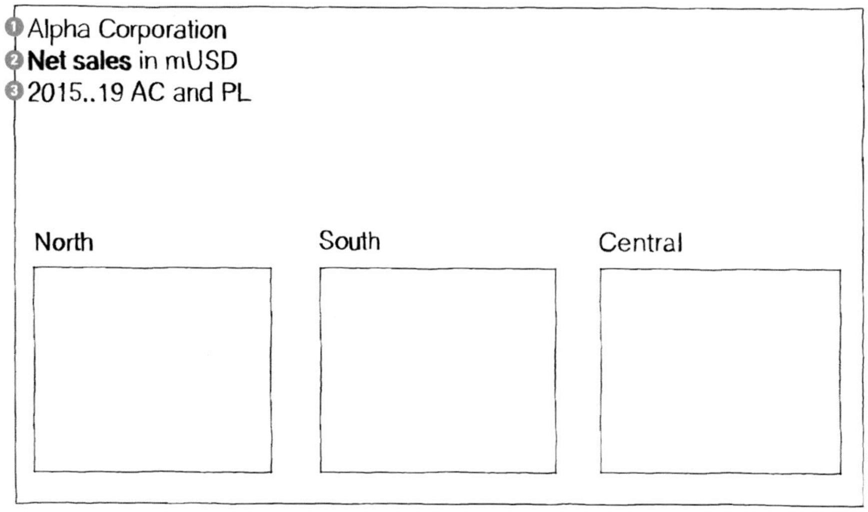

❶ Alpha Corporation
❷ **Net sales** in mUSD
❸ 2015..19 AC and PL

North   South   Central

FIGURE 2.1-12
Page title and subtitle. In this example, the page title is at the top left with the rows:

❶ reporting entity,
❷ measure and unit, and
❸ time reference and scenarios.
The three subtitles refer to the objects on this page, such as charts or tables, for the three regions.

TYPES OF CAPTIONS AND LABELS

We use the above standardized terms in captions and labels of all kinds, such as titles, legends, axis labels and footnotes as well as messages and comments. They should help us express ourselves clearly and unambiguously in charts, tables and on whole screen and paper pages.

TITLE

Some captions serve only to identify the content of a chart, a table or an entire report page. They do not contain any explanations, recommendations or similar statements. Let's call them "titles".

Other disciplines also use titles in this sense: Musicians classify a sheet of music with a few identifying details (computer scientists would call them metadata): What is the name of the piece? Who composed it? Who arranged it if not the composer? Which instrument are the notes for? The latter is indispensable if 60 orchestral musicians are to play different parts of the same piece in a concert.

Fortunately, musicians have also standardized this aspect of their notation: The name of the piece stands centered at the top of each sheet of music. The composer is always to the right, the arranger below the composer. And, if necessary, the intended instrument is on the left side. Always. All over the world and with music of any style.

Engineers and architects are also familiar with such titles in their drawings: They call it a title block and they have even developed a standard for it.

Instead of looking enviously at other disciplines, we should consider how to improve the situation in business reporting. How can we avoid having to search every report, every presentation page, every chart and every table anew for the issue at hand? What can we do, if the descriptions of what we are seeing are wildly distributed and incomplete, such as on the presentation slide shown in FIGURE 2.1-1 (PAGE 54)?

Let's start with titles of full pages: First we agree on its position (e.g. top left) and line spacing, using the same font size as in the rest of the report, see Section 2.7.

Now we have to decide which information is relevant for identifying the page content and how we want to arrange it. Experience has shown that the following three lines are sufficient:

1. REPORTING ENTITY   Which organizational unit (e.g. company, department, cost center) or project are we looking at? If necessary, we also specify further structural information such as region, product area or distribution channel.

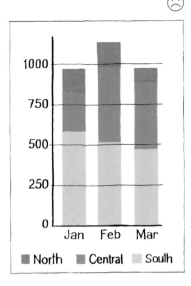

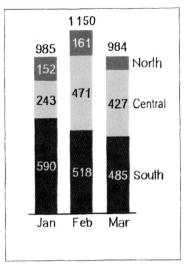

FIGURE 2.1-13
Legends. Integrated legends are easier to read and do not "waste" colors that should be used for more important notation tasks, such as highlighting.
Replacing the y-axis with integrated numerical values also makes it easier to understand.

2. BUSINESS MEASURE Are we looking at headcount, manufacturing costs or sales figures? This information is so critical, we're writing it in bold. This includes the respective unit such as EUR or t (tons) and, if applicable, a multiplier such as k for thousands or m for millions.

3. TIME REFERENCE AND SCENARIOS Without knowing for which date or time period the numbers are valid, charts and tables are worthless. Sometimes it is helpful for understanding to specify the scenarios such as actual or plan and the subsequent variances.

If a report or dashboard page comprises several charts or tables, we mention the references that apply to all objects—for example "Alpha Corporation, Net sales in mUSD, 2015..19 AC and PL"—in the page title. The object-specific additions (and only these) can be found in the sub-titles of the individual objects—for example "North", "South" and "Central" FIGURE 2.1-12.

LEGENDS AND VALUE LABELS

Besides titles and messages, terms defined in our glossary also label data series and chart axes (legends). We also need a consistent way for showing value labels, i.e. the numbers represented by the size of columns, bars, areas or distances.

Legends and value labels are both positioned as close as possible to the corresponding visual elements to avoid "eye ping pong" for the reader. Let's compare the two charts in FIGURE 2.1-13: The left chart, which many software packages generate automatically, requires the eye to bounce not only from the legend at the bottom back up, but also continually over to the values on the left. To interpret the middle of the stacked column on the right, the reader must first note the color, find said color in the legend, remember its meaning and then return to the original object—and then come the number values. Estimating corresponding values of the upper and lower edges of the segment by means of the line grid, the reader then subtracts the lower value from the upper one to approximate the figure represented by the segment. Only now can the eye rest. That's complicated!

In the chart on the right it's different: The legend of the segment stands directly to the right and the segment itself contains the value. Search completed.

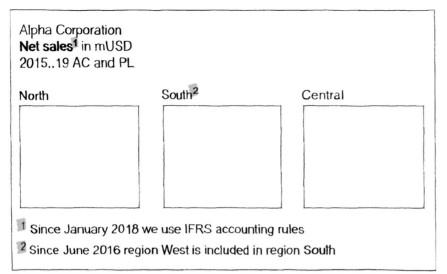

Alpha Corporation
Net sales[1] in mUSD
2015..19 AC and PL

North South[2] Central

[1] Since January 2018 we use IFRS accounting rules
[2] Since June 2016 region West is included in region South

FIGURE 2.1-14
Footnotes. Comments on texts such as definitions, references and explanations are put into footnotes to make the chart easier to read.

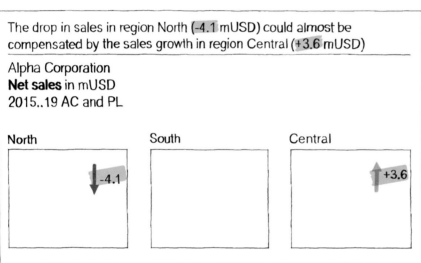

The drop in sales in region North (-4.1 mUSD) could almost be compensated by the sales growth in region Central (+3.6 mUSD)

Alpha Corporation
Net sales in mUSD
2015..19 AC and PL

North South Central

-4.1 +3.6

FIGURE 2.1-15
Messages. By articulating what the reporters have to say, messages—usually at the top of a page—turn a "data collection" or "statistic" into a real "report". The page content explains or proves this message. It is helpful if this is made clear by means of appropriate highlighting (Section 2.5).

We would like to mention in passing that with external legends we also "waste" the powerful stylistic device of color on labeling data series. Additionally, using colors for legends inevitably leads to colors having different meanings in each chart: For instance, in the first chart blue can stand for France, in the second chart for the food product group and in the third for an indirect distribution channel. This fundamentally contradicts our demand for consistency.

FOOTNOTES

Footnotes make texts more readable by "relocating" comments or source references. Since they are less important for comprehension, we usually put them at the bottom of the page. Regarding notation, we have two demands: First, footnotes—like all other text objects—are formatted and positioned uniformly; second, they refer to the relevant text passage using annotation numbers, FIGURE 2.1-14.

MESSAGES

Messages—in contrast to the purely identifying titles and footnotes—make statements about the content presented. They can, at the very least, state a fact, but they can also evaluate, explain, warn of the consequences or even contain a corresponding recommendation. Examples are "In 2018, we were able to improve earnings year-on-year in 4 out of 5 regions" or "We should continue to invest in B to maintain our cost advantage". We know this from journalism: The headlines of editorial articles contain the message.

Messages should be whole sentences to avoid ambiguity; missing verbs are a common shortcoming. As with all text elements, we also recommend defining the position and typography of messages uniformly. With an A4 page in portrait format, we would position the message above the title—like a newspaper article. With dashboards in landscape format (aspect ratio 16:9 or even wider) we can also consider placing the message to the right of the title. Again, the important take away here: There should be rules and they should be followed consistently, FIGURE 2.1-15.

However, not every chart or table serves to reinforce an explicitly formulated message. If they only serve to analyze a situation prior to the formulation of messages, then we omit the corresponding text object. However, we would then be reluctant to speak of a "report", because nothing is actually being reported. The terms "statistics" or "data collection" would probably be more appropriate.

	PY	PL	AC
Switzerland	5 078	5 611	5 509 (1)
France	531	529	484
Poland	1 290 (2)	1 488	1 354
Austria	3 124	2 815	2 850
Denmark	816	818	854
Sweden	809	722	764
Netherlands	604	582	678
Others	5 602 (3)	6 022	5 441
Europe	**17 854**	**18 587**	**17 934**

(1) **Switzerland:** FL data are included for the first time (AC: 256)

(2) **Poland:** PY does not include our new affiliate in Warsaw (AC: 77)

(3) **Others:** PY we were not yet present in Spain and Portugal (AC Spain: 122, AC Portugal: 34)

FIGURE 2.1-16
Comments. We number our comments and assign them to the appropriate places in the report. A term written in bold at the beginning of each comment facilitates an overview.

COMMENTS

Comments are the little brothers and sisters of messages. Similar to messages, comments do not identify the content, but interpret it. They, too, only emerge within an editorial process following the analysis of a situation.

Written comments never pop up on presentation slides because they would be redundant to the spoken word and would distract the listener's attention. For written reports, on the other hand, comments are extremely helpful for understanding. They replace the spoken word of the presenter.

For comments, we recommend not only a uniform typography but also a uniform structure: Every topic gets its own paragraph beginning with a bold term that characterizes its content. This way the report recipient can selectively read those comments corresponding with interest. It is essential that the comments refer to the relevant places in charts and tables by means of connectors. This is the only way to see immediately where comments are placed and to what they refer, FIGURE 2.1-16.

RECAP

The visual language is supplemented by the written language. The uniform notation of titles, legends, axis labels, footnotes, messages and comments helps with orientation and improves the readability of a report or dashboard. In addition to the standardization of the position, format and content structure of captions and labels, the consistent definition and spelling of all relevant terms and their abbreviations also increases understanding. This includes numbers, units, time data, measures, scenarios and the elements of structural hierarchies.

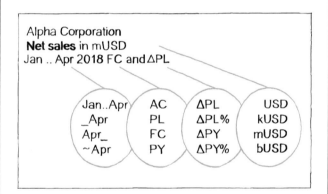

Year:	Cumulative impact Group £m	Year-on-year impact Group £m	UK £m	Spain £m
30 April 2013	5.3	5.3	5.3	–
30 April 2014	4.3	(1.0)	(1.0)	–
30 April 2015	15.7	11.4	8.4	3.0
30 April 2016	12.0	(3.7)	(5.9)	2.2
30 April 2017	6.3	(5.7)	(4.1)	(1.6)
30 April 2018*	2.1	(4.2)	(2.7)	(1.5)
30 April 2019*	–	(2.1)	–	(2.1)

	Group 2017 £000	Group 2016 £000
Operating profit	81,482	90,563
Add back:		
Restructuring costs	2,189	1,777
Intangible amortisation	1,830	1,979
Spain tax settlement	(896)	–
Underlying operating profit	84,605	94,319

	Salary as at 1 May 2016	Salary as at 1 May 2017	Increase
Chairman	£163,200	£163,200	0%
Base fee	£55,000	£55,000	0%
Senior Independent Director	£10,000	£10,000	0%
Audit Committee Chairman	£10,000	£10,000	0%
Remuneration Committee Chairman	£10,000	£10,000	0%

FIGURE 2.2-1

Different time directions. Three tables from the same annual report—with three different directions of time. Source: Northgate plc Annual Report and Accounts 2017

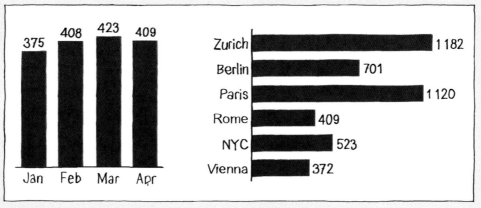

FIGURE 2.2-2

FIGURE 2.2-2
Time development and structural analysis. We draw the category axis horizontally for developments over time and vertically for structural analyses.

2.2
TIME

YESTERDAY IS TO THE LEFT OF TODAY

Every report, every business analysis indicates when it was created and for which period or point in time it applies. Often we also compare facts over time, which usually leads to revealing insights. Without a time reference, nothing really works in financial planning and analysis. If time is always so important, then the need to standardize its notation is obvious. It is less about the visual identification of concrete points in time such as "April 30, 2019 at midnight" or certain periods such as "April 2019". We give them a uniform name and that's it (see Section 2.1.). Here, however, we are primarily concerned with recognizing visually if chronology is our concern and what granularity the periods have. The poor example opening this section, FIGURE 2.2-1, shows that report writers aren't even sure in which direction time should go: left to right, right to left, top to bottom—or maybe bottom to top?

TIME SERIES
VERSUS STRUCTURE COMPARISONS

Even without an explicit rule, people rarely design a chart with a vertical time axis. Time axes usually run horizontally, probably because we write horizontally, FIGURE 2.2-2, LEFT. In tables, too, the categories months, quarters and years tend to be presented in columns rather than rows. But not always.

Conversely, structural dimensions with categories such as products, regions and cost centers are often displayed in a vertical direction in both charts and tables. A chart that arranges articles or locations in the form of bars one below the other along a vertical axis would be a typical representative of a structural chart, FIGURE 2.2-2, RIGHT. That has two advantages: First, names for the structural elements tend to be relatively long and—when written horizontally—don't

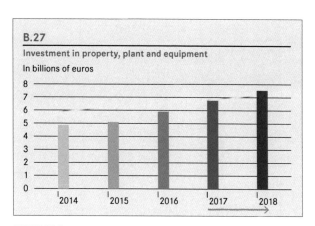

B.27
Investment in property, plant and equipment
In billions of euros

FIGURE 2.2-3

Different time directions. It is incomprehensible that in a report— here even on the same page and on the same topic—time is represented in different directions. Source: Daimler Annual Report 2017, page 111

B.28
Investment in property, plant and equipment by division

In millions of euros	2018	2017	18/17 % change
Daimler Group	7,534	6,744	+12
in % of revenue	4.5	4.1	
Mercedes-Benz Cars	5,684	4,843	+17
in % of revenue	6.1	5.1	
Daimler Trucks	1,105	1,028	+7
in % of revenue	2.9	2.9	
Mercedes-Benz Vans	468	710	-34
in % of revenue	3.4	5.4	
Daimler Buses	144	94	+53
in % of revenue	3.2	2.1	
Daimler Financial Services	64	43	+49
in % of revenue	0.2	0.2	

fit either on the x-axis of a chart or in the column headers of a table. And writing vertically is not a good idea because it's less legible. Second, we frequently want to sort structural elements and the vertical sorting of bars in charts and rows in tables is much more familiar than a horizontal ranking.

So if there is a relatively high probability that time series are displayed horizontally and structural comparisons vertically, why not make it a binding rule? That would have the undisputed advantage of letting us rely on our immediate visual perception: Charts with a vertical category axis[1] always show structure comparisons. Charts with a horizontal axis show time series—with a few exceptions[2]. Here we use the visual variable "orientation"[3] to communicate unambiguously the purpose of the analysis.

Despite all the enthusiasm for the simple rule of showing time series horizontally and structure comparisons vertically, we would like to mention that there are also some charts and tables showing neither time series nor structural comparisons (e.g. charts with two value axes or cross tables). However, analyses by time and structure are by far the most frequent in both internal and external business reports—probably accounting for more than 90 percent.

---

1   By category axes we mean all axes that are not value axes, i.e. have no metric scales we can calculate with. These are axes with nominal scales (without natural order, for example products) and ordinal scales (with natural order, for example months).

2   Statistical distribution curves are also represented with a horizontal category axis, as they are based on an ordinal scale similar to time series and it is obviously easier for us to analyze horizontal curves.

3   See page 25 for definition and discussion of visual variables.

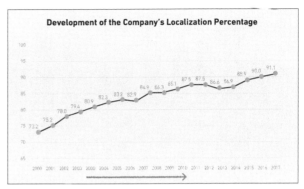

FIGURE 2.2-4

Time direction and writing direction. In the left chart (Arabic report version), the time runs in the same direction as the writing, from right to left. In the right chart (English report version), the same chart runs from left to right. However, there are also charts and tables in the Arabic version where time runs from left to right.

Source: Saudi Electricity Company. Annual Report 2007, page 47

TIME DIRECTION

Now we could think, with "time axis horizontal" everything is regulated. But it's not: Time has a direction, and we mostly show its course from left to right. But in practice there are also cases where time runs from right to left. Where's that coming from? Frequently these are analyses of auditors for whom figures of the current year are naturally more important than the previous. In many annual financial statements, the previous year's figures are therefore to the right of the current year's figures. There is nothing wrong with that either. It makes sense. This practice only becomes questionable if in the same report, sometimes even on the same page, time runs in different directions, FIGURE 2.2-3[4]. Conclusion: A binding rule on time direction would be helpful.

Before we formulate this rule, we take a look at other linguistic and cultural areas, because our standard should also be applicable there. Of particular interest are those regions where the reading direction is not from left to right, but, as in Arabic and Hebrew, primarily from right to left FIGURE 2.2-4. In Chinese, Japanese and Korean there are both the old spelling from top to bottom and today's spelling from left to right. However, it seems that even in these countries there is no fixed rule for the direction of the time axis in a chart. So nothing prevents such a rule from being set up: We consistently display time from left to right—both in charts and in tables. Always. Then we can be just as sure as we are about the orientation in maps: North is up[5]—the future is right.

4   There is a German article in the Frankfurter Allgemeine Zeitung of June 6th 2017 with the title: "Lateinisch, arabisch oder wie der Ochs pflügt". This article addresses statistical surveys on the sequence of periods in annual reports.

5   For the historical development of the rule "North is up" on maps, see page 20.

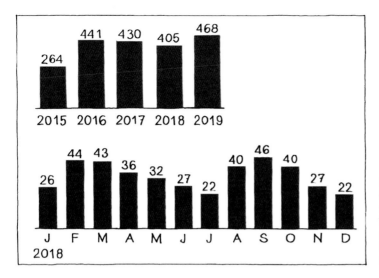

FIGURE 2.2-5
Category width in months and years. The width of the categories on the x-axis indicates the period type: Years are wider than quarters, quarters are wider than months, and so on. This distinction is particularly important because we can rarely use the same scales for months and years.

PERIOD LENGTHS

In business reporting, we usually look at time periods from the calendar, such as months, quarters and years. The recording and presentation of other periods such as the interval from January 17th to April 30th are the rare exception, which only occurs—if at all—in project reports. Even if the information relates to a specific closing date, such as the account balance, we are happy to assign it to the end of a period and then speak of the account balance of that period.

If period types like days, weeks, months, quarters, and years form the basic time grid of our reporting system, then it would be desirable to distinguish these period types from one another visually. Why is this so important? Invariably we won't be able to scale charts with different period types in the same way, and we do not want different things to look the same… The obvious suggestion is to subdivide the x-axis into wider segments (categories) for longer period types (years) and into narrower ones for shorter periods (months). Not strictly proportionally, a year shouldn't be twelve times wider than a month—but, still, wider, FIGURE 2.2-5.

In principle, it would be desirable to assign defined category widths to the different period types in order to best support the recognition effect. This is not a problem with static reports: In an annual report, for example, we would draw the monthly segments with an equal width throughout, the quarters would be slightly wider, and the years wider still. The same would be desirable for all the slides of a presentation.

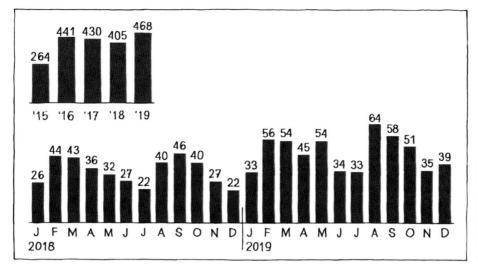

FIGURE 2.2-6

Months and years for interactive analyses. As a result of the interactively selected double period number compared to FIGURE 2.2-5, all categories must be made narrower so that the width ratio of months and years remains the same.

It's harder to implement fixed category widths for period types in dynamic and interactive analyses as it contradicts the desire for flexibility in the analysis. For example, switching the analysis from years to months would lead to presentation problems with fixed widths: Either the chart becomes wider which would mess up the entire report layout, or it needs scroll bars to encompass all the time periods. Neither would be good. In addition, there are problems when displaying a report on different devices with different screen sizes and resolutions (responsive design). That is why we need to compromise on dynamic and interactive reports: For example, when displaying both months and years on a single screen, the x-axis segments representing years should be proportionally wider than those for months, but not with a pre-defined default width[1]. Thus, we only show relative width differences, FIGURE 2.2-6.

Dynamically defined category widths for period types should be valid for an entire screen, i.e. for all charts that are displayed simultaneously. If we increase the number of periods in one chart, which requires narrower categories, this must also result in narrower categories in the other charts on the same page. The situation is similar to the requirement of uniform scaling of the same measuring units on a single screen.

---

1   Caution: When switching from months to years, it's not initially the columns that are drawn wider, but the axis segments (categories). This leads indirectly to wider columns due to the predefined ratio of column width/category width.

RECAP

The time aspect is of central importance in reporting. Not only because of the temporal reference of the information but, above all, because we gain interesting insights from the analysis of developments over time. For this reason, we established three semantic rules for the presentation of time series and the period pattern they are based on:

1. HORIZONTAL TIME AXIS We always display time series as columns, lines or areas on a horizontal axis; structure comparisons always as bars on a vertical axis.

2. TIME RUNS FROM LEFT TO RIGHT Independent of the language and cultural area, we consistently arrange later periods and points in time to the right of earlier ones.

3. WIDER SEGMENTS FOR LONGER PERIODS In order to distinguish annual values visually from monthly values, we display annual values on wider segments of the time axis than monthly values.

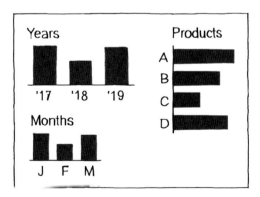

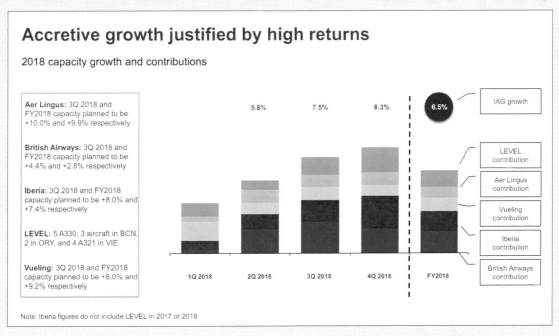

FIGURE 2.3-1
Actual and plan data look the same. All the columns look the same, although the first two represent actual data and the following three plan data. But this isn't clear until after reading the comments. Source: IAG International Airlines Group results presentation quarter two 2018, page 17

2.3
SCENARIOS
DIFFERENT PATTERNS FOR ACTUAL AND PLAN

Analyzing and visualizing business data relies heavily on comparisons: comparing costs and benefits, the figures of several countries, the development over time, or a data constellation—we call it a scenario[1]—with a reference. It is common to compare actual data with the plan data previously created for this period; for example, to compare the results achieved in a fiscal year with those planned.

Scenarios that have different meanings should also look different. It would make sense, for example, to be able to distinguish immediately between actual and plan data, as is shown in the bar chart in FIGURE 2.3-1—or rather: as is *not* shown. Since all five columns are designed in the same way, the chart does not reveal that the first two quarterly columns show actual data while the following two show plan data. We can only ascertain this from the comments. The same comments also state that the column to the right of the line shows plan data for 2018. This is exactly what we want to avoid. Our goal is to create a notation for actual and plan data that can be understood *without* further explanation.

---

1 Scenarios in this sense are also referred to as data types, data categories, or versions. Unfortunately, no clear definition of the term has yet been established.

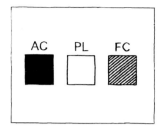

FIGURE 2.3-2

Notation of scenario types.
Actual data (AC) are displayed
"solid", plan data (PL) "outlined"
and forecast data (FC) "partially
solid", i.e. outlined and hatched.

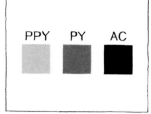

FIGURE 2.3-3

Time scenarios. Previous time
periods such as the previous year
(PY) or the year before the previous year (PPY) are shown lighter
in comparison.

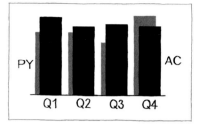

FIGURE 2.3-4

Comparison with the previous year.
The gray reference columns of the previous
year's quarters (PY) are placed slightly to
the left and behind the quarterly columns of
the current year (AC).

CLASSIFICATION OF SCENARIOS INTO TYPES

Scenarios from actual data and scenarios from planning data are fundamentally different: Actual data
has already manifested itself, has been measured
and can be regarded as irreversible. In contrast, plan
data is fictitious, usually invented by someone and
it is unlikely, if not improbable, that all will happen
exactly as planned.

Between actual and plan data, we want to classify a
third scenario type, namely what an extrapolation of
actual data leads us to expect. We often refer to this
data as a *forecast.*

We forecast the annual sales revenue, for example,
by adding the expected values for the remaining
months of the year to the actual values of the past
months. This annual forecast contains both measured and fictitious parts. But even the expected
revenue figures for the remaining months are not
completely fictitious, because they might be based
on existing orders and thus much more reliable than
a pure plan.

VISUAL DIFFERENTIATION OF SCENARIO TYPES

Measured (actual), expected (forecast) and fictitious (plan) data give rise to completely different
expectations on the part of the report recipient. We
propose differentiating the visual representation of
these scenario types.

The basic idea is to visualize measured actual data
with a *solid* fill and to keep fictitious plan data
merely *outlined*. This evokes the association that the
plan still has to be (ful)filled, something easily distinguishable and quite memorable.

The intermediate forecast scenario type is also *outlined* as it is partially fictitious, but, at the same time,
partially filled—not yet solid—since the extrapolation either contains actual data or is based on it. This
is why we show the forecast as partially filled, better:
hatched, FIGURE 2.3-2.

Sometimes the division into actual, forecast and
plan is not sufficient, and it is necessary to distinguish several scenarios of a scenario type. Here is
what we propose:

TIME SCENARIOS

Scenarios can pertain to different time periods; for
example, comparing actual monthly figures with
the prior month or the corresponding month of the
previous year. This comparison is not to be confused
with a time series, rather the earlier period serves
as a reference for the later period. For this reason

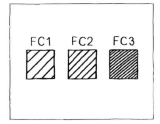

FIGURE 2.3-5

Update scenarios of the forecast scenario type. The more concrete the forecast FC is for a period, the "denser" the hatching will be. FC1 is the first forecast of the year, for example, from the beginning of April for the remaining months of May to December. FC2 is the second forecast of the year, from the beginning of July, FC3 from the beginning of October.

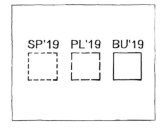

FIGURE 2.3-6

Update scenarios of the plan scenario type. The more concrete the plan is, the "denser" the frame will be: The strategic plan for 2019 (SP'19) was probably drawn up in 2016, the three-year plan (PL'19) in 2017 and the budget for 2019 (BU'19) most recently in October 2018.

we don't show columns and bars representing the reference period *next to* the actual period (as we would do with time series), but slightly offset *behind* it. Different opacity levels distinguish different time scenarios, adhering to the rule "the darker, the later", FIGURE 2.3-3. The application of both of these rules is shown in FIGURE 2.3-4—reference periods behind the actual periods and with a lighter fill.

We use the visual distinction of earlier periods for comparison purposes only. With a pure time series, this distinction would be rather distracting; therefore, in this case all periods have the same opacity.

UPDATE SCENARIOS

Sometimes there is a desire to compare scenarios with different creation dates within a single scenario type. Think of comparing two different plans for the same period; for example, the 2019 budget created in 2018 with the 2019 strategic plan created in 2017. Also, forecasts are often updated several times. Think of the quarterly update of the annual forecast, often referred to as FC1 (in April), FC2 (in July) and FC3 (in October).

We understand update scenarios as "concretizations", meaning we have another sequence to express visually. The obvious suggestion is: "The more concrete, the denser". This means, for example, that the hatching in forecast scenarios becomes denser the closer we get to the (solid) actual data, FIGURES 2.3-5 AND 2.3-6.

While we use the semantic notation of *time scenarios* for comparison purposes only, there may also be a desire to identify *update scenarios* in situations without any comparison. For example, it would be interesting to see whether the plan figures in a report represent the budget or the three-year plan.

VARIANTS AND BENCHMARKS

During planning we often compare several variants of the same plan. Think, for example, of alternative plan variants with and without consideration of a possible trade agreement. We can also represent different action scenarios in such variants: What if we acquire a company, launch a new product line or open a new location?

Sometimes we also use benchmarks as reference scenarios. Think of comparisons with an industry average, a branch average or a main competitor. Normally this is a comparison of actual data. For example, if we want to compare our monthly figures with the industry average, we place the columns for the industry average as a reference scenario overlapped behind the columns for our figures—just as we do with other reference scenarios.

Because of the many different requirements for variants and benchmarks, we don't want to make a proposal for their semantic notation. We would rather recommend developing internal patterns that are appropriate for the respective purpose.

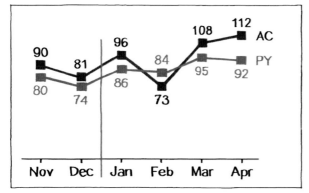

Electronic Inc. **Profit after tax** in kUSD 2018 Countries	PY	PL	AC
Italy	2 316	2 237	2 435
France	479	522	508
Switzerland	779	739	723
Sweden	1 056	930	1 009
Others	889	995	945
Europe	**5 519**	**5 423**	**5 620**

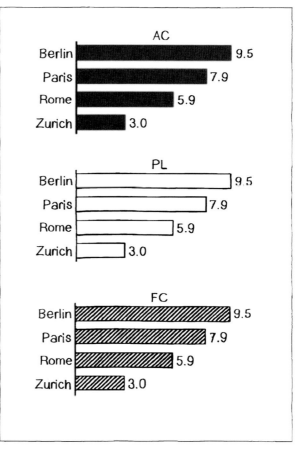

FIGURE 2.3-7
Scenario notation for tables. In this fairly typical table, the lines below the column headers indicate the scenarios for previous year (PY), plan (PL) and actual (AC) figures.

FIGURE 2.3-8
Line chart with scenario notation. Lines and markers are dark for actual (AC) and light for previous year (PY). The vertical line is used here to separate the calendar years.

FIGURE 2.3-9
Bar charts with scenario notation. Actual is displayed solid (AC), plan outlined (PL) and forecast hatched (FC).

APPLICATION OF SCENARIO NOTATION

When applying the semantic notation of scenarios, we must take into account the individual characteristics of the various table and chart types.

TABLES   We generally display time and scenarios in columns. If it is important to distinguish between different scenarios, we display the semantic notation of a scenario in a thick line below the column header, FIGURE 2.3-7.

LINE CHARTS   For scenario comparisons in line charts, the semantic notation can be expressed both by the type of lines and by the marker points, FIGURE 2.3-8.

COLUMN AND BAR CHARTS   For column and bar charts and their variations (e.g. waterfall charts), we suggest providing the areas of columns and bars with the semantic notation, i.e. solid, outlined or hatched, FIGURE 2.3-9.

For all other chart types with points, circles and areas, we must find individual solutions that conform to the proposals presented.

RECAP

Measured (actual), expected (forecast) and fictitious (plan) data are fundamentally different in meaning, so they should look different. For this reason, we suggest that actual data should always be *solid* and planning data *outlined*; the quasi-intermediate forecast data *hatched*.

The application of this semantic notation to charts and tables enables the immediate visual differentiation of these scenario types as well as of individual scenarios if required.

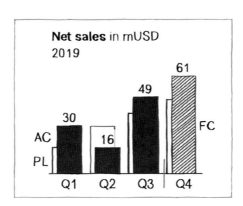

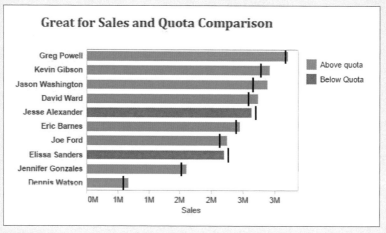

FIGURE 2.4-1

Incorrect visualization of variances. If variances are highlighted, it must be done correctly. Were Mrs. Sanders in this example even one dollar below her quota, her bar would still be completely red. And if she were only one dollar above her quota, her bar would be completely green. It would be more correct to only highlight the variances from the respective quota in red or green, as in our revision on the right.

Source: Tableau Whitepaper "Visual Analysis Best Practices" Page 17 (no date)

2.4
VARIANCES

RED IS BAD

Analysis and reporting are essential tools for controlling business. They support running a company by objectives. And like with control systems in engineering, this control is based on the measured variance between the actual state and a corresponding reference variable. We got to know the states to be compared in the previous section, named them scenarios and provided them with the semantic patterns *solid*, *outlined* and *hatched*.

Now we talk about the notation of *variances* between scenarios. For example, to see where the actual situation differs significantly from the plan, and maybe even *why*. Or to point out which key figures differ from the industry average. The measured variances can be good or bad for the achievement of objectives. Management can use this knowledge to decide on suitable actions. The good news is that a clear variance analysis alone is often sufficient to identify appropriate actions.

The introductory example in FIGURE 2.4-1 shows that even major software vendors make best-practice suggestions that give a false impression: Why color the whole bar to visualize a variance? If we color only the difference to the reference value then we perceive the extent of the variance immediately, FIGURE 2.4-2.

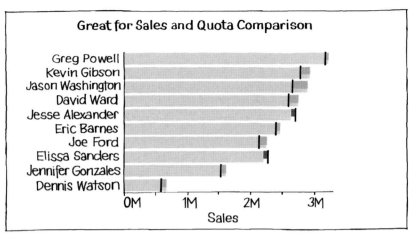

FIGURE 2.4-2

Correct visualization of variances. In contrast to the proposal on the left, only the variances from the respective quota must be red or green. (Which doesn't mean that this chart now fully meets our standards.)

SIGN, COLOR AND DIRECTION

If we want to standardize the visual design of variances, then we must agree on the uniform use of positive and negative signs, colors and the direction of variance columns and bars. At first glance, these three design features look redundant: Wouldn't we always draw negative variances in red and to the left or bottom of the axis? Unfortunately, it is not that simple.

SIGN FOR THE VALUE

The easy thing is the sign: Mathematically a variance is either positive or negative. As already described in the section on labels, we recommend explicitly visualizing positive variances with a plus sign ("+"). This gives the aspect "positive versus negative variances" a certain symmetry (as negative variances also have a sign), and it helps to distinguish variances from the underlying basic measures. A table column containing numbers with plus signs is always a variance column. We will come back to this in Section 2.6 on tables.

COLOR FOR GOOD OR BAD

Variances and their significance are what we look for in most reports and what we want to focus our attention on. Therefore, when visualizing variances the meaning must be clear: Finally we're going for color. Color is like a strong spice in visual design, effective only when administered with restraint and in small doses.

Let's start with those variances we don't like too much because we haven't achieved our goals. We suggest the color red, which in many places signals a stop or issues a warning. Red variances generally have negative consequences for us; they do not indicate successful action. They are bad.

We are aware that red can also be seen as a beautiful color. In ancient Russian, the words for beautiful and red were identical. And for the Chinese the color red carries a largely positive connotation, being associated with courage, joy and summer. But now that we don't talk ancient Russian and drivers in China also stop at red traffic lights, a strict rule for red variances might find international acceptance after all.

It becomes a little more difficult with good variances. We naturally lean towards the color green, as it is the opposite of red on traffic lights. Even more, green and red are complementary colors. But we should also consider the nine percent of men and a much smaller share of women with red-green visual deficiency who distinguish better between red and blue than between red and green. Even though this is not as serious a problem as stated sometimes, we recommend that interactive analytical systems have specific color palettes for users with color deficiencies.

If we stay with red and green, blue is the best color for highlighting neutral variances. This means, though, that the three main RGB colors are already assigned and not too many other colors remain for other purposes.

The proposal to use green and red for good and bad variances should come as no surprise and be quickly accepted. However, many people don't realize that this now makes any other use of green and red taboo. For example, we can no longer color bars in charts green just because green is our corporate design color, or because we like green, or because Excel assigned it by chance. In charts and tables green only means a good variance. Period. If we cannot rely on the fact that green *always* signals a good variance, we will not benefit from pattern recognition.

INTERACTION OF SIGN AND COLOR

As long as we consider sign and color separately, everything seems logical and comprehensible. But what about their interaction? Unfortunately, the algebraic sign does not let us automatically judge something as good or bad. Positive variances are not indiscriminately good nor negative variances bad across the board. This relates to the different notation of bad measures, which we return to in Section 2.8 (Measures).

If we note costs with a negative sign using the *addition method*, negative cost variances are a bad thing because the absolute costs have increased. If, on the other hand, we use the *calculation method* and present costs with positive figures, negative cost variances are a good thing. The costs have dropped, see the box on the right. As a result, we show the cost increase as –9 according to the addition method, +9 according to the calculation method with an additional sign before the measure indicating that we must deduct this item when calculating the result.

As we can see, the sign of the variance alone doesn't allow us to draw general conclusions about its significance in terms of achieving our goals. It is necessary to point out the effect of the number on our corporate goals with green and red color.

ADDITION METHOD

	PL	AC	ΔPL
Software sales	467	479	+12
Support sales	99	93	-6
Consulting sales	145	164	+19
Sales	**711**	**736**	**+25**
Direct costs	-282	-291	-9
Gross result	**429**	**445**	**+16**

CALCULATION METHOD

	PL	AC	ΔPL
+ Software sales	467	479	+12
+ Support sales	99	93	-6
+ Consulting sales	145	164	+19
= Sales	**711**	**736**	**+25**
− Direct costs	282	291	+9
= Gross result	**429**	**445**	**+16**

ADDITION VS. CALCULATION METHOD   In practice, two different methods are used side by side for the notation of measures with a negative effect ("bad" measures). The first—we call it the **addition method**—shows costs and other bad measures with a negative sign. Accountants like to use this method in tables because they can simply add up the figures from the profit and loss statement in the table on the left. But wouldn't it then be logical to speak of "The costs amount to *minus* 282" and to show negative columns downwards in charts?

We prefer the more common **calculation method** used in corporate planning and management reporting, displayed in the table on the right. Here the calculation is separate from the sign of the number, so that cost values display positively (and the corresponding columns in a chart upwards). However, we must ensure that the calculation is understandable. If it is not clear, we add plus and minus signs before the names of the measures.

	PL	AC		ΔPL	
+ Software sales	467	479	+12		+12
+ Support sales	99	93	-6	-6	
+ Consulting sales	145	164	+19		+19
= **Sales**	**711**	**736**	**+25**		**+25**
- Direct costs	282	291	+9		+9
= **Gross result**	**429**	**445**	**+16**		**+16**

FIGURE 2.4-3

When using the calculation method, cost increases are positive. This means that cost increases point to the right, while revenue declines point to the left—although both are red because both reduce gross profit.

	PL	AC		ΔPL	
Software sales	467	479	+12		+12
Support sales	99	93	-6	-6	
Consulting sales	145	164	+19		+19
Sales	**711**	**736**	**+25**		**+25**
Direct costs	-282	-291	-9	-9	
Gross result	**429**	**445**	**+16**		**+16**

FIGURE 2.4-4

In the addition method, cost increases are negative and point to the left. This seems visually more consistent, but is harder to communicate: "Costs have increased by −9", and the corresponding variance bars "increase" to the left.

DIRECTION FOLLOWS THE VALUE …

Now another aspect comes into play: Which variances do we want to draw upwards for horizontal axes and to the right for vertical axes in charts? The "good greens" or the ones with the plus sign? Essentially, we have no choice: Our charts are based on the Cartesian coordinate system and the axes run from bottom to top and from left to right. In concrete terms this means we have to display positive variances upwards or to the right, negative variances downwards or to the left.

As long as we display simple charts with only one measure this is no problem. Not with sales anyway, and with costs we would follow the visualization of the measure: When choosing our preferred calculation method, we notate cost increases positively and display them upwards or to the right; using the addition method, cost increases would have a negative sign and we would display them downwards or to the left.

It only becomes challenging with bar charts that display several measures simultaneously. Typically, this will involve calculation schemes, such as a profit and loss statement. Following the calculation method, an increase in costs would be positive and the corresponding red bar would have to point to the right. As FIGURE 2.4-3 shows, this has unpleasant consequences: Red revenue bars protrude left, red costs bars right. Conversely, if we apply the addition method, a cost increase is negative and points to the left, FIGURE 2.4-4. This might be formally more consistent—but it is

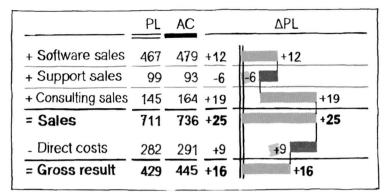

FIGURE 2.4-5
Waterfall for calculation method. When using the calculation method, revenue decreases and cost increases of the waterfall point in the same direction. This makes it visually clear which variance contributes to the total variance of the gross profit and how.

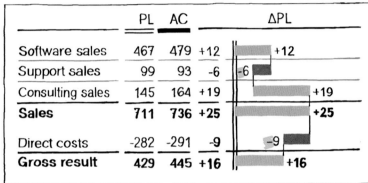

FIGURE 2.4-6
Waterfall for addition method. The waterfall looks the same for the addition method, only the signs of the cost increases are negative.

difficult to interpret the negative cost increase. Who wants to say "Costs have risen by *minus* 9" and refer to a bar that protrudes to the *left*? And from a more abstract view: Isn't it extremely counterproductive for the understanding of a calculation scheme if its visual representation depends on the chosen method for the sign of bad measures? We need to look for another solution.

... EXCEPT FOR WATERFALLS.
Vertical waterfall charts are well suited for the visualization of calculation schemes. They are constructed in such a way that the bars are connected to each other and do not rise in the direction of value, but in the direction of their contribution to a result. With variance waterfalls, a bar that reduces the total variance protrudes from right to left—regardless of its sign.

Let us look at the examples in FIGURES 2.4-5 (calculation method) and 2.4-6 (addition method). In both figures we show the cost increases in red and pointing to the left, because they reduce the total variance of the gross profit. It almost doesn't matter that the sign is a plus in FIGURE 2.4-5 and a minus in FIGURE 2.4-6.

We therefore propose to visualize calculation schemes and their variances as waterfalls.

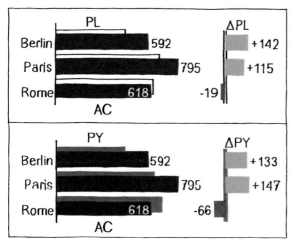

FIGURE 2.4-7

Variances between different scenarios. The upper chart combination shows the base values, actual and plan, on the left. To the right are the absolute variances of the actual values from the planned values (ΔPL). The filled red and green variance bars indicate that these are actual numbers. The variances refer to the respective planned figures, which is indicated by the "outlined" axis. With the lower chart combination, the planned figures are replaced by the previous year's figures—"outlined" becomes "lightly filled", i.e. gray.

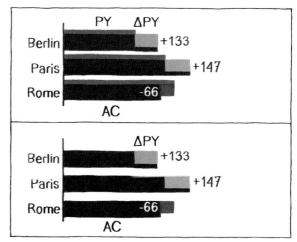

FIGURE 2.4-8

Integrated variances. If the variances are integrated into the base chart, space is saved. However, it is difficult to compare the variances with each other because they do not start at the same zero line. And we have to decide whether to label the base values or the variances. If the reference scenario is also omitted (lower picture), it is no longer visually apparent that the variances are from the previous year.

SCENARIO NOTATION

Typically, we analyze actual data, sometimes forecast data. We have already learned their semantic notation: *solid* and *hatched*. If we combine this with the just-established notation rules for variances, then a positive variance of the actual revenues is a solid green and a positive variance of the forecast revenues a hatched green.

However, what a variance relates to is not yet expressed. Variances always include two scenarios: the scenario to be compared, and whose notation we have just described, and the reference scenario to be compared with. Visually, the variance corresponds to the distance from the end of the variance bar to the axis. So it is obvious we must to provide the axis with the semantic notation of the reference scenario; we call this a "semantic axis". With variances from the previous year, we draw the axis in gray, which corresponds to the scenario notation for previous periods. If there are variances from the plan, we draw an "outlined" axis instead, preferably a double line. Thus, in both cases we see both the scenario being compared and the reference scenario, FIGURE 2.4-7.

Semantic axes are somewhat thicker than regular axes allowing for easy recognition of the reference scenario. Regular bars have to begin at the center of the semantic axis so that they scale correctly, even if some bars are crossing the axis, as in waterfalls.

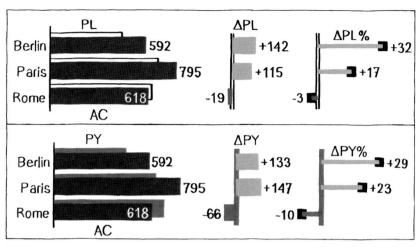

FIGURE 2.4-9

Relative variances. Relative variances are represented as pins. The pinheads identify the scenario to be compared—mostly "solid" for actual or "hatched" for forecast. The reference scenarios can be recognized, as with the absolute variances, by the axis shape—here oulined for plan and gray for previous year.

INTEGRATED VARIANCES

Instead of displaying variances in an additional chart next to or above the corresponding basic data, we can also integrate them directly into the basic chart, FIGURE 2.4-8, UPPER CHART. While it saves space, this makes it harder to compare the individual variances, as they do not start at the same zero line.

We could further simplify the chart by omitting the reference scenario. However, it becomes more difficult to recognize the values of the reference scenario, and no visualization indicates what the reference scenario is FIGURE 2.4-8, LOWER CHART.

RELATIVE VARIANCES

So far, we have considered the notation of absolute variances. Relative variances have a completely different meaning and should consequently look different.

Figuratively, relative variances have lost their volume: 2 percent variances are 2 percent variances—regardless of whether it's a volume of 100 or 100 million Dollars. Therefore, our proposal for the semantic notation of relative variances strips away the volume or, more precisely, the area from the corresponding columns and bars. What remains are red and green pins.

However, the pin shape is too thin to show the scenario notation. We solve this by marking pins with a "pinhead" carrying the semantic notation. We locate this mark behind the pin so that the length of the pin remains clearly visible, FIGURE 2.4-9. The semantic rules are the same: A solid pinhead means that we compare actual data, a hatched pinhead forecast data—mostly to the reference scenarios previous year (gray axis) or plan (outlined axis). Simple, actually.

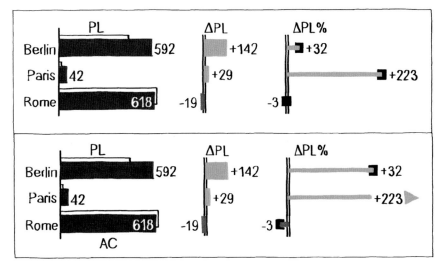

FIGURE 2.4-10
Outliers for relative variances. Large relative variances almost always occur when the reference base is small—large variances from large numbers are quite unlikely. It is therefore inappropriate to scale the other relative variances to this large one, as in the picture above.
The outlier indicator (green triangle in the lower picture) expresses that this pin is "cut off", i.e. not true to scale.

OUTLIER

With relative variances there is an exception to the otherwise strict taboo of cutting columns and bars (see section 2.10 on scales). Think of a relative variance that is very large because the associated reference value is tiny. This large relative variance from a very small value is usually of minor interest and, as it is almost insignificant, it is not appropriate that the smaller—but possibly more important—relative variances from *large* values scale to this larger but unimportant relative variance, becoming almost invisible, FIGURE 2.4-10 ABOVE.

Therefore, in this—and only in this—special case of oversized relative variance, we permit cutting the pin, FIGURE 2.4-10 BELOW. However, we must visualize this fact with a standardized indicator for "outliers". First, we omit the pinhead, because the value being marked is not visible. Instead, the pin grows a small arrowhead indicating that the pin should be much longer. We could even attach several arrowheads to identify different orders of magnitude.

RECAP

The analysis and communication of variances from plan, previous year or other reference scenarios is a central task of business analysts. This is why we use a powerful design tool for the visualization of variances: color. Green for good variances, with respect to our corporate goals, and red for bad ones. We mark algebraic positive variances with the sign "+" to distinguish them from base values. The additional application of scenario notation makes it clear which scenarios are being compared with each other.

While we typically draw absolute variances as columns or bars, we represent relative variances as pins with heads. In the case of large relative variances from small values, we make an exception and permit the cutting of pins, marking them as outliers.

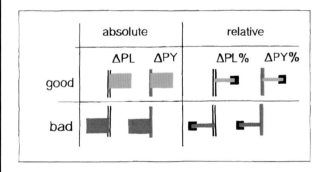

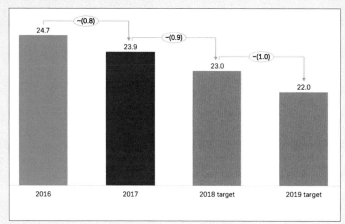

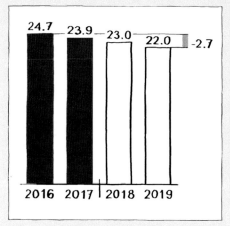

2.5
HIGHLIGHTING
COLORED POINTERS FOR MESSAGES

Compared to the rather demanding section on the semantic notation of variances, a section on highlighting seems almost incommensurate. This is wrong, as this seemingly marginal issue has a significant impact on the speed of understanding the message of a report. The left side of FIGURE 2.5-1 shows a poor real-life example: The lengths of the green arrow do not represent the difference between the corresponding two columns, especially not with the incorrect scaling used. In contrast, we clearly understand the highlighted difference on the right side.

Highlighting emphasizes the most interesting aspects of a report. However, before turning to the "how" of highlighting and then proposing semantic notation for its most important types, we address the interesting "who" and "why" of highlighting.

WHO HIGHLIGHTS AND WHY?

In Section 2.1 on captions and labels, we have already briefly mentioned the two different types of reports: There are reports that have been created to convey a message, such as a statement, warning, explanation or recommendation. And there are reports that do not actually report anything yet, serving analysis purposes only. We should instead call them data collections or statistics. We see the same difference in everyday life: If we want to make a doctor's appointment and ask someone for the phone number, they might do us a favor by looking it up and writing the number on a piece of paper. Alternatively, they could hand over the phone book and ask us to help ourselves. In the first case their "message" answers our question: The note with the phone number is a "report". In the second case, they provide us with a

FIGURE 2.5-1, LEFT PAGE

The clumsy highlighting of differences. So-called "total difference arrows" are not a good solution for highlighting differences because they do not support visual perception. The highlighting of the total variance in the image on the right is a marked improvement—especially when scaled correctly. Source: Deutsche Bank, European Financials Conference, 6.6.2018, page 9, "Adjusted costs in EUR Bn", excerpt

FIGURE 2.5-2

Difference arrow. If a direction can be assigned to the variance—like here the positive development from 2017 to 2018—an arrowhead can be attached to the difference marker. This is not applicable if the differences are very small.

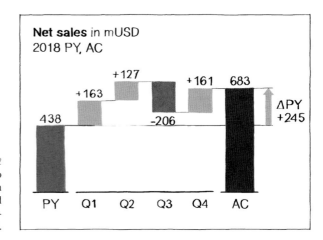

data collection, namely the telephone book, where we have to find the answer ourselves. This is what the providers of reporting software call "Self Service BI"[1].

As a compromise, they could have also given us the telephone book opened to the page with the number highlighted with a marker. "Highlighting", then, seems a creative act, or at least an editorial process, in which we elevate the core of a message to be conveyed over the context. Consequently, we find highlighting mainly in "real" reports conveying a message in a concrete situation.

Most interactive analysis systems, often referred to today as dashboards, have no messages. Just like an electronic phone book, they help us discover messages ourselves. So we would probably not expect highlighting in dashboards. Advocates of applied statistics and artificial intelligence might disagree: Highlighting is not exclusively a manual process performed by an analyst. An electronic system can also generate highlighting to support the search for interesting aspects in a data collection. In such automated highlighting, the "why" of a tag doesn't depend on the message of the reporting party, but on the purpose of the analysis covered by the highlighting algorithm.

[1] BI stands for Business Intelligence, the internationally common umbrella term for analysis and reporting.

NOTATION OF HIGHLIGHTING TYPES

With a standardized notation of highlighting we aim for immediate recognition—ideally with a reference to the type of peculiarity. Differences and trends are most frequently highlighted. In addition, we mark single values in charts and tables that are the subject of the message. This spares the reader time-consuming searches.

And because highlighting is so important for the visual conveyance of messages, it is again appropriate to use one of the strongest visual means: color.

DIFFERENCE MARKERS

We use difference markers to highlight the difference between two values; for example, the increase from the previous year in a column chart. To visually detect the extent of the difference, the length of the marking should correspond to the value. The frequently used "total difference arrow" in FIGURE 2.5-1, whose length, however, does not correspond to the variance, contributes little to visual perception.

Since the differences are usually variances, the same rules apply regarding labeling and coloring: Positive differences receive a plus sign; green stands for a positive, red for a negative and blue for a neutral effect. To emphasize not only the effect (good/bad) but also the direction (increase/decrease) of the change, an arrowhead can mark the difference, FIGURE 2.5-2.

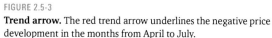

FIGURE 2.5-3

Trend arrow. The red trend arrow underlines the negative price development in the months from April to July.

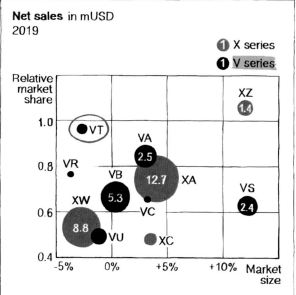

FIGURE 2.5-4

Highlighting of individual values. Positive numbers are framed in green, negative numbers in red. Neutral numbers and general references—here to the product group VT—are framed in blue. Alternatively, a coloured background is also possible—the main thing is a uniform concept.

HIGHLIGHTING OF TRENDS

We use trend arrows to underpin messages regarding a certain development over time. Similar to difference markers, the color of these arrows indicates whether the change has a positive, negative or neutral impact on the set goals. It is important to display the slope of the arrow correctly, because the observer associates the extent and pace of the change with it, FIGURE 2.5-3. Statistical methods such as linear regression can ensure accuracy.

HIGHLIGHTING OF INDIVIDUAL VALUES

The classic example: With a portfolio chart projected behind him, a speaker reports that the relative market share of the VT product group has risen to almost 1.0. Without exception, everyone in the audience will try to find VT in the chart—they are suspicious, after all.

In principle, the means of highlighting doesn't matter as long as we always highlight similar things in the same way. For example, we can highlight the numbers mentioned in the message with the already familiar "neutral" highlighting color blue using a fluorescent marker (or its electronic equivalent). Alternatively, we could draw a blue ellipse around the value, FIGURE 2.5-4.

RECAP

What do we do after extensive analysis? We underline what we have found. What we take for granted
in paper reports is not yet standard with all their
electronic cousins: The message of a report is much
easier to understand if we highlight it. Standardizing
the visual appearance of highlights aids recognition. With colored difference markers, trend arrows,
markings or ellipses we cover the most important
applications.

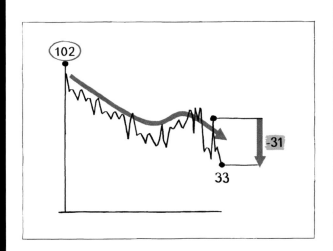

Particulars (Rs. Crs)	Q1 FY19	Q1 FY19 (without effect for Ind AS 115)
Revenue	**93.88**	**98.82**
Other Income	4.12	4.12
Total Income	**98.00**	**102.94**
Construction Expenses / Material Consumed	69.67	72.28
Employee Cost	11.86	11.86
Other Expenses	7.97	7.97
EBITDA	*8.50*	*10.83*
EBIDTA Margin (%)	*9%*	*11%*

GROSS MARGIN (S IN MILLIONS & MARGIN PERCENTAGE)	NON-GAAP without IP	IP	NON-GAAP	STOCK-BASED COMPENSATION (A)	PRODUCT WARRANTY (B)
FY 2015	$2,367	(244)	$2,611	(12)	–
	53.6%	(2.2)	55.8%	(0.3)	–
FY 2016	$2,602	(244)	$2,846	(15)	(20)
	54.8%	(2.0)	56.8%	(0.3)	(0.4)
FY 2017	$3,844	(244)	$4,088	(15)	–
	57.8%	(1.4)	59.2%	(0.2)	–
FY 2018	$5,821	(23)	$5,844	(21)	–
	60.2%	–	60.2%	(0.3)	–

thousand vehicles / € million	2018
Vehicle Sales [3]	5,575
Sales revenue	119,377
Operating profit before Special Items	9,794
% of sales revenue	8.2
Operating profit	8,160
% of sales revenue	6.8
Financial result	813
of which: At-equity result [3]	1,680
of which: Other financial result	-867
Profit before tax	8,972
% Return on sales before tax	7.5
Profit after tax	6,613

NET OPERATING REVENUES	$	**8,245**	$
Cost of goods sold		3,059	
GROSS PROFIT		**5,186**	
Selling, general and administrative expenses		2,505	
Other operating charges		155	
OPERATING INCOME		**2,526**	
Interest income		171	
Interest expense		206	
Equity income (loss) — net		347	
Other income (loss) — net		9	

FIGURE 2.6-1

Table diversity. There is no uniform layout concept for tables.
Source (excerpts), clockwise: Vascon Engineers, Investor Presentation, August 2018;
NVIDIA at GPU Technology Conference Investor Day 2018; Coca-Cola Company,
Quarterly Report Form 10-Q per 29.6.2018; Volkswagen, Half-Yearly Financial Report
vom 1.8.2018

2.6
TABLES AND THEIR STRUCTURE
BOLD SUMS BELOW

Thus far it may seem that semantic notation only applies to business charts. But reports comprise more than charts, they also contain text and tables. We now turn to special semantic notation rules for tables. The compilation of tables in FIGURE 2.6-1 perfectly illustrates the need: Each table looks different. The design of column widths and row heights, fonts, background colors, frames, etc. follows the preferences of the individual table creators and/or the applicable corporate design concept. If we want to understand what a table is all about, we first have to decode its specific formatting. This is time consuming and impedes understanding. The following section shows how to avoid this unnecessary step.

The only reason for a different table layout is different content. Therefore, we first want to format the rows and columns of tables in such a way that the visual appearance reflects the meaning of their content. Then we will examine whether tables would be easier to understand if we arrange sums consistently above or below their summands. This leads us to the

SoftCons International Corp. **Profit and loss statement** in mUSD 2019, PY, PL, AC			AC						
	PY	PL	DE	Of which Berlin	UK	% of Corp.	Other	**Corp.**	ΔPL
+ Software	487	561	243	181	153	27%	164	**560**	-1
+ Support	135	140	53	37	29	22%	49	**131**	-9
+ Consulting	187	199	71	43	48	23%	94	**213**	+14
Of which implementation	56	72	25	12	18	24%	32	75	+3
= **Sales**	**809**	**900**	**367**	**261**	**230**	25%	**307**	**904**	**+4**
- Direct costs	219	221	91	45	57	21%	119	**267**	+46
= **Gross result**	**590**	**679**	**276**	**216**	**173**	27%	**188**	**637**	**-42**
% of sales	73%	75%	75%	83%	75%		61%	70%	-5%
- R&D	111	123	42	17	28	23%	54	**124**	+1
- Sales and administration	32	44	15	10	13	30%	15	**43**	-1
- Other costs	11	9	3	1	2	25%	3	**8**	-1
+ Other income	17	32	17	9	12	22%	26	**55**	+23
= **Operating result**	**453**	**535**	**233**	**197**	**142**	27%	**142**	**517**	**-18**
% of sales	56%	59%	63%	75%	62%		46%	57%	-2%

FIGURE 2.6-2

Sample table. We propose a uniform layout concept for tables. The consistent application of just a few rules ensures that tables look the same.

visualization of hierarchical structures before we finally get into the integration of bar charts and the representation of calculation schemes in tables.

ROWS AND COLUMNS WITH MEANING

How do we recognize the total row in a table? It's usually written in bold. Most report writers at least agree on this point. But why stop here? There are other row and column types that occur frequently. Why not make them look alike too? We have seen this before: Everything that has the same meaning should look the same…

Row types include (but are not limited to) standard rows with base values, totals rows containing sums and other results, header rows for column headers, "of which" rows for non-exhaustive parts of a whole, and share rows showing the figure in percent of another figure (e.g. in % of sales). The same applies to columns.

It's probably impossible to make these five row and column types look the same in all the tables of all the companies worldwide. But uniform formatting within a single company would already reduce the variety of table styles significantly. Readers of tables don't have to contend with other people's personal design preferences anymore, and table writers don't have to bother with styling. A win-win situation.

In order to clarify what we mean by defining a semantic notation for row and column types, we would like to outline the rules we have used for the design of the table in FIGURE 2.6-2. The consistent application of only a few rules ensures that all tables look pretty much the same. Things get even better if we further observe the rules in Section 2.7 on the relationship between font size and layout.

	PY	PL	AC						ΔPL
			DE	Of which Berlin	UK	% of Corp.	Other	Corp.	
SoftCons International Corp. **Profit and loss statement** in mUSD 2019, PY, PL, AC									
+ Software	487	561	243	181	153	27%	164	560	-1
+ Support	135	140	53	37	29	22%	49	131	-9
+ Consulting	187	199	71	43	48	23%	94	213	+14
Of which implementation	56	72	25	12	18	24%	32	75	+3
= **Sales**	**809**	**900**	**367**	**261**	**230**	25%	**307**	**904**	**+4**
- Direct costs	219	221	91	45	57	21%	119	**267**	+46
= **Gross result**	**590**	**679**	**276**	**216**	**173**	27%	**188**	**637**	**-42**
% of sales	*73%*	*75%*	*75%*	*83%*	*75%*		*61%*	*70%*	*-5%*

Left margin labels (top to bottom): Header rows, Standard rows, Of which rows, Totals rows, Share rows

FIGURE 2.6-3

Row types. The five most important row types occurring in practice can be visualized with different formatting.

ROWS

FIGURE 2.6-3 shows the most important row types:

HEADER ROWS We separate the column headers from the rows below by a black or dark gray line. For columns that represent scenarios such as actual or plan, we replace this line with a thick semantic line representing the scenario type (e.g. outlined for plan, see Section 2.3). Multi-level headers are also separated by lines.

STANDARD ROWS Normal rows with base values always have the same height and are separated by very thin, light gray lines.

OF WHICH ROWS We place a row containing non-exhaustive parts of another row (e.g. the additional information for a sales row "of which export") below the corresponding parent row in a slightly smaller font. Above an "of which" row there is no intermediate line to emphasize the affiliation to the parent row.

TOTALS ROWS We display rows with totals or other calculation results in bold below their arguments. A dark line above a totals row clarifies the structure.

SHARE ROWS We display rows with percentage shares (e.g. "in % of sales") in a slightly smaller italic font below the row of absolute values. Again, there is no intermediate line above the row to emphasize the affiliation to the parent row.

In addition, we clarify the row structure by vertical gaps, which we insert above and below a group of related rows.

SoftCons International Corp. **Profit and loss statement** in mUSD 2019, PY, PL, AC	Standard columns		Of which columns		Share columns		Totals columns		
Header columns					AC				
	PY	PL	DE	Of which Berlin	UK	% of Corp.	Other	**Corp.**	ΔPL
+ Software	487	561	243	181	153	27%	164	**560**	-1
+ Support	135	140	53	37	29	22%	49	**131**	-9
+ Consulting	187	199	71	43	48	23%	94	**213**	+14
Of which implementation	56	72	25	12	18	24%	32	75	+3
= **Sales**	**809**	**900**	**367**	261	**230**	25%	**307**	**904**	**+4**
- Direct costs	219	221	91	45	57	21%	119	**267**	+46
= **Gross result**	**590**	**679**	**276**	216	**173**	27%	**188**	**637**	**-42**
% of sales	73%	75%	75%	83%	75%		61%	70%	-5%

FIGURE 2.6-4

Column types. The five most important column types occurring in practice can be visualized with different formatting.

COLUMNS

In FIGURE 2.6-4 we show the most important column types:

HEADER COLUMNS   In most tables there is a column with row headers on the left side of the table. In contrast to the otherwise right-aligned numerical values, here the text is left-aligned. Although it is a kind of heading, the format of this column is not uniform, but determined by the type of the respective row.

STANDARD COLUMNS   Standard columns show base values whose number of digits should not exceed five. The column width is only slightly wider than the longest number, so the column headers are often split or abbreviated. Both the numerical values as well as the headers are right-justified. This allows us to omit vertical lines and get a cleaner table layout.

OF WHICH COLUMNS   We place "of which" columns (e.g. the additional information for a sales column "of which export") to the right of the corresponding parent column in a slightly smaller font. As a result, these columns are narrower than the standard ones.

SHARE COLUMNS   We place columns with percentage shares (e.g. "in % of sales") to the right of the reference column in italics. Again, the font is somewhat smaller, narrowing the column width.

TOTALS COLUMNS   We arrange columns with totals or other calculation results to the right of their arguments and display them in bold.

Additionally, we use horizontal gaps of different widths to support column perception and to group columns.

Trends in the IT Market – Accelerated IT Spending Year Over Year			
Growth in % at constant currencies	2016e	**2017p**	2018p
World			
Total IT	2.0	3.4	3.2
Software	6.5	8.6	8.3
Services	4.1	4.3	4.4
Europe, the Middle East, and Africa (EMEA)			
Total IT	1.7	2.2	2.1
Software	6.3	8.1	7.9
Services	2.8	3.3	3.7
Americas			
Total IT	2.0	3.6	2.9
Software	6.9	8.5	8.2
Services	5.5	5.2	5.1
Asia-Pacific-Japan (APJ)			
Total IT	2.3	4.5	4.7
Software	5.8	9.6	9.8
Services	3.0	3.7	3.7

e = estimate, p = projection

Total Expense for Share-Based Payment		
€ thousands	**2017**	2016
Bill McDermott (CEO)	7,684.4	6,525.3
Robert Enslin	2,181.9	1,185.8
Adaire Fox-Martin (from May 1, 2017)	309.7	-
Michael Kleinemeier	1,509.8	635.2
Bernd Leukert	2,287.4	1,237.2
Jennifer Morgan (from May 1, 2017)	309.7	-
Luka Mucic	2,059.0	1,123.5
Stefan Ries	1,049.3	367.5
Steve Singh (until April 30, 2017)	1,676.5	465.3
Total	**19,067.7**	**11,539.8**

FIGURE 2.6-5

Row totals above or below. We recommend that you generally position the row totals below the arguments. For the readers it is hard to understand when the sum is sometimes added up and sometimes down (here even in the same report).

SUMS AT THE TOP OR BOTTOM?

If it is only about pattern recognition, i.e. the primary goal of semantic notation, then it doesn't really matter whether we arrange sums and other calculation results above or below the rows (or to the left or right when it comes to column sums). Again, the most important thing is consistency. Sometimes this way and sometimes that, as in the two tables shown in FIGURE 2.6-5, makes it hard to understand.

We have to make up our minds: Always up or always down. Both have their advantages and disadvantages. From our daily life we are used to sums being below. We learn this in school: Arithmetic runs from top to bottom corresponding to our reading direction. It's the same with receipts in the supermarket.

Conversely, having the sum above speaks to the idea of seeing the important numbers first and then the associated details. This is especially true if the summands don't fit on one page, only turning the page or scrolling reveals the total. Having the sums above also eliminates the need for subheadings showing hierarchical structures (see next section).

As already seen from the table in FIGURE 2.6-2 (PAGE 95), we clearly favor "totals below". One reason is that we are used to it and habit is particularly important for pattern recognition. The decisive second reason is that it is difficult to put "sums above" in all circumstances. Look at a tabular presentation of a profit and loss statement: Sums and other calculation results above would require the profit to be at the top and the

	€ million
	2017
Turnover	~~53,715~~
Operating profit	8,857
After (charging)/crediting non-underlying items	~~(543)~~
Net finance costs	(877)
Finance income	157
Finance costs	(556)
Pensions and similar obligations	(96)
Net finance cost non-underlying items	(382)
Share of net profit/(loss) of joint ventures and associates	155
Other income/(loss) from non-current investments and associates	18
Profit before taxation	8,153
Taxation	(1,667)
After crediting tax impact of non-underlying items	~~655~~
Net profit	6,486

FIGURE 2.6-6

Different calculation directions. Without a calculator, the calculation process in this table is hardly comprehensible. From "operating profit" to "net profit", the figures are calculated downwards, while "net finance costs" add up upwards. Three elements are not included in the bill at all. Source: Unilever Annual Report and Accounts 2017, page 86, excerpt ("Consolidated Income Statement for the year ended 31 December")

revenues and costs below. This is very unusual. We might be tempted to show at least partial sums above. Like in the *income statement* in FIGURE 2.6-6, where the *net finance costs* are added up upwards while the *net profit* is calculated from top to bottom omitting three positions (!). Pretty confusing.

So the sums of rows at the bottom; the sums of columns to the right. But the problem of long tables with the totals on the following page or below the edge of the screen remains. Well, to begin with, tables over several pages are difficult to read and do not belong in management reports. Our first recommendation would be to create an overview on the first page by grouping rows that belong together into subtotals and displaying only those. Another

recommendation is to sort the rows in descending order according to their significance and group the less important rows that don't fit on the page into an "Others" row. This way the totals are complete and recipients are guided to the important details. If required, the "Others" items can be analyzed more precisely on the next page of a paper report or in the drill-down on the corresponding detail page of a dashboard.

	Q1	Q2	Q3
» Germany	5 078	5 611	5 509
» Switzerland	531	529	484
» Others	1 290	1 488	1 354
› **Europe**	**6 899**	**7 628**	**7 347**
» China	517	609	588
» Australia	2 107	1 925	2 399
» Others	67	87	144
› **Rest of world**	**2 691**	**2 621**	**3 131**
World		**9 590**	**10 249** **10 478**

FIGURE 2.6-7

Indentations. Indenting the row headers clarifies the row hierarchy, but this is only visible in the title column, not the numbers.

	Q1	Q2	Q3
Germany	5 078	5 611	5 509
Switzerland	531	529	484
Others	1 290	1 488	1 354
Europe	**6 899**	**7 628**	**7 347**
China	517	609	588
Australia	2 107	1 925	2 399
Others	67	87	144
Rest of world	**2 691**	**2 621**	**3 131**
World		**9 590**	**10 249** **10 478**

FIGURE 2.6-8

Horizontal gaps. Additional horizontal gaps clarify the hierarchy of the rows, but require a little more vertical space.

HIERARCHICAL STRUCTURES

Consistent rules for the representation of hierarchical structures are helpful for a quick understanding of more sophisticated tables. For this purpose, different design means are available, such as indentations, gaps, font attributes (size, color, style, etc.) and subheadings. The result will always be a combination of these stylistic devices. Again though, the decision should not lie with the individual table writer, but be based on uniform specifications.

Next, we will look at the advantages and disadvantages of the different stylistic devices for the visualization of hierarchies based on table rows.

INDENTATIONS

When indenting, we move the row headers to the right: The deeper the hierarchical level, the greater the indentation, FIGURE 2.6-7. This simple and popular principle has disadvantages:

(1) Indented row headers are less legible than those left-justified.

(2) The space required for the header column increases with the number of indentations.

(3) The indentations are only visible in the row header itself, but not in the columns with the corresponding numbers.

GAPS

If we insert gaps between blocks of related rows, the hierarchy is actually visible in every column, FIGURE 2.6-8. We see the structure particularly well when we omit the horizontal lines above and below the gaps. With gaps, we can legibly present up to three hierarchical

	Q1	Q2	Q3
Germany	5 078	5 611	5 509
Switzerland	531	529	484
Others	1 290	1 488	1 354
Europe	**6 899**	**7 628**	**7 347**
China	517	609	588
Australia	2 107	1 925	2 399
Others	67	87	144
Rest of world	**2 691**	**2 621**	**3 131**
World	**9 590**	**10 249**	**10 478**

FIGURE 2.6-9

Background color. Coloring the background with different shades of gray can also help to express the hierarchy. However, make sure the shading is not too dark, as light writing on a dark background is more difficult to read.

	PY	PL	AC
Overhead costs			
Indirect labor	5 078	5 611	5 509
Social security	531	529	484
Auxiliary materials	1 290	1 488	1 354
Working materials	231	235	238
Office supplies	1 205	1 254	1 314
Third party repairs	629	656	718
Energy	494	446	421
Transport	457	328	410
Depreciation	517	609	588
Interest	231	209	255
Taxes	67	87	144
Others	1 102	996	1 341
Overhead costs	**11 832**	**12 448**	**12 366**

FIGURE 2.6-10

Subheadings. If the totals for tables are arranged below, a subheading above the rows provides the proper context.

levels (base rows, subtotals and grand total), which will suffice for most management reports. If we need to differentiate more levels, we use gaps with the first three and then from the fourth levels onwards deploy indentations, shaded backgrounds or gradations of the font color (see an example on page 203).

TEXT FORMATS

In principle, text formats are suitable for underlining the visual perception of a table structure. We already use a bold font for sums. And we use smaller font sizes and italics as stylistic devices to mark both of which and share rows. However, we must keep the variety of font formats to a minimum, as too many sizes and styles make a table look busy and impair legibility. We fundamentally advise against the use of colored fonts, reserving color for the representation of variances and other highlighting.

BACKGROUND COLORS

Lightly colored backgrounds in different shades of gray can illustrate the structure of a more detailed table, FIGURE 2.6-9. However, since we usually read in bright rooms—both on the screen and on paper—we shouldn't work with light writing on a dark background.

SUBHEADINGS

With our recommendation to put sums at the bottom, we somewhat addressed the issue of subheadings. With the sum below its summands, the reader may miss the hierarchical context higher up. If, for example, overhead costs are totaled from several cost elements, the fact that the rows represent overhead costs only becomes clear when you read the label of the totals row. Adding a subheading before a block of related rows might be helpful, FIGURE 2.6-10.

	Jan	Feb	Mar	Q1	Apr	May	Jun	Q2	H1
Netherlands	507	561	550	**1 618**	243	237	480	**426**	**2 044**
Belgium	531	529	484	**1 544**	423	264	687	**527**	**2 071**
Luxembourg	1 290	1 488	1 354	**4 132**	735	658	1 393	**1 534**	**5 666**
Benelux	**2 328**	**2 578**	**2 388**	**7 294**	**1 401**	**1 159**	**2 560**	**2 487**	**9 781**

FIGURE 2.6-11
Hierarchies in table columns. The design concept for row hierarchies can also be translated to columns.

	PY	AC	ΔPY
Austria	5 078	5 509	+431
Belgium	531	484	-47
France	1 290	1 354	+64
Italy	3 124	2 850	-274
Poland	816	854	+38
Sweden	809	764	-45
Switzerland	604	678	+74
Others	5 602	5 441	-161
Europe	**17 854**	**17 934**	**+80**

FIGURE 2.6-12
Integrated charts. In many spreadsheet applications, visual elements can improve readability.

When mapping hierarchies in table columns, similar considerations apply, FIGURE 2.6-11.

INTEGRATED CHARTS

We can significantly increase the expressiveness of tables if we enrich them with visual elements. In particular, embedding semantically noted variance charts[1] proves extremely useful for drawing the reader's attention to the most significant rows of a table FIGURE 2.6-12. We therefore recommend already including the option of embedding bar charts when defining company-wide table standards.

SIGN AND ARITHMETIC OPERATION

Finally, let's revisit the topic of the addition vs. the calculation method[2], because this leads to considerable uncertainties, contradictions and incomprehension in tables: Are expense figures negative and added in the table (addition method), or are they positive and subtracted in the calculation (calculation method)? We spoke already in favor of the calculation method with the clear recommendation to make it more comprehensible by adding plus and minus signs before the measures. Then even less experienced report readers can better understand tabular calculation schemes.

---

1 See section 2.4 on page 86.

2 See section 2.4 on page 83.

RECAP

Tables are an important and frequently used part of reports. Through the consistent application of company-wide rules for the notation of row and column types, for the positioning of totals and other calculation results (top or bottom) and for the representation of hierarchical structures, all tables end up looking similar. When there is no longer the need to become acquainted with the individual design concepts of various report writers, time is saved and understanding facilitated. The embedding of standardized variance charts additionally supports the reader in concentrating on the essentials.

These are the basic rules for table design:
- A) Numbers and column headers right-justified
- B) Calculation results bold
- C) Calculation results below
- D) Gaps between groups
- E) Thicker lines before calculation results
- F) Gaps instead of vertical lines
- G) Display calculation scheme

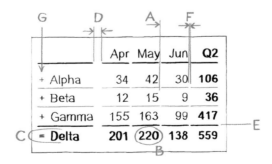

	Apr	May	Jun	Q2
+ Alpha	34	42	30	**106**
+ Beta	12	15	9	**36**
+ Gamma	155	163	99	**417**
= **Delta**	**201**	**220**	**138**	**559**

Group operating result
in mEUR

Net Interest Income
in mEUR

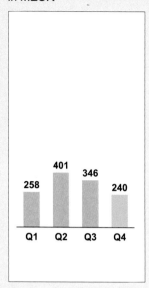

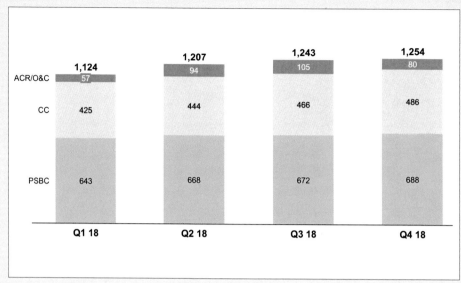

FIGURE 2.7-1

Uneven proportions. Perception is thrown off when the ratio of font-size to visual elements—here columns—is out of proportion.
(It is also confusing if the color yellow highlights both the current quarter and a data series.) Source: Commerzbank Analyst conference—Q4 2018 / FY 2018, pages 8 and 9

2.7
FONT SIZE-BASED LAYOUT

FIXED PROPORTIONS

In this section, we'll consider how we can promote pattern recognition using standardized proportions for the layout of report pages along with the chart and table objects they contain, like with sheet music and circuit diagrams. This requires not only uniformly designed visual elements such as lines and rectangles but also certain rules on how to uniformly label these elements and the resulting report objects and how to arrange them on report pages. Again, specific elements of reports should look the same, regardless of their author and the software used. In the negative example in FIGURE 2.7-1, however, not even the labels are proportional to the size of the visual

elements. Not only does this look unattractive, it also makes the comparison more difficult. And isn't easy comparison what visualization is all about? FIGURE 2.7-2 gives a much clearer impression.

FONT SIZE AS THE UNIT OF MEASUREMENT
To standardize our reporting layout, we use the same trick as designers who want to achieve a consistent look and feel for websites: We make all dimensions of the geometric elements and their arrangement in relation to each other dependent on the size of the most frequently used font. In accordance with the

Group operating result
in mEUR

Net Interest Income
in mEUR

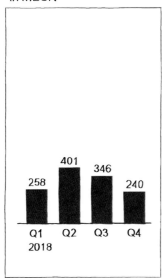

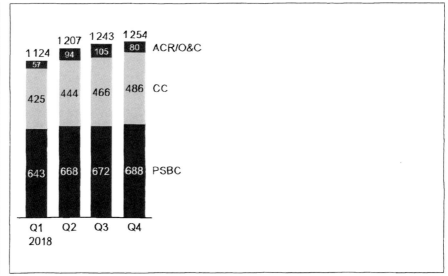

FIGURE 2.7-2
Same proportions. Unlike Figure 2.7-1, here the column widths for the quarters are all the same and proportional to the font-size. (In addition, both charts get the same scale and axis designations).

CSS[1] standard, which is fundamental for the design of websites, we call the size of this font "em". For example, if the main font size is 10 points and we want to show a line of 1 point, we set the line width to 0.1 em.

Incidentally, the size of most fonts does not correspond to the height of the capital letters, but often includes space at the bottom for the descenders of

lowercase letters such as g or p. Sometimes it also reserves space above for accents or letters such as k or h, which—though not immediately visible to laypeople—can extend somewhat higher than the corresponding capital letters.

Different fonts like Arial, Tahoma or Verdana can be "cut" quite differently, i.e. run wider or be higher than others. We don't want to consider this here, as we do not strive for absolute accuracy. A relative orientation to the respective font size is sufficient for our purposes.

---

1   Cascading Style Sheets (CSS) define the layout of web pages. The standards for CSS are defined by the World Wide Web Consortium (W3C).

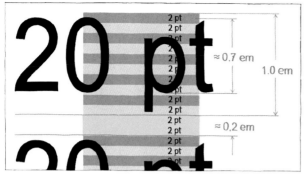

FIGURE 2.7-3

Line spacing and font size. The line spacing for single-line fonts is about 0.2 em. Example: Arial 20 pt (not to scale)

	PL	AC	ΔPL
United States	1 042	1 010	-32
Canada	427	448	+21
Brazil	311	297	-14
Mexico	12	26	+14
Others	77	70	-7
Americas	**1 869**	**1 851**	**-18**

FIGURE 2.7-4

Line spacing for tables. By default, the line spacing for tables is 1.5 em.

It is important for the legibility of texts that there is some space left between the lines. This space— referred to in typography as "leading"—is approximately 0.2 em for normal continuous texts, FIGURE 2.7-3. For tables, a uniform ratio of font size and row spacing is crucial—not only for a pleasant appearance but also for legibility. We use a default row spacing of 1.5 em for tables, FIGURE 2.7-4.

DIMENSIONING OF ELEMENTS

A few geometric elements suffice as "basic equipment" for the design of reporting objects: For tables a few lines and spaces are enough, for charts different rectangles and circles are added. That's all.

Since most reports and their objects are created by using reporting packages, this software should also regulate the uniform dimensioning depending on the font size. The line width of frames, the width of table columns or the size of arrowheads—everything should be expressed and standardized as multiples of the font size em, FIGURE 2.7-5. Such a design detail is often left to the personal taste of report writers or the default settings of different software packages, but this leads to unnecessary variety that demands more time for interpretation.

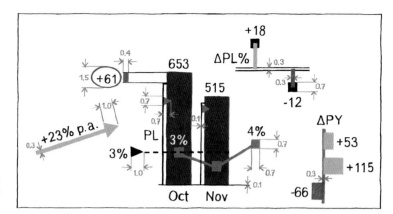

FIGURE 2.7-5

Dimensioning the elements. From the line width of the frames to the size of arrowheads—everything should be expressed as a multiple of the font size em so that a uniform image is created.

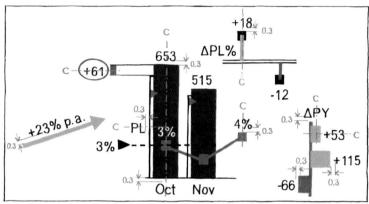

FIGURE 2.7-6

Distance and orientation of the labels. All inscriptions should have the same distance from the inscribed elements; for example 0.3 em. The arrangement is also regulated: C stands for centered.

ARRANGEMENT OF THE ELEMENTS

In addition to the font size-dependent dimensioning of the elements themselves, there should also be a defined relationship between the selected font size and the distance between the elements. This means that all labels have a uniform distance from the respective reference elements and it also means that the geometric elements occupy defined positions relative to each other. Besides the distance of labels, we must also specify their alignment (right-justified, left-justified or centered). Other aspects address the degree of overlap of columns or bars in charts and the row height and column width in tables, FIGURE 2.7-6.

In addition to these general settings, we also have to check the dimensions of the visualization elements such as columns and bars. Of course, the length of these elements is proportional to the represented numerical value. But there are still degrees of freedom in the width of these elements and their arrangement along the category axis, which we talk about later when it comes to the visualization of different business measures. Here's a taste: We make columns and bars of basic measures two-thirds as wide as the category width, while broken ratios are only one-third as wide[1]. And the category width? We have already shown in the section on the semantic notation of time how to distinguish different periods such as months and years by different category widths.[2]

1   See page 122 in section 2.8.

2   See page 72 in section 2.2.

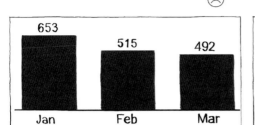
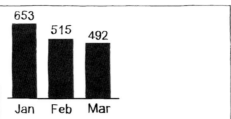

FIGURE 2.7-7
Positioning of objects on a page. The arrangement and size of the objects on a page is not determined by the available space, but by the font size. Nobody would even think of fitting maps to the available space.

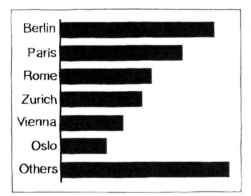
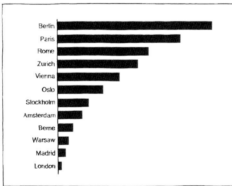

FIGURE 2.7-8
"Others" position or smaller font. If there is not enough space to show all the elements in the selected font-size, we can either create an "Others" element or reduce the font-size.

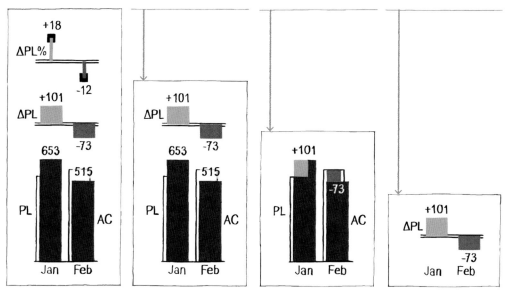

FIGURE 2.7-9

Changing the analysis. If there is not enough space, the analysis may be simplified to convey a similar message.

PAGE LAYOUT

If we as the report writers along with the software we use follow the rules outlined above, our charts and tables will have a uniform design that is easy to understand. But will they also fit into the available space on a (static) report page or a (dynamic) dashboard?

What we *don't* want is to stick with the bad practices inherited from tools like MS-Excel where the space available defines the layout of charts and tables: the more space available, the larger their respective objects—usually with the same font size. The relationship between font size and the size of visual elements constantly changes. This would be like stretching or collapsing a map to fit the space available, FIGURE 2.7-7.

Given a standard font size, we want, for example, that the width of the bars in a chart remains the same regardless of whether we display 3, 6 or 10 bars. This means that the height of the entire bar chart depends on the number of bars, i.e. it is variable. So we are probably left with some white space if we show less bars than the space allocated to the widget might allow. And what if the space available is not sufficient? Either we can sort the bars according to their significance, showing as many bars as we can and fit the rest into an "Others" bar. Or we choose a smaller font size so that the proportions remain the same, FIGURE 2.7-8. A third option is to adapt the type of analysis, e.g. to simplify it, FIGURE 2.7-9.[1]

There are other rules for a uniform page layout, but we won't go into more detail here. It goes without saying that we need defined positions and font sizes for titles, messages, footnotes, etc. Some rules from the corporate design framework might help to achieve a consistent overall impression.

---

[1] We refer to the adaptation of charts and tables to different space situations according to business criteria as *business-responsive design* (see page 164 in Section 3.2).

RECAP

Patterns in reports are much easier to identify if the proportions of the report elements remain constant. Therefore, we suggest standardizing all dimensions and making them dependent on the font size used. This not only ensures that our report objects look similar and is consequently easier to read; we also feel the arrangement to be more "aesthetic". It just looks better.

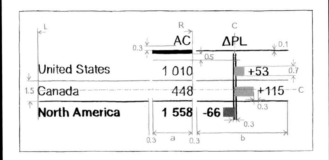

CONCEPTS FOR FURTHER SIGNS

HOW FAR DO WE WANT TO GO?

By applying the concepts of semantic notation described so far, reports, presentations and dashboards become more understandable. However, they cannot yet be fully grasped visually—i.e. they need labeling. For example, sales still look just like costs, products like regions and millions like billions. In this excursus, we want to dedicate ourselves to the semantic notation of these open aspects, knowing that further development and a good deal of persuasion still needs to be done.

MEASURES

Revenue, headcount and quality metrics: everything looks the same in today's reports. We want to succeed in making the meaning of business measures visually recognizable and propose a kind of symbolic language for this purpose.

STRUCTURE DIMENSIONS AND ATTRIBUTES

Due to the diversity and company-specific individuality of structure dimensions such as products and regions as well as their elements (e.g. cars and trucks for products or Canada and France for regions), comprehensive visual standardization is a challenge. Nevertheless, we are putting forward a proposal that would make it possible for a report by product to avoid looking the same as a report by region.

SCALES

We can only compare similar things. But how can we know if the scaling of two charts is really the same? We make a proposal where non-comparable scales look different in order to avoid making false comparisons.

GROUP REVENUE

£10.7bn +0.7%

14/15	10.3
15/16	10.4
16/17	10.6
17/18	**10.7**

Group revenues increased as a result of new Food store openings, offset by a reduction in International revenues as we completed the exit from ten loss-making markets.

GROUP PROFIT BEFORE TAX (PBT) & ADJUSTING ITEMS

£580.9m -5.4%

14/15	661.2
15/16	684.1
16/17	613.8
17/18	**580.9**

Group PBT before adjusting items was down on last year, largely due to the reduction in Food gross margin and the increase in operating costs associated with new space, volume growth and channel shift.

RETURN ON CAPITAL EMPLOYED (ROCE)

14.0%

14/15	14.7
15/16	15.0
16/17	13.7
17/18	**14.0**

The increase in ROCE largely reflects the reduction in the carrying value of property, plant and equipment.

ADJUSTED EARNINGS PER SHARE (EPS)

27.8p -8.6%

14/15	33.1
15/16	34.8
16/17	30.4
17/18	**27.8**

Basic EPS before adjusting items decreased primarily due to the lower adjusted profit generated in the year. The weighted average number of shares in issue during the period was 1,624.0m (last year 1,623.1m).

2.8
MEASURES

KEY FIGURES NEED TO BE RECOGNIZED

We have grown accustomed to not understanding the content of a chart until we have read the labels in and around the chart. And even then, we often still don't understand …. This is because the columns, bars or lines look exactly the same, regardless of whether they represent revenue, group result or return on capital as in the example in FIGURE 2.8-1.

This is not satisfactory at all; it is actually an imposition. Haven't we already shown in Chapter 1 that it makes perfect sense for different things to also look different? The aim of a notation concept must be to visually identify the content of a report, perhaps even understand it, without needing to read detailed descriptions.

Same notation of different measurs. These four charts look the same but they are four completely different measures. As a side note: The time direction from top to bottom is not exactly standard either.
Source: Marks & Spencer Annual Report and Financial Statement 2018, page 11

In this section, we will consider what to do to make a bar chart of employee numbers by department look different from a chart of the cost of those same departments. We first discuss the question of which basic measures, such as revenue and equity, ought to be distinguished from each other in principle. Then we design a concept for their visualization. Finally, we extend this concept from basic measures to ratios such as sales per employee or earnings per capital employed.

CONTENT CLASSIFICATION

At first glance, the requirement that each measure should look different seems unattainable. Financial reporting alone involves many hundreds of basic measures and several dozen ratio figures used in practice. In addition, there is a multitude of functional sales, logistics, production and personnel metrics—to name just a few. And even if we managed to make each key figure look different who could remember all these different visualizations?

To deal with this challenge we don't initially visualize the measure itself, but rather certain classes of measures that are similar in content. We want to proceed according to the Pareto principle: At first we only consider those 20 percent of the measures that cover 80 percent of management reporting.

FINANCIAL MEASURES

Let's start with the income statement, where we can group the measures to three classes:

1. REVENUES   It feels like at least one third of all report content in business revolves around revenues, and in most industries these are sales revenues. When looking at revenues we immediately see the performance of our product portfolio, our sales regions and our distribution channels—a good overview of our activities.

2. COSTS   Different types of costs, such as "wages and salaries" or "marketing costs", make up the lion's share of the items in a profit and loss statement.

3. RESULTS   The classic result items are called "EBIT" or "Net income". However, we also want to include "Gross profit" or various "Contribution margins" in this class.

The situation is similar for the balance sheet items where we also manage with three classes:

4. ASSETS   The balance sheet comprises all the assets of a company. For the time being we don't want to differentiate between fixed and current assets.

5. LIABILITIES   No matter whether short-term or long-term liabilities, we pool the entire debt capital.

6. EQUITY CAPITAL   The equity capital is the result of the balance sheet, the difference between assets and liabilities—the third class of our balance sheet items.

NON-FINANCIAL MEASURES

There is a greater diversity of non-financial measures because they reflect the specific characteristics of each industry. But we want to concentrate on three common classes:

7. OUTPUT QUANTITIES This refers to the number of cars sold by the car dealer as well as the number of operations in the hospital and the kilowatt hours of the energy supplier. For the time being we don't distinguish between production and sales volumes.

8. STOCK QUANTITIES In the case of storable products, these are the stocks. Not in dollars, but in tons, hectoliters or number of units.

9. NUMBER OF EMPLOYEES No matter whether men or women, wage workers or salaried employees, calculated in heads or full-time equivalents (FTE), initially there is no differentiation.

Of course, there are also reports on production capacities and their utilization, market shares, credit lines, lot sizes and much more. Physical metrics such as temperature, pressure and sunshine hours can also be important for certain reports—but they are not typical for management reports. We estimate that the nine classes of measures defined above cover 80 percent of the classic reporting topics.

DESIGN PRINCIPLES

Before we assign colors, patterns or shapes to measures, we have to define the requirements for these visual variables.

SELECTIVITY

The nine classes described should look so different as to make visual confusion impossible. So we need a visual variable that can have at least nine clearly distinguishable characteristics. We say *at least* because we want to be open for more classes in the future.

RESEMBLANCE

As different as the measures may be, familial relationships, as it were, still exist between them. For example, the sales volume is the non-monetary counterpart to the sales revenue. A good visualization would represent this semantic proximity, i.e. it would ensure that service volumes and sales revenues look similar, but not the same.

Resemblance also means that measures with diametrically opposed meanings are visually recognized as such. Costs and revenues, for example, are such a pair of opposites—just like assets and liabilities.

EXPANDABILITY

The visualizations we assign to the nine classes must be expandable in two respects: First, the "breadth" of the nine classes do not cover all measures; for example in sustainability reports, we need additional functional and physical measures. And second, we must prepare ourselves for the fact that at some point we will want to refine the classes in "depth". Instead of visualizing costs alone, we might want to visually distinguish personnel costs from material costs and further subdivide personnel costs into wages, salaries and ancillary wage costs. It would be awkward if the form of visualization we chose now didn't allow for later refinement.

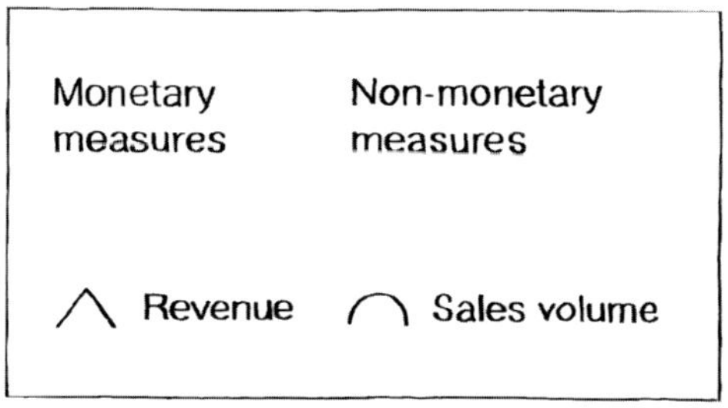

FIGURE 2.8-2
Monetary and non-monetary measures.
The symbols for monetary measures are *square,* the symbols for non-monetary measures are *round.*

IDENTIFICATION BY SYMBOLS

We assume that the application of "primary" visual variables such as shape, color or pattern cannot cover all these requirements. The development of a symbolic language is most likely the only feasible solution for the visualization of measures. We know that the visual impression of symbols is weaker than that of primary visual variables. But only a symbolic language offers the necessary flexibility for later extensions. A carefully chosen symbolic language also does not rule out that certain design features of the symbols can also be applied directly to elements such as columns or line markers.

A particular advantage of symbols is that we can represent the similarity of related or opposite measures by combining the shape, fill level, line width and alignment of the symbols.

In the following, we will examine the properties of measures more closely and make suggestions for their symbolic visualization.

MONETARY AND NON-MONETARY

Each measure has a unit of measurement. It makes sense then to visualize measures with the same units of measurement in a similar way: Monetary figures with the unit "currency" such as net sales would then look different from non-monetary figures such as headcount. And for quantity figures we could later differentiate between pieces, square meters or hectoliters.

At first glance, it looks like percentages form a class of their own. However, percentages only occur in ratios, i.e. quotients such as export share, equity ratio, capacity utilization or index figures. These quotients are dimensionless and usually lie between 0 and 1. In this respect, we regard percent not as a unit of measurement but as a kind of multiplier.

We want that charts with sold cars (in units) differ from those representing the revenue generated by them (in USD). At the same time, suitable semantics should make the close relationship of these two measures clear. We have already decided on a symbolic language and here comes the first rule for the design of the symbols: We show monetary measures in a square form, while non-monetary measures have a round form, FIGURE 2.8-2. Our first concrete suggestion here is to use the symbol $\wedge$ for sales revenue and $\cap$ for sales volume.

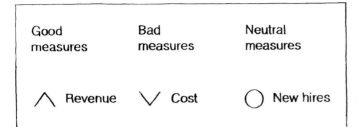

FIGURE 2.8-3

Good, bad and neutral measures. The symbols for good measures point *upwards,* those for bad measures point *downwards.* Neutral measures point neither up nor down.

GOOD, BAD AND NEUTRAL

An important question to ask is "Would an increase in that measure be good or bad for our company goals?" Increased revenue is usually good, more costs bad. However, we cannot answer this question unequivocally for some measures. Are more personnel good or bad for the company? What about more investments? "Well, it depends" is what we would like to answer. And that's why, in addition to good and bad, we need a third expression: neutral.

Now we might think that good measures would already be presented as positive and bad measures as negative across the board. If only. As we have already explained in Section 2.4 (Variances), in practice there are two different procedures for the notation of bad measures:[1]

With the *addition method* often found in annual financial statements, costs and other bad measures get a negative sign so that we can simply add them up.

In management reporting it's more common to use the *calculation method*, in which we separate the calculation procedure from the sign of the number so that cost values are represented positively and deducted by the calculation procedure.

As we can't conclude from the sign of a number or from the direction of a bar whether a measure is good or bad, we also assign a visual variable to this property.

Good and bad measures often form pairs with opposite meanings. That's why we looked for a visual variable suited to mapping opposites and landed on orientation: If the symbol $\wedge$ stands for *revenues,* wouldn't $\vee$ be the obvious visualization for a *cost* figure? So *good* points up and *bad* points down. For results calculated from good and bad measures, the character follows the minutiae: Earnings resulting from the difference between revenues and costs can be both profits and losses. But an increase in earnings is generally regarded as good. Therefore, it is advisable to characterize results with the symbol $\diamondsuit$, which combines the symbols of revenues ($\wedge$) and costs ($\vee$), but still, on the whole, points upwards.

---

1   For a distinction between addition and calculation method, see page 83.

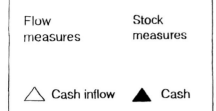

FIGURE 2.8-4

Flow and stock measures. The symbols for flow measures consist of *lines,* those for stock measures of *areas.*

In addition to good and bad, there are also measures for which it is not possible to determine whether an increase is a priori good or bad. Typical representatives of this category of neutral measures are headcounts whose circle symbol does not point in any direction. FIGURE 2.8-3 shows suggestions for good, bad and neutral measures.

FLOW AND STOCK

A further distinguishing feature arises from the question of whether a measure refers to a time period or to a closing date. Period-related measures, also known as flow measures, can accumulate over time. Revenues for the first quarter are the sum of monthly revenues from January to March. The amount of money in our bank account, on the other hand, is a closing date-related stock measure. Unfortunately, the account balance at the end of the first quarter is not equal to the sum of the monthly amounts.

We want to express this difference by representing flow measures with line symbols, while giving stock symbols an area fill. The symbols proposed so far for sales volumes, revenues, costs and results all concerned flow measures. We can find stock measures in the balance sheet, for example. Let us look at assets: it is monetary, i.e. angular. Greater asset value is good for the company, so the symbol points upwards. And as a stock measure it is flat, which almost inevitably results in our proposal for the visualization of assets: ▲. The opposite of assets is liabilities. We represent them by the symbol ▼ accordingly. For the resulting balance sheet item, equity, we consequently propose the symbol ◆. FIGURE 2.8-4 shows our proposals for flow and stock measures.

We have now visualized 7 of the 9 measure classes. The remaining two are almost self-evident:

INVENTORY   Monetarily valued inventories are part of the assets in the balance sheet, so they get the symbol ▲. Inventory volumes are the non-monetary counterpart and are consequently represented as ◖.

NUMBER OF EMPLOYEES   Headcount is non-monetary, hence rounded. They're not clearly good or bad, so they have no direction. And they're stocks, so they get an area fill. This almost inevitably results in the symbol ●.

	Monetary ($)		Non-monetary (#)	
	Flow	Stock	Flow	Stock
Assets	△ Investment, etc.	▲ Fixed assets, etc.	⌓ Inventory decrease, etc.	◖ Inventory, etc.
Liabilities	▽ New debts, etc.	▼ Bank debts, etc.		
Equity	◇ Capital increase, etc.	◆ Share capital, etc.		
Revenue	∧ Net sales, etc.		⌒ Sales volume, etc.	
Cost	∨ Material cost, etc.		∪ Material use, etc.	
Result	⩔ Net profit, etc.			
Capacity			○ New hires, etc.	● Headcount, etc.

FIGURE 2.8-5

Symbols for measure classes. This table provides an overview of our symbol suggestions for the most important basic measures.

FURTHER MEASURES

We have now added symbols to all 9 measure classes we consider important. Perhaps it is better to speak of symbol classes, as they are supposed to make it possible to incorporate further measures.

Incorporating further measures is almost self-explanatory in some cases; For example, we can represent stock changes by the hollow variants of the corresponding stock symbols, that is, changes in headcount by ○ and changes in inventory volume by ⌓. The similarity of the symbol for changes in

inventory volume (⌓) with the symbol for sales volume (⌒) is nice here, because there is indeed a close relationship between these two measures. FIGURE 2.8-5 shows an overview of the measure classes visualized so far including a few typical examples.

If we want to refine these measure classes, e.g. differentiate between net and gross sales or personnel and material costs, we suggest varying the respective basic forms in a meaningful way: adding, for example, points at different places on the symbol or using different line styles, FIGURE 2.8-6.

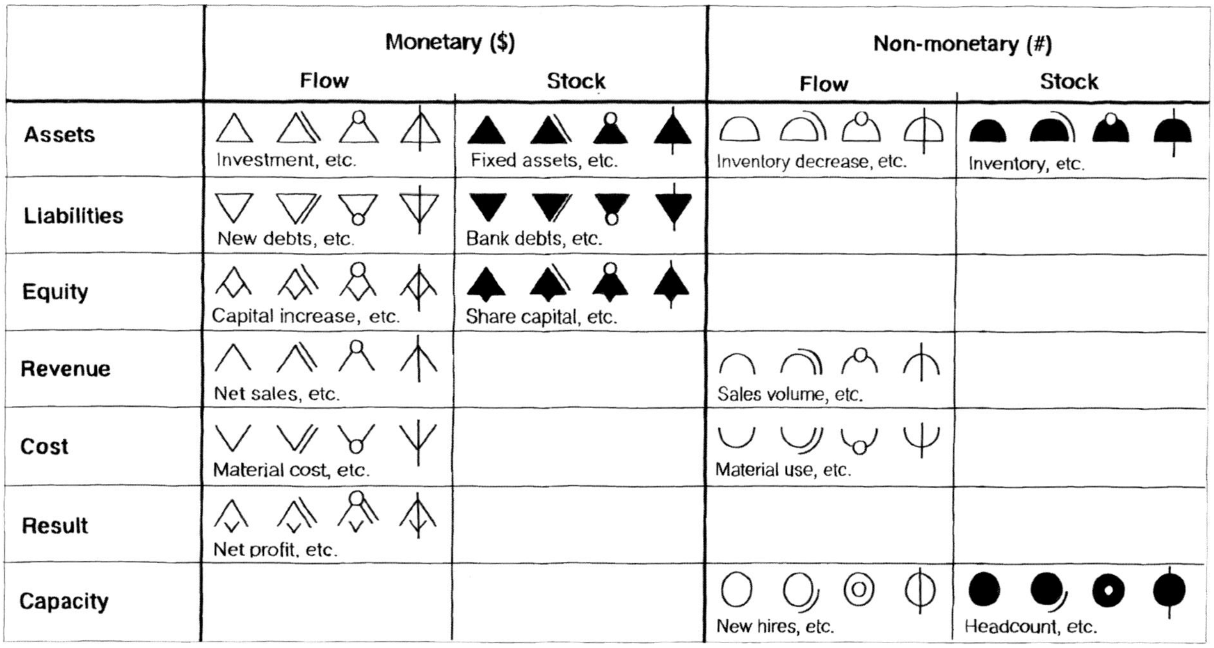

	Monetary ($)		Non-monetary (#)	
	Flow	**Stock**	**Flow**	**Stock**
Assets	Investment, etc.	Fixed assets, etc.	Inventory decrease, etc.	Inventory, etc.
Liabilities	New debts, etc.	Bank debts, etc.		
Equity	Capital increase, etc.	Share capital, etc.		
Revenue	Net sales, etc.		Sales volume, etc.	
Cost	Material cost, etc.		Material use, etc.	
Result	Net profit, etc.			
Capacity			New hires, etc.	Headcount, etc.

FIGURE 2.8-6

Further symbols for measures. Concrete proposals for different types of revenue, cost, liabilities, etc. do not yet exist. This overview is only intended to show how easy it is to create further variants using our symbol concept.

Are such small differences sufficient for an understandable differentiation? Considering how a small comma can completely change the meaning of a sentence, the answer is definitely yes. We can easily recognize the slightest differences in the symbols and classify them correctly.

But is this all way too complicated? Is this level of differentiation meaningful at all? And is there a reasonable balance between efforts and benefits? The future will show whether a symbolic language for business measures—in this or another form—is adopted in practice. But let's be realistic: No one learns traffic signs and music notes in just a few minutes. Demanding a certain amount of learning work for our subject area is not unreasonable.

There is another reason to think about this topic at an early stage: There will always be users who look for visual distinctions for special measures, "invent" corresponding solutions and use them successfully within the company. But then it becomes more and more difficult to gather these different visualizations under one roof.

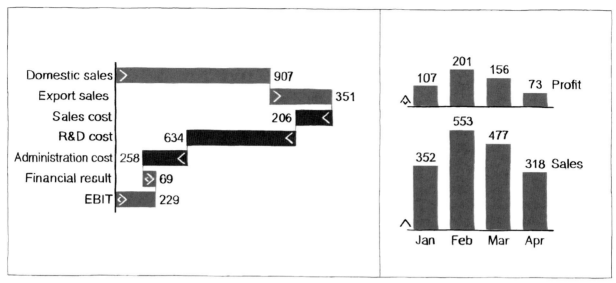

FIGURE 2.8-7
Measure symbols in charts. Measure symbols can fit into the chart; either directly in the visual elements (left) or on the axes (right).

POSITIONING THE SYMBOLS

Now that we have designed the symbols for the most important measures the question arises: Where and how should we place them?

In charts, we typically mention the measures in the title; we could also add the corresponding symbol there. However, we always strive to position the identifiers as close as possible to the associated visual elements in order to avoid unnecessary eye movements. This calls for a direct positioning e.g., in the columns and bars; see the lefthand chart in FIGURE 2.8-7. In the usual case of all columns and bars of a chart showing the same measure, we could also attach the corresponding symbol to the category axis; see the righthand chart in FIGURE 2.8-7.

We can also use these symbols in tables; for example, in the title or in the row or column headers. Even in continuous text it might be possible to integrate symbols so that even skimming creates a general impression of the measures being reported on.

BASIC MEASURES AND RATIOS

With the previous proposals for the visualization of measures, we have limited ourselves to basic measures. Many *key performance indicators* (KPIs) used for the evaluation of operational performance are created by bringing two basic measures in relation to each other. Typical examples are return on sales (profit/sales) or return on equity (profit/equity).

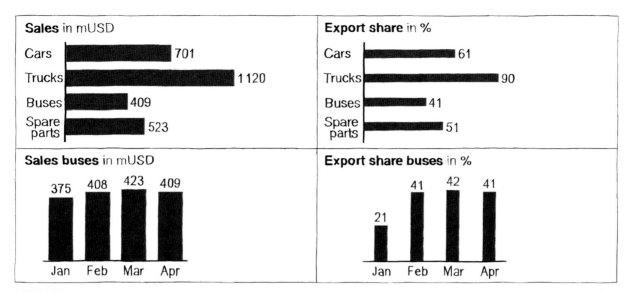

FIGURE 2.8-8

Different visualization of basic measures and ratios. For the basic measures, the column or bar width is two thirds of the category width, for the ratios only one third. This enables us to distinguish between these two fundamentally different groups of measures.

Typically, we cannot conclusively assess these ratios without knowledge of the underlying basic measures. An increased return on sales may sound positive at first glance, but it is not so great when both profit and sales have reduced. Unfortunately, return on sales doesn't reflect this. We should therefore treat ratios with caution.

Since ratios differ completely from basic measures, we recommend making them look significantly different. Here is our suggestion: The width of columns and bars that represent *basic measures* should be two-thirds of the category width.[1] This results in the following visual pattern: two-thirds filled, one-third empty, two-thirds filled, one-third empty, etc.; see the two charts on the lefthand side of FIGURE 2.8-8. It could be the other way round for ratios: columns and bars occupy only one third of the category width. The visual pattern is then: one-third filled, two-thirds empty, one-third filled, two-thirds empty, etc.; see the right two charts of FIGURE 2.8-8.

---

1   See page 72 for the concept of period differentiation through categories of different width.

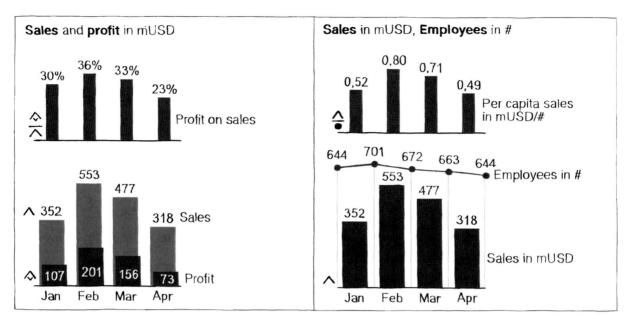

FIGURE 2.8-9

Measure symbols for basic measures and ratios. These examples show how our measure symbols work not only for basic measures but also for ratios. (Since the employees are end-of-month stock figures, the markers of the line chart are put on the right edge of the month categories.)

With this rule, we manage to avoid confusing ratios with basic values. However, this doesn't yet support their identification in terms of content. To that end, we use the symbols of the basic measures from which the respective ratio is calculated and show the calculation rule. In most cases, we will simply separate the symbols of numerator and denominator with a slash or fraction line: ◇ / ∧ (Profit/Sales) would then be the return on sales. FIGURE 2.8-9 demonstrates the practical use of measure notation.

RECAP

The semantic notation of measures poses a particular challenge because of their multitude. One possible solution is to develop a symbolic language to represent the most important classes of measures. Contextual affinities or contrasts between these classes are marked by symbols with either the same or opposite visual properties depending on the relationship. The resulting symbolic language then follows a certain logic that facilitates the learning of the symbols.

Using symbols also ensures the expandability to additional classes and the subsequent detailing of already symbolized classes. In addition, the position of the symbols can be flexible: on the axes of charts, in labels of all kinds and even in continuous text.

In contrast to other proposals in this chapter, the semantic notation of measures is still a vision of the future, as we haven't yet gained any practical experience in this area. But if we want to visually differentiate measures at *all,* we should agree on a concept sooner rather than later. Otherwise, we will get uncontrolled development that we cannot codify into a helpful standard any more.

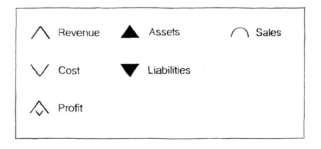

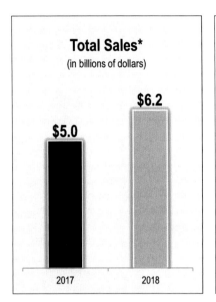

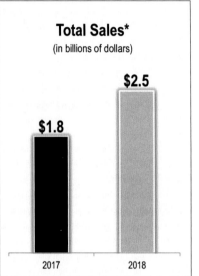

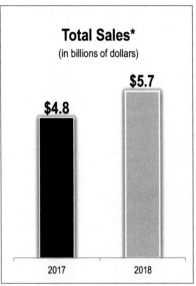

PAGE 6 **(Construction Industries)**   PAGE 7 **(Resource Industries)**   PAGE 8 **(Energy & Transportation)**

FIGURE 2.9-1
**Diagrams for different structural elements that look exactly the
same.** The three revenue charts shown here come one after the
other on slides in a quarterly presentation. The fact that each chart
pertains to a wholly different branch is only given by the title of
the slide—there is no visual indication. This is, however, normal in
today's reporting. The uneven scaling (!) as well, unfortunately.
Source: Caterpillar Second Quarter 2018 Financial Review of 2018, July 30.
Excerpt of pages 6, 7, and 8.

2.9
STRUCTURE DIMENSIONS AND ATTRIBUTES

ICONIC REPRESENTATION OF PRODUCTS, REGIONS AND ORGANIZATIONAL UNITS

Products, regions, organizational units, distribution channels—we use these and many other, sometimes deeply structured dimensions to obtain as comprehensive a view of the data as possible. To distinguish these hierarchical dimensions from the dimensions of time, scenarios and measures, we call them structure dimensions.

Software helps us combine these structure dimensions into multi-dimensional views and we can navigate our analysis along the hierarchies within these dimensions.

But what is the use of all that multidimensional data and analytics software if everything looks the same to the viewer—no matter whether it is a product analysis, a country analysis, or product area A or B within a given country? FIGURE 2.9-1 shows a bad example reflecting a typical practice in many reports. Okay, we can recognize the displayed structure dimension and its elements by reading the inscription, but this requires using our System 2[1]—pattern recognition doesn't work this way. Our System 1 would need visual differentiators so that we could see whether it was an analysis of products or regions. And it would

require a different design of the individual elements of these dimensions so that we could also distinguish two charts placed next to each other: one showing the numbers of Europe, the other the numbers of America. These distinguishing features need a consistent design that does not conflict with the features already presented.

In the following, we first consider which structure dimensions we frequently encounter in reporting and how we want to distinguish between them. Then we think about whether and how we could visualize individual elements and their attributes within the most important structure dimensions.

STRUCTURE DIMENSIONS

We usually organize management reports according to the same dimensions. Sales, for example, are most frequently reported according to unit, region, product, customer, and sales channel. Take headcount: We report it by organization unit, region and functional area. Costs, as another example, are broken down into functional areas and cost centers.

---

1 To differentiate between System 1 and System 2 in our brain, see page 36.

Organization units

 Products

 Customers

 Distribution channels

 Projects

 Regions

 Functional areas

FIGURE 2.9-2

Icons for identifying structure dimensions and attributes.
Most companies use the same structure dimensions and attributes
of their elements. We propose using icons to identify them.

We believe that with the following structure dimensions we can cover most reporting requirements:

ORGANIZATION UNITS, from the corporate group to business units, companies, departments, cost centers and individual employees;

PRODUCTS, from product areas to product groups to individual articles;

CUSTOMERS, from the customer group to individual customers to their branch offices;

DISTRIBUTION CHANNELS, e.g. the distinction between direct and partner sales or between bricks-and-mortar stores and online business

PROJECTS, e.g., in development, IT, marketing or production.

There are also attributes that we can assign to these structure dimensions in order to set up alternative summarization hierarchies and to analyze them in more detail:

REGIONS, e.g., countries for organization units and customers;

FUNCTIONAL AREAS, such as production, sales or administration for organization units.

Since we generally structure our reports and analyses according to only a few dimensions and attributes, we could assign standardized pictograms (icons) to these views, FIGURE 2.9-2.

STRUCTURE ELEMENTS AND ATTRIBUTE CHARACTERISTICS

In many cases, it is not enough to know whether the analysis is about, say, countries or products. We probably also want to see *which* countries and *which* products are involved. So we also have to find a solution for the visualization of individual structure elements and their attribute characteristics.

COMPANY-SPECIFIC STRUCTURES

The elements of the structure dimensions mentioned above, such as products or distribution channels, depend on the company under consideration. We

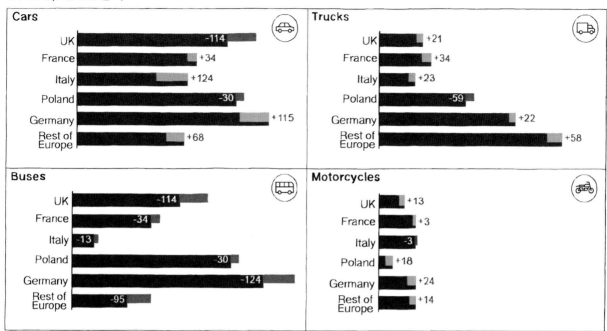

Vehicle Company
Sales in mUSD
Q1 2019, AC and ∆PY

Cars

UK	-114
France	+34
Italy	+124
Poland	-30
Germany	+115
Rest of Europe	+68

Trucks

UK	+21
France	+34
Italy	+23
Poland	-59
Germany	+22
Rest of Europe	+58

Buses

UK	-114
France	-34
Italy	-13
Poland	-30
Germany	-124
Rest of Europe	-95

Motorcycles

UK	+13
France	+3
Italy	-3
Poland	+18
Germany	+24
Rest of Europe	+14

FIGURE 2.9-3

Icons for marking elements of a structure dimension. To identify individual elements of a structure dimension, we recommend the use of similarly designed icons, such as here for the divisions cars, trucks, buses and motorcycles.

cannot standardize them across industries. At most we could consider industry-specific concepts. Within a company, however, we would visualize them in a consistent way.

The choice of suitable visual variables is difficult. Most hierarchically structured dimensions have too many elements to distinguish them by patterns, forms or similar features. In particular, we caution against the use of those colors already put to use elsewhere: red, green, blue, black and gray. This leaves only a few clearly distinguishable colors and even then we don't have enough colors left for future expansions.

Let us also be cautious using company and product logos to visualize companies and product areas. They often do not allow for clear identification. For example, the logo of a group of companies is most probably the same for each single company.

Considering the variety and individuality of elements, we again recommend the use of icons. Whether, how and where we display these icons in reports and dashboards depends on the expected benefit. In tables, icons in every single row are likely to impede visual comprehension; here we might limit ourselves to one icon for the entire structure dimension. With the simultaneous display of many small charts for product groups (Small Multiple), a small icon in the corner of a chart can help with orientation, FIGURE 2.9-3.

Delta Corporation
Sales by country in mUSD
H1 2019

Germany

	Jan	Feb	Mar	Q1	Apr	May	Jun	Q2	H1
Licenses	507	561	550	1 618	243	237	480	426	2 044
Services	531	529	484	1 544	423	264	687	527	2 071
Others	1 290	1 488	1 354	4 132	735	658	1 393	1 534	5 666
Software	**2 328**	**2 578**	**2 388**	**7 294**	**1 401**	**1 159**	**2 560**	**2 487**	**9 781**
Computer	312	281	285	878	143	143	286	375	1 253
Printer	816	818	854	2 488	424	476	900	935	3 423
Others	604	582	678	1 864	275	366	641	368	2 232
Hardware	**1 732**	**1 681**	**1 817**	**5 230**	**842**	**985**	**1 827**	**1 678**	**6 908**

Switzerland

	Jan	Feb	Mar	Q1	Apr	May	Jun	Q2	H1
Licenses	45	64	87	196	65	88	80	233	429
Services	98	92	57	247	87	80	46	213	460
Others	345	421	430	1 196	457	321	350	1 128	2 324
Software	**488**	**577**	**574**	**1 639**	**609**	**489**	**1 098**	**1 574**	**3 213**
Computer	24	82	54	160	53	50	98	375	535
Printer	56	80	70	206	109	61	86	935	1 141
Others	34	32	29	95	111	123	48	368	463
Hardware	**114**	**194**	**153**	**461**	**273**	**234**	**507**	**1 678**	**2 139**

Austria

	Jan	Feb	Mar	Q1	Apr	May	Jun	Q2	H1
Licenses	145	164	187	496	165	188	180	533	1 029
Services	198	192	157	547	187	180	146	513	1 060
Others	34	32	29	95	111	123	48	368	463
Software	**377**	**388**	**373**	**1 138**	**463**	**491**	**954**	**1 414**	**2 552**
Computer	34	42	24	100	53	50	98	375	475
Printer	56	80	70	206	109	61	86	935	1 141
Others	54	32	22	108	87	88	48	368	476
Hardware	**144**	**154**	**116**	**414**	**249**	**199**	**448**	**1 678**	**2 092**

FIGURE 2.9-4
Flags used to identify regions. The visual identification of known countries by flags works well. With individually tailored regions, creative solutions have to be found.

 Production

 Marketing and sales

 Research and development

 Administration

FIGURE 2.9-5
Icons for standardizable functional areas. The icons for the four functional areas of the cost-of-sales method could also look same.

STANDARDIZABLE ATTRIBUTES

Regions and functional areas are typical attributes valid across companies. It makes sense to standardize the values of these attributes:

REGIONS The popular flag symbols work well as long as they represent known countries, FIGURE 2.9-4. But if regions are individually tailored—e.g., "Lake Constance region", "Central sales region", "Middle East"—we have to make do with our own creative constructs.

FUNCTIONAL AREAS Unlike departments, functional areas are not organization units. Rather, it is a matter of allocating personnel and costs to specialist areas, as required for the presentation of an income statement using the cost of sales method within the International Financial Reporting Standards (IFRS). There we find the four functional areas of production, marketing and sales, research and development, and administration. FIGURE 2.9-5 shows suggestions for the corresponding icons.

RECAP

If we want to visually differentiate the figures shown in charts and tables according to structure dimensions and their elements, then we should also consider standardization here. We propose the use of icons for both the identification of structure dimensions and their elements. Since management reports and dashboards always report according to a similar set of structure dimensions, the icons for the identification of the dimension (e.g., sales by *product* or by *region*) can be standardized across the board. The elements within the structure dimensions (e.g., *trucks* or *Middle East*), on the other hand, are so special that we recommend the development of company-specific icon sets.

 Production

 Organization units

 Marketing and sales

 Products

 Research and development

 Customers

 Administration

 Distribution channels

 Projects

 Regions

 Functional areas

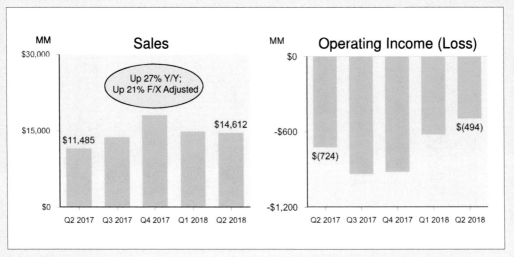

FIGURE 2.10-1

Incorrect scaling. One gets the impression that Amazon has made more losses (right) than revenues (left). With the same scaling, one would have seen that the losses were relatively small—and also reduced from 6.3% to 3.4%.

Source: Amazon Q2 2018 Financial Results Conference Call Slides, Segment Results – International (page 13, excerpt)

2.10
SCALES

RECOGNIZABLE SCALING
AVOIDS FALSE COMPARISONS

Visual analysis means comparison. Yet we can only make comparisons if we compare the same thing. This applies in the particular to the scaling of charts.

At least since Edward Tufte[1], every creator of business charts should actually know to observe certain basic rules of scaling to enable the visual comparison of values. This includes, for example, not "cutting off" either the value axis or any single column

or bar in a chart. This also means that charts being compared must use the same scaling. However, in today's charts we can't even tell if they are scaled completely differently: They always look the same. The practical example in FIGURE 2.10-1 gives the impression that Amazon made more losses than sales.

If we apply the notation of measures presented in Section 2.8, it is at least possible to determine whether these charts use the same unit of measurement or not. Key figures with different units of measurement, such as USD and kg, would be notated

---

1 Tufte, Edward R.: The Visual Display of Quantitative Information, Graphics Press, Cheshire 2001.

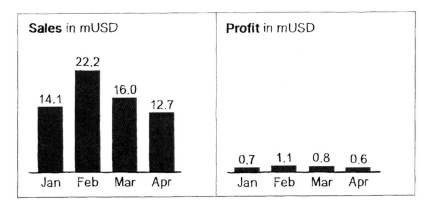

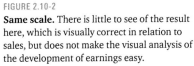

FIGURE 2.10-2
Same scale. There is little to see of the result here, which is visually correct in relation to sales, but does not make the visual analysis of the development of earnings easy.

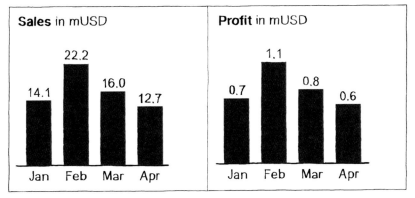

FIGURE 2.10-3
Different scales, same thousand multipliers. Although the earnings trend can be analysed well here, the comparison with sales gives a completely wrong impression.

differently, ensuring no one would even think of comparing the values of these charts with each other.

But what do we do if we need to display two charts with large and small values of the same unit of measurement next to each other on a report page? Take, for example, the revenue and operating result of a retail company where operating result is 5 percent of revenue. Should we really scale the two charts the same to make the values visually comparable, FIGURE 2.10-2? Or would we resort to different scales to better analyze the development of earnings? If we do this

it looks as if we generate the same amount of earnings as sales, FIGURE 2.10-3. Therefore, if we don't scale the two charts the same, we must at least ensure we adhere to sentence 2 of the basic rule for semantic notations[2]: *Things that don't mean the same must not look the same.* The different scaling of the two charts must be visually recognizable so we won't be tempted to compare their values.

2   See page 40.

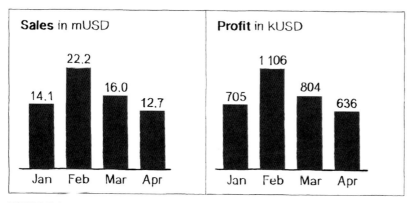

FIGURE 2.10-4

Charts not scaled equal (2). This comparison hardly offers more visual differentiation than the one in FIGURE 2.10-3.

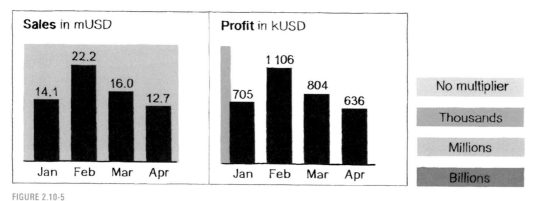

FIGURE 2.10-5

Different colors. Colored markings can help to distinguish thousand multipliers and thus prevent us from comparing incomparable charts. (On the left with a completely colored area, on the right only with a hint of it).

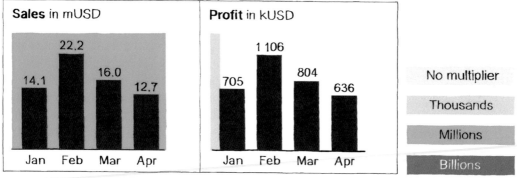

FIGURE 2.10-6

Different opacity. Markers with different opacities show the order of the different thousand multipliers (the larger the darker) better than colors (left with completely colored area, right only with a hint).

This brings us to the semantic notation of scales: Charts you are allowed to compare should look the same; charts you are not allowed to compare, should not. This pertains to the visualization of thousands, millions and billions, which we refer to as thousand multipliers in the following[1]. This also encompasses the visualization of different scales within these multipliers, if, for example, we cannot represent single-digit million profits on the same scale as triple-digit million revenues. Finally, we will deal with scaling aids, combining different scales to at least get a feeling for the different sizes of values.

THOUSANDS, MILLIONS AND BILLIONS

At first we might think we can solve the problem shown in FIGURES 2.10-2 AND 2.10-3 (PAGE 133) by changing the thousand multiplier, i.e. showing the *operating result* in thousands, while showing the *revenue* in millions. But as easily seen in FIGURE 2.10-4, this doesn't help much with visual differentiation: Our intuitive System 1[2] still perceives two identical looking charts. We only notice that the two charts are not comparable when our rational System 2 recognizes the other multiplier (kUSD) in the title on the right and reads the numbers. So in order to prevent System 1 from comparing the two charts, we have to make them look different, i.e. assign different values of a visual variable to them. In the following we will discuss the suitability of different visual variables for this purpose.

COLOR

Different coloring would express the diversity of the multipliers quite well. We could color the entire chart area, FIGURE 2.10-5 LEFT or just a suggested part of it, FIGURE 2.10-5 RIGHT. Partial coloring would be preferable because it conveys the same information with less printing ink[3] and because it also works well in charts with two differently scaled value axes (e.g., bubble charts).

However, colors have only limited capacity in representing the sequence of multipliers (thousands, millions, billions). We could assign the colors "from cold to warm", but it's not really intuitive.

OPACITY

Opacity as a visual variable maps sequences better. The lower the thousand multiplier, the brighter the chart area, FIGURE 2.10-6 LEFT or part of it, FIGURE 2.10-6 RIGHT.

A problem with the use of opacity is the identification of the thousand multiplier in only one chart, if no comparison in opacity is possible. On the other hand, we are primarily concerned with making non-comparable charts look different. Opacity would be a suitable stylistic device for this.

SYMBOLS

In general, symbols are not a visual variable according to Jacques Bertin[4]. They play a hybrid role between the visual patterns being quickly recognized by System 1 and the texts being read and processed by System 2. Still, in the absence of a "real" visualization, a well recognizable symbol is still better than a pure label. Musicians also use symbols, namely clefs, to identify their scales.

---

1 We don't want to use the more general term "unit prefix" or "prefix" here because in the International System of Units (SI) this is used not only for the thousand steps like kilo, mega, giga, terra etc., but also for ten steps like Deka and Hekto as well as Dezi and Zenti.

2 For the definition of System 1 and System 2, see page 36.

3 For the advantages of a better *data ink ratio,* see the comments on Edward Tufte on page 26.

4 Bertin, Jacques: Sémiologie graphique, Editions Gauthier-Villars, Paris 1967.

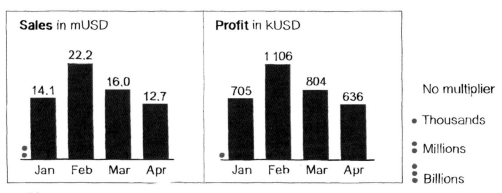

FIGURE 2.10-7
Different symbols. Also blue dots lined up here are suitable for the differentiation of thousand multipliers.

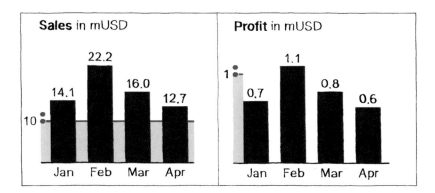

FIGURE 2.10-8
Scaling lines. Within the same multiplier (here millions), scaling lines with corresponding labels could draw attention to different scales.

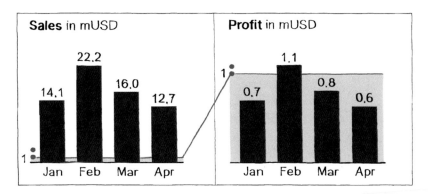

FIGURE 2.10-9
Connected scaling lines as scaling aids. If the scaling lines in two adjacent charts mark the same amount, they can be connected. Such a scaling aid allows us to kind of zoom into the larger scale.

So what could such clefs look like for scales with different multipliers? We could, for example, attach blue dots to the value axis: No point means no multiplier, 1 point equals thousands, 2 points equals millions and 3 points equals billions, FIGURE 2.10-7. We already know this in a similar form from the number format in reporting tools such as Excel[1]. And this would also work quite well with charts with two value axes (e.g., dot and bubble charts). This stylistic device would also be suitable for black and white reports.

The only problem with this symbolism is that the choice of "no point" for "no multiplier" is ambiguous: Are there no points because it is no multiplier, or are the points perhaps missing because the scale was not at all semantically notated? This problem disappears if we add the scaling lines described below to the point symbols.

DIFFERENT SCALES WITHIN THE SAME THOUSAND MULTIPLIER

The visualization of thousand multipliers is not enough. Sometimes it is also necessary to use different scales within a thousand multiplier: If the numerical difference of FIGURE 2.10-2 (PAGE 133) was even more extreme, we would no longer see the result at all.

If we cannot work with the same scales within the same thousand multiplier, we have to make sure that we can perceive the difference. We suggest scaling lines drawn in blue to distinguish them from other line types such as average, target or index lines. In addition, the area below the scaling line or a suggested part of it could also be lightly colored, FIGURE 2.10-8. The height and labels of the scaling lines indicate the scale of the chart.

One thing should be clear to us in all these considerations about the visualization of scales: With systematic use and some practice, these will help us *distinguish* different scales. But it doesn't allow us to visually *compare* values that differ by orders of magnitude. To a limited extend, this would only be possible by comparing area and volume representations (FIGURE 1.5-1 ON PAGE 46).

SCALING AIDS

If, however, the scales in two charts do not differ too much, then it would be desirable to get at least a feeling for their relationship. Our example with sales and earnings in FIGURE 2.10-9 shows such a case: Both the development of earnings—the reason a different scale is chosen—and the ratio of earnings to sales are of interest.

The obvious idea is to provide two adjacent charts with scaling lines representing the same value (here 1 mUSD). By connecting these lines, we create a kind of magnifying glass function: The line in the left chart represents the same value as the (higher) line in the right chart.

Scaling aids facilitate the comparison of charts whose numerical values differ by a factor of 10 to about 30—depending on the size of the display. If the factor is smaller than 10, we usually scale the two charts the same. If it is greater than 30, then the scaling line of the chart with the larger values is so close to the category axis that we cannot perceive its height any more.

[1] Note by Andrej Lapajne during a presentation at the IBCS Annual Conference 2018 in London.

RECAP

Correct scaling is the basic requirement for any visual comparison, but it is also the most difficult to fulfill. Semantic notation can at least help to prevent the visual comparison of values between charts with different scaling. For charts with the same unit of measurement and the same thousand multiplier (e.g., millions) but an unequal scale, we recommend scaling lines that are placed and labeled at a suitable height. For different scales of similar size, we can connect these scaling lines to give an impression of the relationship between the scales. For charts with different multipliers (e.g., thousands and millions), point symbols can be used to make them look different.

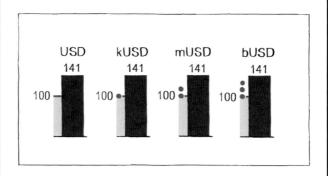

CHAPTER 3

TEMPLATES FOR REPORT OBJECTS, ANALYSES AND BUSINESS TOPICS

OUR REPORTS HAVE STANDARDS

Now we want to bring together the various concepts of semantic notation developed in the second chapter and apply them. We design charts and tables, combine them into analyses and create reports for entire business topics—proving that these concepts work not only on their own but also in combination.

In these design tasks we will find that there is a second level of standardization and thus also a second level of pattern recognition: Templates that serve a specific purpose and always look similar. We also find this second level of pattern recognition in other disciplines. In music notation, for example, there are templates for big band or symphonic orchestra, which already take into account the required instruments, their grouping and specific notation, such as transposition and clef. The same applies to architects who can make use of templates for building elements (e.g., windows) and complete plan sets for garages or detached houses. The aim of these sample templates is always the same: to minimize the effort in creating them and to present the readers with a familiar presentation so they understand them as quickly and as correctly as possible. That is why we want to use this second level of pattern recognition in reporting as well.

In the individual sections of this chapter we will always proceed in the same way: We first describe the situation to be presented in order to visualize them afterwards. This creates—quite deliberately—exercises to be solved before looking at the sample solution.

CHARTS AND TABLES

We start with the design of column, line and bar charts as well as simple tables, which—besides the texts—are by far the most important report objects in practice. It is primarily about the semantically correct design of these objects so we can recognize their meaning by their format.

COMPARISONS AND VARIANCES

From an analytical point of view, charts and tables are particularly exciting when they serve a specific purpose. We find that management reports are primarily about comparisons and the analysis of variances. For the most important forms of comparisons and analyses, we develop sample templates that should cover a large part of the practical requirements.

FINANCE AND MORE

We can standardize not only comparisons and analyses but also reporting on entire business topics to a certain extent. For example, each company reports on its balance sheet, income statement and cash flow. Best practices for the visual analysis of this financial triad would significantly speed up not only the production of reports but also their understanding.

In principle, we can also develop templates for topics more company-specific than balance sheets and income statements, albeit less standardized. However, we are happy to leave this to the respective specialists.

3.1
CHARTS AND TABLES

SEMANTICALLY DESIGNED REPORT OBJECTS

Let's start with the design of the most important reporting objects: charts and tables. After a brief look at the various overviews on the selection of chart types in the relevant literature, we ask ourselves: Should we strive for the widest possible variety of chart types in our reporting or are we satisfied with a handful? Since some authors[1] compile well over 50 different chart types, it may seem boring to use the same ones over and over again. However, this repetition significantly helps us quickly understand the contents through recognizing known patterns. And since this is exactly where our interest lies, we restrict the application of semantic notation to the most important chart types: column, line and bar charts. We can easily derive the semantic notation of the equally important XY charts (e.g., dot and bubble charts) from this. And for most other chart types (e.g., pie, radar and funnel charts) there are usually more suitable alternatives based on columns, lines and bars.

In the first step of the semantic notation of charts and tables, we settle for very simple representations for demonstration purposes only, though in practice they are hardly suitable for a profound analysis or even for conveying an exciting message. We save the suggestions for practical templates for the next section.

Let's start with the description of facts we want to visualize. Assume that we received the following task at the beginning of August 2019:

EXERCISE #1 Presentation of the monthly net sales of Alpha Corporation from January to July 2019 and the expected development to the end of the year.

First it is not a question here—nor with the following exercises—of conveying a specific message, such as: "The lower net sales in the summer months are explained by the vacation period".[2] We only show the numbers and leave their interpretation to the reader. Because there is no message to convey, we begin directly with the formulation of the title to identify the content of the chart[3]:

Line 1 of the title contains the reporting entity, i.e. Alpha Corporation.
Line 2 contains the measure and its unit, i.e. Net sales in mUSD.
In line 3 we write the time reference and, if necessary for understanding, the scenarios presented (e.g., actual or plan). In our case the mention of the year should suffice for identification, i.e. 2019.

We place the title in the upper left corner in a font size our target group can read comfortably on the intended presentation medium (paper, screen, canvas)—let's say 10 pt (i.e. 1 em = 10 pt[4]). We choose Arial as the default font.

Now we have to consider which form of presentation to choose: chart or table. We choose a chart because

---

2 For the definition of messages, see page 65.

3 For the notation of titles, see page 62.

1 In its Visual Vocabulary, for example, the Financial Times shows 70 different chart types (www.ft.com/vocabulary).

4 To use "em" as a unit for dimensioning visual elements, see page 105.

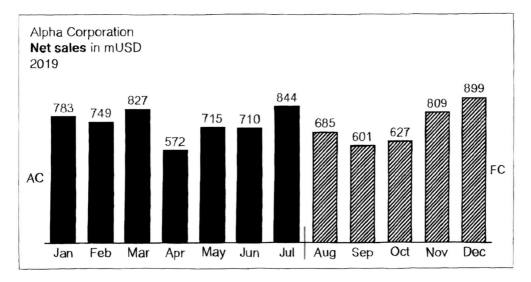

FIGURE 3.1-1 | SOLUTION EXERCISE #1
Period values of a time series. Time series are shown with a horizontal category axis, period values are shown preferably with columns. The columns show basic measures and are therefore two thirds as wide as the categories. Columns with a dark fill represent actual data, outlined and hatched columns respresent forecast data.

it makes it easier to visually understand the facts. Since we want to represent a time series, the chart inevitably runs along a horizontal category axis[5]. Now we still have the choice between columns and lines. This decision depends on whether it is more about the presentation of the individual monthly values or the analysis of a longer temporal pattern. As this is about the individual months of a year we opt for columns.

COLUMNS

So we draw a horizontal chart with twelve columns. We choose a width of 3,0 em[6] for the month categories. The columns within these categories represent basic measures, and according to our semantic notation of measures we draw them at two thirds of the category[7] width.

Actual data is available for the months January to July, so we fill these seven columns in black or dark gray. The five columns from August onwards represent the future and show the forecast, so they are outlined and hatched[8]. An additional vertical separator line marks the split between actual data and forecast. With the category width of 3.0 em, we can abbreviate the monthly designations with three letters: Jan, Feb, Mar, etc.

The length of the monthly columns naturally corresponds exactly to the amount of the monthly revenue. Now we add the value labels[9] above the columns, so we don't need a value axis (y-axis). The chart in FIGURE 3.1-1 can't really look any other way.

5 For distinguishing time series analyses from structural comparisons, see page 69.

6 For the concept of linking the period length to the category width, see page 72.

7 For a visual distinction between basic measures and ratios, see page 122.

8 For scenario visualization, see page 76.

9 For the notation of value labels, see page 63.

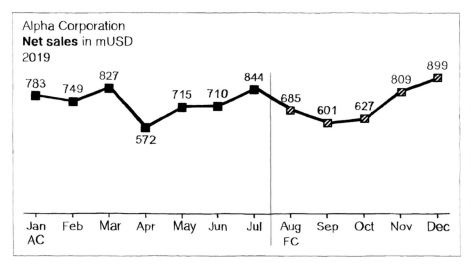

FIGURE 3.1-2 | SOLUTION EXERCISE #2
Progression pattern of a time series. We use lines if the progression pattern is more important than the period values or if there are a lot of values.
The markings of the points are provided with scenario notation; the corresponding designations (AC, FC) can be attached either to the lines or to the axis (as shown here).

LINES

EXERCISE #2 We continue to look at the monthly net sales for 2019, but now we are less interested in the individual monthly figures than in their time pattern. We want, for example, to identify seasonal influences.

There are two main criteria that would entail lines instead of columns in time series analyses: Either a large number of data points, e.g., the weeks of a year, or when the analysis of the pattern in time is more important than the comparison of the individual period values. The latter is given here so we create a line chart.

The category axis with months is identical to the column chart, we only add 12 axis tick marks to position the values exactly. Instead of the columns, we draw points equal to the monthly net sales and connect the points with a line. To avoid misinterpreting the line as a continuous evolvement, we mark the twelve measured monthly values with small squares. These markers simultaneously become carriers of semantic scenario notation: The markers from January to July get a dark fill (actual data), while the markers from August on are hatched (forecast). Now we label the markers with the values—and the line chart is ready, FIGURE 3.1-2.

STACKED BARS

EXERCISE #3 We now want to differentiate net sales by the following regions: Germany, Rest of Europe, USA and Rest of World. The chart should show sales broken down by machinery and accessories in all regions for the second quarter of 2019.

In contrast to the time series above, this situation relates to the single period Q2 2019, where we want to compare the revenue types structurally. According

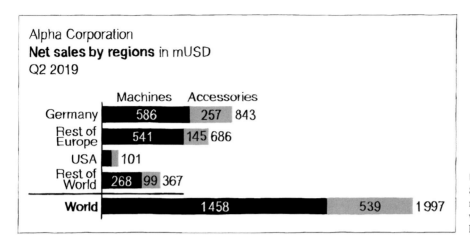

FIGURE 3.1-3 | SOLUTION EXERCISE #3
Structure comparison. For the representation of structures we use charts with vertical axes—here stacked bars.

to our semantic rules we present the facts on a vertical category axis, i.e. with a bar chart stacked according to the two types of revenue.[1]

Again we have no message, so we start directly with the title: Building on the first two exercises, we add the references "Q2" and "by regions" to the title.

Now we draw a chart with bars for the four regions. We choose 1.5 em as the category width, because this width is also suitable as a row height for tables and we can therefore combine tables and bars easily. Net sales is a basic measure, meaning bars are again two-thirds as wide as the categories[2].

Now we have to divide the bars into "machines" and "accessories". As our primary interest lies with the machines, we draw them as the lowest or leftmost segment of the bar, using a solid fill because it is actual data. On top (here: to the right) we stack the accessories in a lighter gray. We add the figures inside the bars and write the totals to the right.

In this specific case, there is enough space to show a total bar. This is not possible with many bar charts due to a much larger total. If this is the case, we still write the total values (without bars) below the bold total line. Better than nothing. FIGURE 3.1-3 shows the finished bar chart.

1 For distinguishing time series analyses from structural comparisons, see page 69.

2 For a visual distinction between basic measures and ratios, see page 122

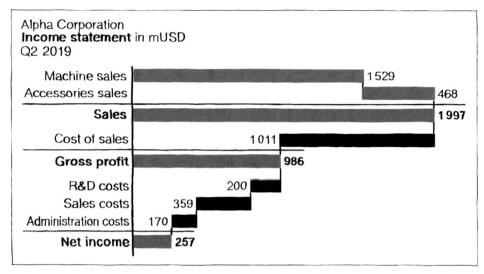

FIGURE 3.1-4 | SOLUTION
EXERCISE #4
Calculation scheme. The
waterfall chart visualizes the
contributions of individual
elements to the (intermediate)
results. For better differentiation, we notate the "good"
values somewhat brighter than
the "bad" ones.

VERTICAL WATERFALL

EXERCISE #4 **In this exercise we want to present a simplified income statement of Alpha Inc. for the second quarter of 2019. We calculate the profit from the total sales of machines and accessories, subtracting the manufacturing costs to arrive at the gross profit. This result is then reduced by the costs for development, sales and administration.**

The title is obvious again: We change the second line to "Income statement in mUSD", the third line is "Q2 2019".

The contents are also quite similar to the previous exercise: Again, structure elements—here measures. So we just draw the same chart, only with nine bars (from machine revenue to the result) instead of four? Not quite.

In contrast to the last exercise, we link the individual items of the income statement to a calculation scheme with additions and subtractions. We therefore need to enhance the bar chart by visualizing this

calculation scheme: We arrange the bars as a waterfall, i.e. we append bars on the right of the previous bar for values to be added, and to the left for values to be subtracted. For a better differentiation we draw the "good" bars (here sales) a little lighter than the "bad" ones (here costs). Bars that are added to the right are labeled on the right. Bars that are deducted, i.e. which protrude to the left, are labeled on the left. Result bars start at the axis and receive bold-faced labels, as with tables. The length of a bar naturally corresponds to the value of the respective measure. FIGURE 3.1-4 shows the resulting vertical waterfall.

TABLE

As tabular presentations of Exercises 1 to 4 would be trivial, we combine them as follows:

EXERCISE #5 **We want to present the items of the income statement in a table on a quarterly basis: Q1 and Q2 with the actual figures, Q3 and Q4 with the expected figures.**

If possible, we also represent time periods in tables horizontally, i.e. in columns. We arrange the quarters from left to right with the extrapolation to the annual value on the far right. We show the calculation of the income in the rows. So far the structure of the table is clear.

The title is also simple again: It basically remains the same as for the waterfall in FIGURE 3.1-4. We simply adjust the time period in line 3, simply 2019.

The design of the table details is less obvious. If we want the readers to recognize patterns, the design details cannot follow the personal taste of the creator. They must follow fixed rules.

The font type for the table is the same as for the title and the font size remains 10 pt.

The first column contains the left-justified designation of the measures. The column width can still be a little flexible according to the length of the designations. However, we should avoid long row headers so that the table remains clear. If necessary, we would use abbreviations or shift details into footnotes.

The following columns with the quarterly values and their sum (extrapolation to the annual value), on the other hand, are by default just wide enough for four digits and one sign to fit comfortably into them.

To clarify the column structure, we insert a gap between the column with the row headers and the columns with the numerical values. The same between the individual quarters. The year column on the far right is separated by a little wider gap. These gaps break-up the horizontal lines of the table.

Alpha Corporation **Income statement** in mUSD 2019		AC				FC
		Q1	Q2	Q3	Q4	**2019**
+	Machine sales	1 820	1 529	1 578	1 758	**6 685**
+	Accessories sales	539	468	552	577	**2 136**
=	**Sales**	**2 359**	**1 997**	**2 130**	**2 335**	**8 821**
-	Cost of sales	1 123	1 011	1 099	988	**4 223**
=	**Gross profit**	**1 236**	**986**	**1 031**	**1 347**	**4 600**
-	R&D costs	256	200	345	408	**1 209**
-	Sales costs	599	359	436	523	**1 917**
-	Administration costs	234	170	222	256	**882**
=	**Net income**	**147**	**257**	**28**	**160**	**592**

FIGURE 3.1-5 | SOLUTION EXERCISE #5
Calculation scheme over several periods. Calculation schemes are best displayed vertically in a table, time periods horizontally. Semantic lines indicate the scenarios. The algebraic signs on the left show the arithmetic operation. Horizontal and vertical gaps clarify the table structure.

We write the column headers in bold font and align them according to the data displayed below: Headers for number columns are therefore right-aligned, even if this seems a bit unusual at first. It helps with the visual perception of the column structure and removes the need for any vertical lines. For the designations of the quarters, we agree on the abbreviation with two letters.

Below the column headers, we draw a line that marks the beginning of the numeric block. If the columns show values for different scenarios, we make these lines slightly thicker to show the corresponding scenario: In our case, this semantic line is solid (actual) for the first two quarters, outlined and hatched (forecast) from Q3 on.

The numeric block starts with a gap of half a line height, which we always use when there is a kind of group change. Then comes—without a horizontal line—the first sales row. The row height for tables remains 1.5 em. A discreet horizontal line (preferably gray and thin) separates the first sales row from the second. After listing all sales revenues and

manufacturing costs we draw a black line and show the gross profits below the line in bold[1].

We do not draw a line below the gross profit, but insert a gap of half a line height to mark the beginning of a new group. This group begins with development costs. Below this group follows another line and then the result in bold font.

When discussing the notation of signs for "good" and "bad" measures and their effect on tables, we presented two possible methods: The *calculation method* that presents costs positively, and the *addition method* that presents them negatively[2]. We want to use the calculation method as the standard, as we already did with the vertical waterfall. For better traceability of the calculation process, we add the algebraic sign to the designation of the measures in the row headers — in other words, a minus sign for the manufacturing costs. And the table shown in FIGURE 3.1-5 is finished.

---

1 For the question of whether to display totals above or below their summands, see page 98.

2 For the sign problem in the notation of measures and their consequences for table design, see page 83.

RECAP

When drawing column, line and bar charts, and when designing tables, we adhered to the semantic rules presented in Chapter 2—and we were like a train on its tracks. Every design decision was made unambiguously. It is hard to imagine that another person following the same rules would have arrived at a completely different visual result. We have thus achieved our goal: The appearance of charts and tables no longer depends on the personal preferences of the creator and the reporting software used—just as the appearance (not the content!) of sheet music is independent of the composer and the music notation software used. You grow accustomed to the appearance, recognize it and understand it much faster.

In addition, the examples have shown that the rules presented in Chapter 2 not only work in isolation but also in combination with each other. At least for very simple charts and tables. In the next section we will try our hand at more complex exercises.

3.2
COMPARISONS AND VARIANCES

TEMPLATES FOR ANALYSES

The charts and tables in the previous section were limited to showing actual and forecast data in their basic form. We often find such "one-dimensional" representations in reports and dashboards. They do not, however, say much because they only show a temporal course or a simple structural juxtaposition. Imagine the return on sales rising from 3.3% in January to 3.9% in June. Reliably assessing this increase demands further comparisons. In the previous year, for instance, return on sales never fell below 4.5%. The same with the plan for the current year. Important competitors are even seeing double-digit figures. This additional information reveals that we cannot be satisfied with our growth.

When defining the semantic notation of variances in Section 2.4, we referred to the control loop in business management: We measure actual values, compare them with a reference such as the plan, and finally calculate the variance and evaluate it. From this, we derive actions which—at least in the case of variances with negative effects—aim to close the gap between actual and plan.

That's why we are less concerned with the pure representation of the situation than with its analysis; its comparison with a reference and the visualization of the variances. This applies to both time series and structural comparisons.

We see the following illustrations as an attempt to develop sample templates for various forms of variance analysis. In doing so, we increase the information density of the charts and tables developed in previous exercises.

COMPARISON OF PERIOD VALUES
We extend the situation from Exercise #1 as follows:

EXERCISE #6 **We want to compare the monthly net sales and the expected future development with the corresponding plan figures and the previous year.**

We can take the title from FIGURE 3.1-1 (PAGE 143), after all we want to analyze the same numbers already shown there.

The structure of the column chart also remains unchanged: We still consider twelve months, five being forecasts.

Now it is a matter of staging everything in such a way that it is easy for the reader to compare the actual data with the planned and previous year's data. Since we typically base the plan for the year to come on data from the previous year, we use it as the primary reference for comparison. We address the comparison with the previous year later on.

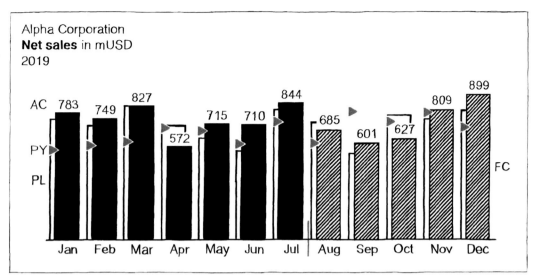

FIGURE 3.2-1 | SOLUTION EXERCISE #6A

Time series analysis. We place the plan data in outlined columns behind and to the left of the actual data columns without changing the category width. The previous year's values are represented by gray triangles.

OVERLAPPED COLUMNS

We suggest positioning plan columns to the left behind, and overlapped by, the actual columns. *Overlapped* because fitting a complete column beside the actual column requires adjusting the category width, which we want to avoid for pattern recognition reasons. *Behind* because the actual data is more important to us. And to the *left* because the plan was created before the actual data[1].

In order to immediately recognize the reference columns as a *plan*, we use semantic scenario notation and draw them outlined—next to both the actual and forecast columns.

---

1   There is another important reason for this arrangement of the planning columns: For horizontal waterfalls, the reference value (here plan) must be arranged on the left (for vertical waterfalls, above). Otherwise it isn't possible to draw it.

SCENARIO TRIANGLES

Now we are looking at the second reference required: the previous year. We advise against a further column because this would easily become messy and spill over the category width. Instead, we propose reducing the less important reference—here the previous year's figures—to small triangles marking the height of a virtual third column. We use the surface of these triangles again for the semantic scenario notation and draw them in previous year's gray. We label the triangles only in exceptional cases—details are rarely the issue here, after all.

FIGURE 3.2-1 shows the results of the above considerations. With the help of this chart we can already compare actual with plan and previous year to obtain an initial snapshot of the "performance". But that's not enough for us to call it a sample template.

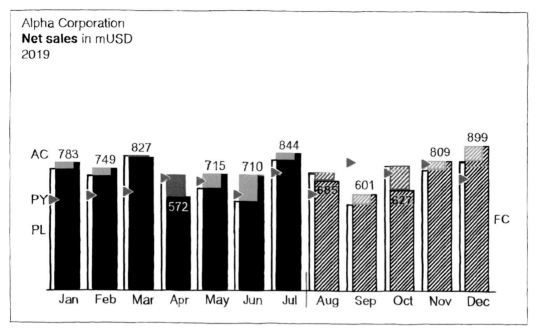

FIGURE 3.2-2 | SOLUTION EXERCISE #6B

Time series analysis with integrated variances. Here the variances between actual and plan are "integrated" into the basic chart. This saves space, but sometimes leads to labeling problems. This representation is also not quite as meaningful as what follows in FIGURE 3.2-3 because there is no baseline for comparing the monthly variance. Expected variances are shown hatched.

ABSOLUTE VARIANCES

When comparing actual and plan, the reader tries to quantify the difference between the corresponding columns. We can help with this task: Why not show these variances right away? Either directly in the column as an *integrated variance* or as a separate *variance chart* on a second tier above the original chart. Integrated variances require less space. They have the added charm of making it possible to dispense with the overlapped plan columns without any loss of information, FIGURE 3.2-2. Independent variance charts, on the other hand, are easier to read. They allow for comparison of variances over time, because in contrast to the integrated representation, all variances start at the zero line, FIGURE 3.2-3. We can also use additional charts to visualize further variances, such as the variance from the previous year.

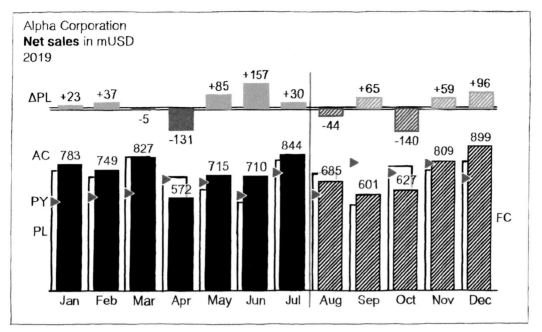

FIGURE 3.2-3 | SOLUTION EXERCISE #6C

Time series analysis with separate variances. Here the variances between actual and plan (ΔPL) are shown with an additional chart. The reference for the variances is the plan, therefore the axis receives the semantic notation "outlined".

wIn both cases the visual design of these variances follows the rules set out in Section 2.4: We show variances with a positive effect on our corporate goal in green and with a plus sign. Variances with a negative effect are correspondingly red. For variance charts, the x-axis bears the semantic notation of the reference scenario (semantic axis). And the scaling of the variances is of course identical to the scaling of the base numbers.

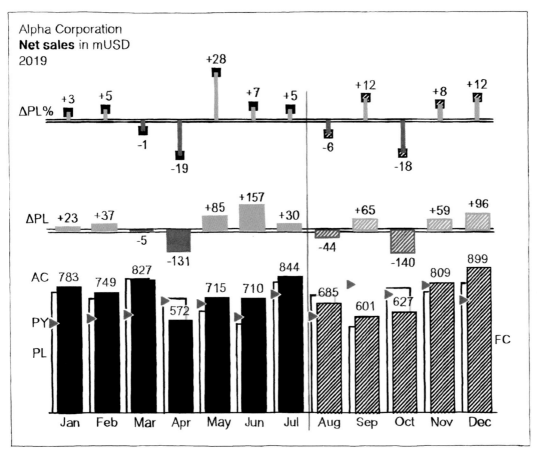

FIGURE 3.2-4 | SOLUTION EXERCISE #6D
Time series analysis with absolute and relative variances. In this figure, we add relative variances to the representation of FIGURE 3.2-3. Since percentages are a different unit, we are free to scale it. The pin heads represent the scenario to be compared; the pinheads are set back so that the colored pins show the correct length and small values are still visible.

RELATIVE VARIANCES

When looking at time series, the analysis of relative variances is actually only of interest if the monthly values are subject to strong seasonal fluctuations, which we eliminate via relative consideration. To represent it, we would supplement the absolute figures with a relative variance chart on a further tier. We use pins instead of columns with pinheads carrying the semantic scenario notation—as described in section 2.4.

FIGURE 3.2-4 summarizes all we have addressed until this point. Now it becomes clear for the first time why we so vehemently fight to use colors exclusively for highlighting, here variances: The green and red colors are striking and tell you which months went well, and which did not.

Nevertheless, we aren't yet satisfied. We would like to add another aspect before declaring the template complete.

ACCUMULATION

When looking at the twelve-monthly figures presented in FIGURE 3.2-4, managers wanting to adhere to a budget will inevitably ask what the monthly

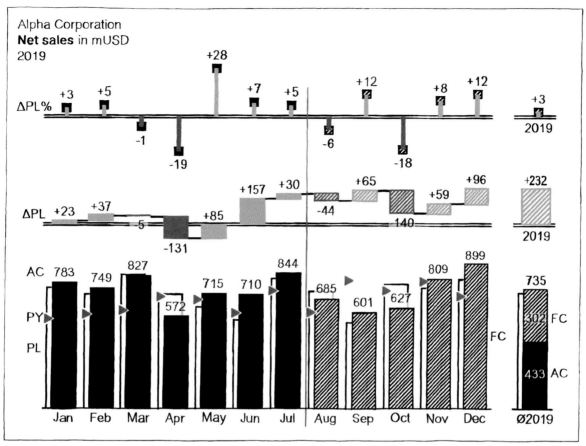

FIGURE 3.2-5 | SOLUTION EXERCISE #6E

Time series analysis with monthly and annual variances. We would like to call this representation a sample template for a time series analysis with columns. In comparison to FIGURE 3.2-4, we show the absolute variances as a waterfall so we can also identify the cumulated variances. We have also added the monthly average, which we—in contrast to the annual value—can display correctly scaled and thus better compare with the monthly values.

variances mean for the year as a whole. Accumulating the 12 monthly values would require a substantially larger scale. As a result, the individual monthly values get very small, and their variances even more so.

An additional chart with the average of the monthly values would solve this problem. This single column on the right comprises actual and forecast data, preceded by the reference column with the average monthly plan, FIGURE 3.2-5. This way we can see by how much we are likely to be above or below the plan at the end of the year—at least for an average month.

If we want to see exactly by what amount we are likely to exceed or fall short of the plan, we would choose a waterfall representation instead of a simple variance chart. This adds up the monthly variances to the total annual variance.

FIGURE 3.2-5 shows both solutions: on the right the average month as an extended chart, and on the second tier the variances in a waterfall. Now we are satisfied and offer the result as a sample template for time series analyses with columns.

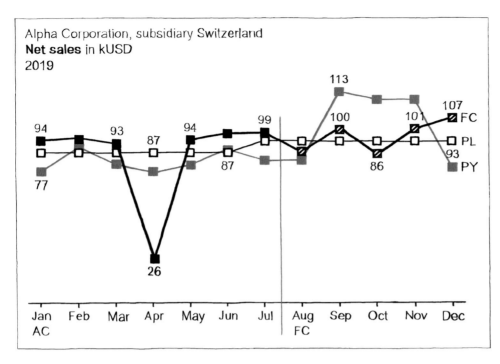

Alpha Corporation, subsidiary Switzerland
Net sales in kUSD
2019

FIGURE 3.2-6 | SOLUTION
EXERCISE #7A
Time series comparison.
The representation of
multiple lines that overlap
several times, as here, can
easily become a confusing
"spaghetti chart".

COMPARISON OF TEMPORAL PATTERNS

EXERCISE #7 **We want to compare the monthly
sales of the Swiss subsidiary in 2019 with plan
and previous year. We focus more on the temporal course than on the individual monthly values.**

We add "Switzerland" to the first line of the title and
opt for a line chart. Line charts are better suited to
unveiling temporal patterns than columns, especially if we are investigating more than one data
series.

MULTIPLE LINES
We start with a chart with only one line, as in FIGURE
3.1-2 (PAGE 144), and consider how we can add a reference scenario to evaluate the actual values. The solution is obvious: We put the plan values on a second
line with *outlined* markers making them recognizable as a plan. A third line with gray markers could

represent the previous year's values—but, as we see
in FIGURE 3.2-6, this can quickly turn into a confusing
"spaghetti chart". It might be helpful to highlight specific lines, parts of them or the differences between
two lines in order to get a message across.

ABSOLUTE VARIANCES
To display the absolute variances, we could consider coloring the area between the two lines green
and red, FIGURE 3.2-7; unless we want to display an
additional variance chart above the line chart, as we
have done in FIGURE 3.2-3 (PAGE 153).

This integrated coloring looks appealing, but
we should be aware of three problems with this
approach:

FIRST, there is the fundamental problem of all area
charts representing single values and not a continuous course: The colored areas between the lines

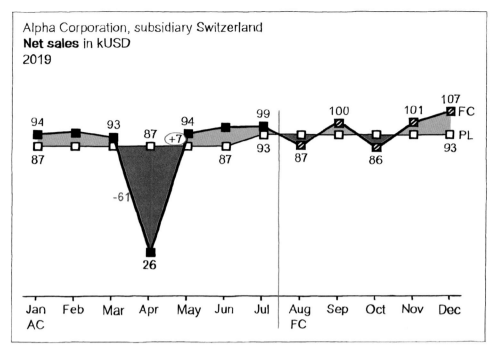

Alpha Corporation, subsidiary Switzerland
Net sales in kUSD
2019

FIGURE 3.2-7 | SOLUTION
EXERCISE #7B
**Time series comparison
with difference areas.**
The colored difference
areas between actual and
plan values look nice,
but they are not quite
correct as the areas are not
proportional to the vari-
ances measured at specific
points: The very small
green area below the 94
in May and the large red
area above the 26 in April
do not represent the ratio
of the actual variances
between +7 and −61.

represent only an approximation of the proper values. A closer look reveals, for example, that the
corresponding red and green areas do not show
the right proportion of the two variances in April
$(26 - 87 = -61)$ and May $(94 - 87 = +7)$. The
numerical ratio $(61/7 = 8.7)$ is considerably smaller
than the ratio of the small green triangle below the
94 in May to the large red triangle above the 26 in
April $(61^2/7^2 = 75.9)$[1]. The area comparisons are
only correct if the variances upwards and downwards are the same, as is the case from August to
October.

SECOND, this representation creates intersections
between two measuring points—for example,
between September and October—that do not even
exist in the data. In the case of stock measures, we

could argue that this is an interpolation of the stock
values at the end of the month—but in the case of
flow measures like here with revenue? The outlier in
April has nothing to do with the May figure, but in the
chart it looks as if the target figure was only reached
shortly before May, which cannot be justified.

THIRD, there is a problem with stock measures: Let
us imagine a line chart assessing the development
of a stock market price from the beginning of the
year until today. The areas above the initial value
are marked green, the areas below the initial value
are marked red. Our share price rose by 10% at the
beginning of January. The price remained there until
yesterday, when it fell to 10% *below* the initial value.
The chart shows a large green area. Is this visualization helpful with regard to a sales decision? We don't
think so. So we always have to ask ourselves what we
actually want to show.

---

1   With two values x and y above and below a horizontal reference
     line, the areas of the corresponding triangles behave like x^2 to y^2.

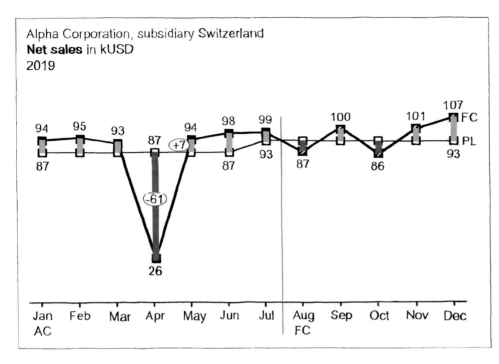

Alpha Corporation, subsidiary Switzerland
Net sales in kUSD
2019

FIGURE 3.2-8 | SOLUTION
EXERCISE #7C
Time series comparison with difference markers. Highlighting the differences at the points of measurement is—in contrast to highlighting the difference areas in FIGURE 3.2-7—safer. With this representation, we visualize variances correctly for both stock and flow measures, but they are not as eye-catching due to the smaller amount of color.

If we want to avoid these problems safely, we have only one option: We highlight the differences in color only at those points where values were actually measured, FIGURE 3.2-8; not quite as appealing as the colored areas in FIGURE 3.2-7—but always correct. And we have another sample template.

COMPARISON OF CUMULATIVE FLOW MEASURES

EXERCISE #8 **We now want to compare the cumulative monthly net sales of the French subsidiary for 2019 with the plan. At the same time, we want to determine whether the development of sales is based on a trend.**

For cumulative flow measures, we can interpret the connecting lines between two measured points as linear interpolation, similar to the case for stock measures. For this reason, a so-called Z-chart is a suitable solution for this task: We present the individual monthly values as columns and the cumulative values as ascending lines above them. Note:

While drawing the columns in the middle of a month category, we position the line markers at the end of the month, i.e. between two months. The corresponding cumulative value represents the revenue accrued up to the end of the month.

Now we want to analyze whether there is a trend here. We cannot see this from the individual monthly figures because they are subject to seasonal fluctuations. The cumulative values do not show whether there is a trend either. So we add a line with Moving Annual Totals ("MAT") to the chart which gives the chart the shape of a "Z" and its name, FIGURE 3.2-9. The fact that twelve months are always added up on a rolling basis means that seasonality is eliminated and a trend is visible. For clarification, we prefix an underscore to the marks of the cumulative values and a tilde to the marks of the MAT values as suggested in Section 2.1.

We also add the planning data to this chart in order to evaluate the sales achieved. Again, we place the columns to the left of and behind the actual and

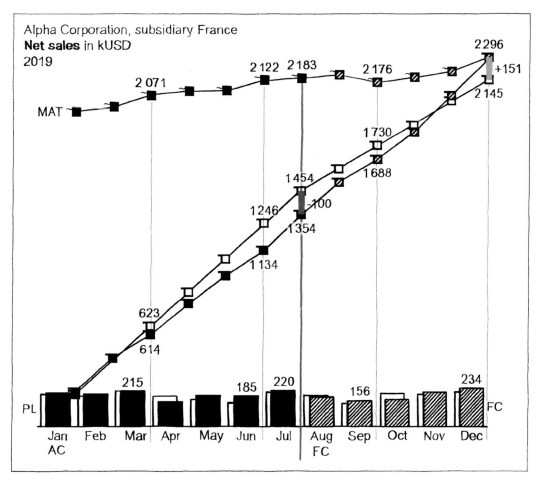

FIGURE 3.2-9 | SOLUTION EXERCISE #8:
Comparison of cumulated flow measures. In this Z-chart we present actual and forecast data as columns. The Z is calculated from the cumulative values up to the end of the year (marked with an underscore) and the Moving Annual Totals (MAT) of the past (marked with a tilde). The green and red difference markers show the variances from the plan.

forecast columns. We also draw a second line with outlined markers for the cumulative plan values, but not for the planned MAT values.

As with the variances between two "normal" lines, we don't color the area between the two cumulative lines green and red. Instead, we mark the differences between actual and plan, or forecast and plan, on two particularly interesting dates[1]: the variance

as of today and the expected variance at the end of the period under review. An advantage arises from our placing the line markers at the end of the month: The difference markers lie exactly on the separator line between actual and forecast values and at the end of the year.

We believe that the Z-chart has the potential to become a standard for the visualization of variances from cumulative flow measures. And we've got another template.

1 For the definition of difference markers, see page 91.

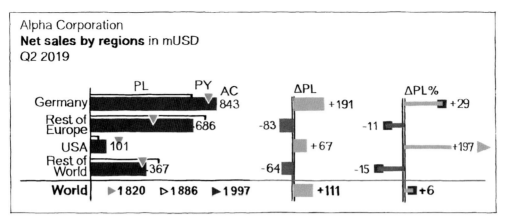

FIGURE 3.2-10 ⋮ SOLUTION EXERCISE #9

Structural comparison with variances. This representation of the absolute variances ΔPL and ΔPL% corresponds to the time series analysis of FIGURE 3.2-4, but rotated 90°. Due to the small planned value of the USA, the percentage variance is very large here. As this value is of low importance, we make an exception and cut the pin so that the relative variances of the other regions do not look so small.

COMPARISON OF STRUCTURES

EXERCISE #9 **We want to compare the sales of the same four regions (Germany, Rest of Europe, USA, Other) in the second quarter of 2019 with the plan and the previous year.**

This is not a time series question, but one of structural comparison, so we start with the bar chart of Exercise #3, FIGURE 3.1-3 (PAGE 145), where we don't need to subdivide the bars into machines and accessories. We change the third title line to "Q2 2019".

OVERLAPPED BARS AND SCENARIO TRIANGLES

To compare actual and planned net sales, we draw outlined plan bars slightly above the actual bars and overlapped by them—analogous to Exercise #6. For the previous year's values, we likewise reduce the display to light gray scenario triangles; see the base values on the left of FIGURE 3.2-10[1].

ABSOLUTE AND RELATIVE VARIANCES

The visualization of the variances follows the same considerations as in Exercise #6—only rotated 90°. We opt for variance charts on additional tiers. The semantic design of the bars for the absolute variances, the pins for the relative variances, and the associated axes is the same as before.

Additionally we are interested in the variance of the total revenue. Due to a lack of space we cannot visualize the total revenue as we did in FIGURE 3.1-3 (PAGE 145), so the bold totals below the total line must suffice. Visualization of the absolute and relative variances of the total revenue is most likely not going to be a problem: Absolute variances are usually smaller than their underlying base values, and outliers for relative variances can mostly be truncated and highlighted with a marker[2], FIGURE 3.2-10.

We have now developed our fourth sample template for the scenario comparison of structural elements.

---

1   We have increased the category width from 1.5 em to 1.8 em to make room for the overlapping bars.

2   See page 88.

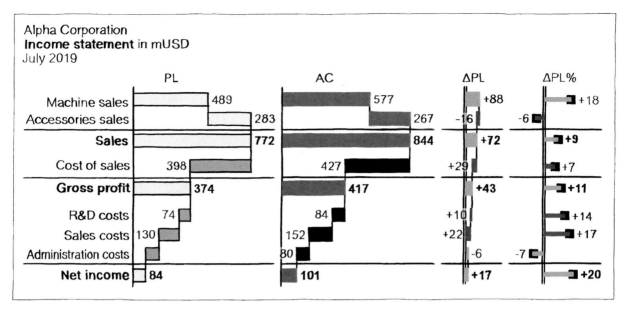

Alpha Corporation
Income statement in mUSD
July 2019

	PL	AC	ΔPL	ΔPL%
Machine sales	489	577	+88	+18
Accessories sales	283	267	-16	-6
Sales	772	844	+72	+9
Cost of sales	398	427	+29	+7
Gross profit	374	417	+43	+11
R&D costs	74	84	+10	+14
Sales costs	130	152	+22	+17
Administration costs	80	80	-6	-7
Net income	84	101	+17	+20

FIGURE 3.2-11 | SOLUTION EXERCISE #10

Comparison of a calculation scheme. Calculation schemes are best visualized by vertical waterfalls—plan with outlined bars, of course. We also show absolute variances of calculation schemes as a waterfall due to the sign problem.

EXERCISE #10 Now we want to compare not only the sales but also the complete income statement of Alpha Corporation with the corresponding plan for July 2019.

We take the title from Exercise #4 FIGURE 3.1-4 (PAGE 146) without adding the scenarios (PL, AC) and variances (ΔPL, ΔPL%) to the third line because it's obvious.

WATERFALLS

As in Exercise #4, we present the income statement for July 2019 as a vertical waterfall. But where to put the plan? Overlapping bars would be too confusing. Even integrated variances don't work properly with waterfalls. There is no other option than to create a second waterfall for the planned figures. We show the plan to the left of the actual waterfall because time goes from left to right and plan figures were there first. The bars are outlined—as they are plan—and lightly tinted so we can distinguish the good from the bad, FIGURE 3.2-11.

ABSOLUTE VARIANCES

We recommended presenting absolute variances in calculation schemes as variance waterfalls[3]. We draw yet a third waterfall to the right of the actual numbers, showing the contribution of the various variances to the total variance of the operating result.

RELATIVE VARIANCES

As we cannot add up relative variances, a waterfall display is not an option. If we need relative variances at all, we extend the representation using a regular variance chart with pins. We knowingly accept that red pins in the revenues point *left* as they represent negative values, while red pins in the costs show positive numbers and therefore point *right*.

FIGURE 3.2-11 shows the resulting sample template for vertical waterfalls representing variances of a calculation scheme.

---

3   For the problem of variance bars in calculation schemes, see page 84.

Alpha Corporation
Income statement in mUSD
2019

	Q1+Q2			Q3+Q4			2019			
	PL	AC	ΔPL	PL	FC	ΔPL	PL	FC	ΔPL	ΔPL%
+ Machine sales	3 165	3 349	+184	3 321	3 336	+15	6 486	6 685	+199	+3
+ Accessories sales	1 025	1 007	-18	1 078	1 129	+51	2 103	2 136	+33	+2
= **Sales**	**4 190**	**4 356**	**+166**	**4 399**	**4 465**	**+66**	**8 589**	**8 821**	**+232**	**+3**
- Cost of sales	2 163	2 134	-29	3 132	2 087	-45	4 295	4 221	-74	-2
= **Gross profit**	**2 027**	**2 222**	**+195**	**2 267**	**2 378**	**+111**	**4 294**	**4 600**	**+306**	**+7**
- R&D costs	428	456	+28	756	753	-3	1 184	1 209	+25	+2
- Sales costs	969	958	-11	984	959	-25	1 953	1 917	-36	-2
- Administration costs	441	404	-37	433	478	+45	874	882	+8	+1
= **Net income**	**189**	**404**	**+215**	**94**	**188**	**+94**	**283**	**592**	**+309**	**+109**

FIGURE 3.2-12 | SOLUTION EXERCISE #11A
Tabular variance analysis. The variance table is a classic in management accounting. Of course, you can use other periods if required or add further relative variances.

TABULAR VARIANCE ANALYSES

EXERCISE #11 **Finally, we want to compare both the actual and forecast values of the income statement with the respective plans by quarter.**

Again, we use the simple table from Exercise #5 FIGURE 3.1-5 (PAGE 148)—at least in terms of title and row structure. However, we will not create three additional columns for each of the five periods (four quarters plus one year) with the plan, the absolute and the relative variance. The analysis of both past quarters is of secondary importance, so we condense them into the first half of the year. We also consolidate the two forecast quarters into one value. Together with the annual value, this means we only have three periods to compare with their respective plans.

ABSOLUTE VARIANCES
Now we insert a plan column in front of each of the three actual columns and a column with the absolute variance after each. The gaps between the columns of such a triple block are narrow while the gaps between two blocks are slightly wider.

Alpha Corporation
Income statement in mUSD

2019		Q1+Q2			Q3+Q4			2019		
	PL	AC	ΔPL	PL	FC	ΔPL	PL	FC	ΔPL	
+ Machine sales	3 165	3 349	+184	3 321	3 336	+15	6 486	6 685		+199
+ Accessories sales	1 025	1 007	-18	1 078	1 129	+51	2 103	2 136		+33
= Sales	**4 190**	**4 356**	**+166**	**4 399**	**4 465**	**+66**	**8 589**	**8 821**		**+232**
- Cost of sales	2 163	2 134	-29	2 132	2 087	-45	4 295	4 221		-74
= Gross profit	**2 027**	**2 222**	**+195**	**2 267**	**2 378**	**+111**	**4 294**	**4 600**		**+306**
- R&D costs	428	456	+28	756	753	-3	1 184	1 209	+25	
- Sales costs	969	958	-11	984	959	-25	1 953	1 917		-36
- Administration costs	441	404	-37	433	478	+45	874	882	+8	
= Net income	**189**	**404**	**+215**	**94**	**188**	**+94**	**283**	**592**		**+309**

FIGURE 3.2-13 | SOLUTION EXERCISE #11B
Tabular variance analysis with integrated bars. In this representation we replaced the column ΔPL of FIGURE 3.2-12 with a variance waterfall to direct the reader's attention to the most important numbers.

RELATIVE VARIANCES

For the two half-years we don't make any relative variances, but we want to see them in the annual figures. FIGURE 3.2-12 shows the table created so far. It is suitable as a sample template for variance tables.

INTEGRATED BARS

We've already talked about this: Tables need to be read. They engage our system 2, but we want to accelerate our recognition with the help of system 1. Therefore, in many cases it is a good idea to enrich tables with visual elements that draw our attention to the important figures.

Now we see the advantage of choosing exactly the same value (1.5 em) for the category width in bar charts as we have for the row height in tables. We can easily replace the important annual variance column with a variance waterfall as in Exercise #10. This completes our sample template for a variance table with integrated bars, FIGURE 3.2-13.

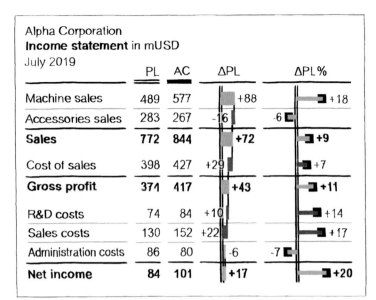

FIGURE 3.2-14
Business-responsive design (tablet). This is the first reduction of FIGURE 3.2-11, for when less space is available—like on a tablet. The selection of the information to hide (waterfalls AC and PL reduced to figures) was based on their business importance and not on technical or visual criteria.

FIGURE 3.2-15
Business-responsive design (smartphone). In the second reduction of FIGURE 3.2-11, e.g., for a smartphone, only the most important columns remain: the actual figures and their visualized variance from the plan.

BUSINESS-RESPONSIVE DESIGN

Our sample templates work well as long as we create static reports for a fixed format. With interactive dashboards it's different: The screen size of the device (computer, tablet, smartphone) is variable as is the data constellation a user navigates (e.g. the number of products to be displayed). This is why the designers of user interfaces try to map the content differently depending on the screen size of the device in use (responsive design). The smaller a screen gets the more content moves to additional pages.

We suggest considering business management aspects in responsive design. This *business-responsive design* would never spread a variance analyses across several pages. On a large screen we would show two waterfalls for actual and plan: the corresponding waterfall for the absolute variances and pins for the relative variances, FIGURE 3.2-11 (PAGE 161). For the smaller screen size of a tablet, we would replace the two absolute waterfalls with table columns, FIGURE 3.2-14. On a smartphone, we would also remove the plan column and the relative variances. What remains are the actual figures and the variance waterfall, indicating the contributions of the individual measures to the total variance of the result from plan, FIGURE 3.2-15.[1]

---

1   We first saw the practical implementation of this form of business-responsive design during the IBCS certification of the Zebra BI software.

RECAP

While the charts and tables in the previous section were one-dimensional and not intended for practical use, we have expanded them in this section to include comparisons and variances. The result is practical sample templates. We believe that just these few templates for time series analyses, structural analyses and tables cover a large part of the requirements in business.

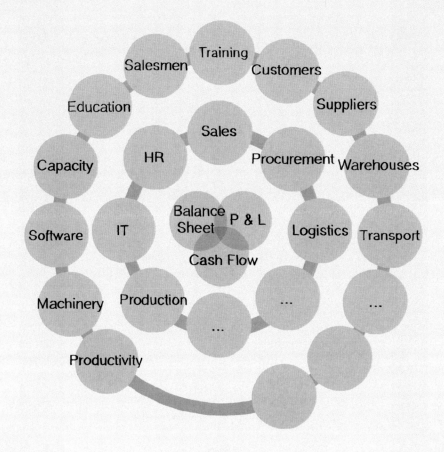

3.3
FINANCE AND MORE

BEST PRACTICES FOR SPECIALIST TOPICS

We could stop at this point or perhaps develop a few more templates for generic topics such as portfolio or geographic analysis. But shouldn't we go one step further and try to provide *best practices* for frequently used analyses of specialist topics? Proven functional templates would save millions of creators the trouble of having to design the same thing over and over in an attempt to render the best possible representation of the same facts. We would grow accustomed to such templates and be able to evaluate them in seconds. Or is there a particular reason the reports used to analyze a company's balance sheet, plant productivity, or customer retention should differ completely from those of other companies within the same industry?

We are well aware that we are now moving out of pure data visualization into areas for which there are specialists who understand more about their subject than we do. We are also far from writing a textbook on balance sheet analysis or industry-specific topics. The proposals in this section are intended to be suggestions on how to develop templates for specialist topics in principle. We are happy to leave the competition for the best solution to the specialists.

FIGURE 3.3-1

Reporting universe. The financial triad of balance sheet, profit and loss statement, and cash flow statement comprises the center of the reporting universe. Their visual representation can be largely standardized. The further a topic is from this center, the more individual its design. Already the second ring can be standardized industry-wide at best. The outer ring always remains company-specific, but can be oriented towards templates.

THE REPORTING UNIVERSE

We consider which topics are, in a conceptual sense, largely independent of the reporting company and its industry. We arrange the topics in a kind of *mind map* in such a way that the distance from the center is a measure of how company-specific we consider the respective topic. The result is the reporting universe shown in FIGURE 3.3-1.

At the center of the universe are the three interdependent reports of the financial triad: balance sheet, income statement and cash flow. Conceptually these reports are almost independent of the reporting company. The contents presented are—at least as far as *external* reporting is concerned—largely regulated by commercial law.

Standardizing *internal* financial reporting is somewhat more difficult. For example, the structure of the internal income statement can vary from company to company, reflecting company-specific value-adding processes in the best possible way. The basic structure, however, remains similar. The same applies to a company's cash accounting.

If you move further away from the financial center of the universe, you will find reports on topics such as personnel, sales or logistics. The reports in this second ring differ significantly from company to company. Take sales, for example: It makes a huge difference whether we sell our products via a web shop, our own direct sales or a partner network. The corresponding reports will clearly look different. At best,

industry-specific report templates may make sense. We might imagine, for example, that bed occupancy reports from two different hospitals could look the same—perhaps even similar to the occupancy report of a hotel or the seat occupancy report of an airline. But as we said, we will leave that to the specialists.

In the following, we will try to use sample templates as examples for the analysis of balance sheet, income statement and cash flow, where a standardized design seems to make sense. Don't get us wrong: We are not interested in developing templates for the calculation schemes of the measures used. The relevant accounting standards (e.g., US GAAP or IFRS) already regulate this in external reporting, and we are happy to leave this to accountants and auditors. Here it's only about the visualization of the topic.

BALANCE SHEET

The analysis and evaluation of a balance sheet, as with any analysis, requires a reference for comparison. Experienced balance sheet analysts may have their own yardstick when comparing the balance sheet ratios with empirical benchmarks. We would like to create a visual reference to objectify the analysis and make it understandable even for less experienced readers.

Possible references for balance sheet analysis are the previous years' figures as well as industry averages—we rarely see plan balances. So let's start with time series analyses and industry comparisons.

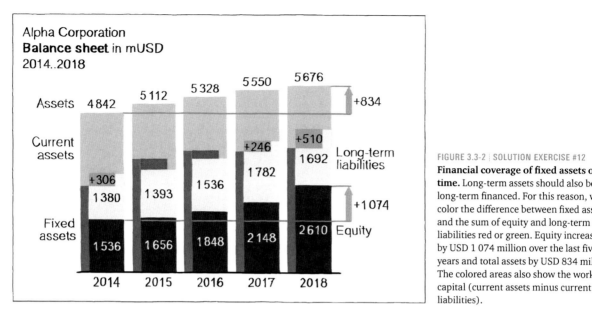

Alpha Corporation
Balance sheet in mUSD
2014..2018

FIGURE 3.3-2 | SOLUTION EXERCISE #12
Financial coverage of fixed assets over time. Long-term assets should also be long-term financed. For this reason, we color the difference between fixed assets and the sum of equity and long-term liabilities red or green. Equity increased by USD 1 074 million over the last five years and total assets by USD 834 million. The colored areas also show the working capital (current assets minus current liabilities).

BALANCE SHEET STRUCTURE

EXERCISE #12 **We want to analyze the balance sheet structure from 2014 to 2018 with our primary focus being the development of total assets and the origin of the required financial resources. We are also interested in the solvency of the company: To what degree are the fixed assets covered by equity and long-term liabilities?**

As we are comparing periodic values, we revert to our arguments made in Exercise #6 (time series analysis, page 150) and opt for a column chart. In the second row of the title we write "Balance sheet in mUSD", in the third row we enter the time interval "2014..2018"[1].

Now we present the long-term capital, comprising equity and long-term debt, as stacked columns. We put the equity at the bottom of the stack because it is the most interesting part and the lowest segment of a stacked column is the easiest to analyze in terms of development over time.

We do not compare long-term capital with a corresponding plan, but with fixed assets visualized by an overlapped column. According to the silver rule for balance sheets, the fixed assets should be long-term financed. This means that the long-term capital should be larger than the fixed assets. We show the surplus or deficit in coverage as an integrated variance in green or red. This results in a visual indicator for the asset coverage ratio II (equity plus long-term debt divided by fixed assets). We can also see the level of coverage by pure equity (golden rule for balance sheets, asset coverage ratio I) in this chart.

---

1 Two points ".." are the recommended notation for intervals in the labeling of time periods, see page 61, section 2.1.

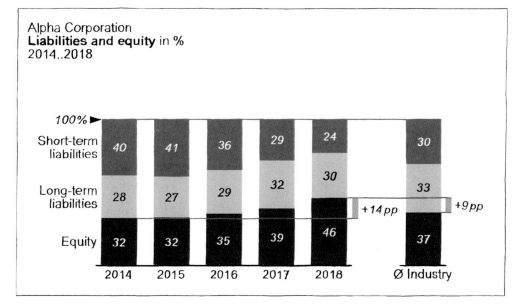

Alpha Corporation
Liabilities and equity in %
2014..2018

	2014	2015	2016	2017	2018	Ø Industry
Short-term liabilities	40	41	36	29	24	30
Long-term liabilities	28	27	29	32	30	33
Equity	32	32	35	39	46	37

+14 pp   +9 pp

FIGURE 3.3-3 ¦ SOLUTION
EXERCISE #13
Analysis of the capital structure. By normalizing the balance sheet total to 100%, we get a visual impression of the change in capital structure over the last five years. The equity ratio rose by 14 percentage points to 46%, 9 percentage points above the industry average.

In the same chart, we also illustrate the development of total assets, i.e. the balance sheet total. As a consequence we can now also perceive the current assets and the current liabilities. This way we get a visual impression of the shares of fixed and current assets in total assets (asset intensities). Now the green and red variances have an additional meaning: They also correspond to the working capital which is the difference between current assets and current liabilities.

Finally, we highlight the changes in shareholders' equity and total assets over a 5-year period and see the development of the balance sheet shown in FIGURE 3.3-2

CAPITAL STRUCTURE

EXERCISE #13 **Now we are interested in the capital structure, not only how it develops over time but also how it compares to the industry average. What is the company's financial independence and indebtedness?**

We return to the column chart and show the liabilities side of the balance sheet: equity, non-current and current liabilities. Since we are now interested in *structural* comparisons, we normalize the columns to 100% and can immediately see the degree of financial independence from the equity ratio (equity through total capital). The complementary debt ratio (liabilities through total capital) is also immediately clear. Besides the temporal development of these variables, the comparison with the industry average is also of interest. Therefore, we extend the chart to the right and show an additional column—set off from the others by a wider gap—with the average values of the industry. Finally, we highlight the change in the equity ratio over five years and its variance from the industry average and end up with FIGURE 3.3-3.

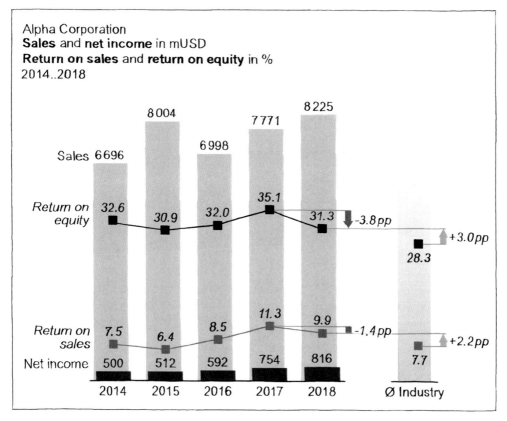

Alpha Corporation
Sales and **net income** in mUSD
Return on sales and **return on equity** in %
2014..2018

FIGURE 3.3-4 | SOLUTION
EXERCISE #14
Development of sales and net income. The success of a company is reflected in the development of sales and net income as well as the ratio of net income to sales and equity. Here, the return on sales fell compared to last year but is still higher than the industry average. The same applies to return on equity.

INCOME STATEMENT

EXERCISE #14 **Now we want to analyze the income of the company during the same period in terms of both sales and results. Once again, along with the development over time we are interested in the comparison with the industry average.**

We stick to the structure of the category axis in FIGURE 3.3-3, i.e. five annual periods and the industry average set off to the right. For the five years, we are drawing columns for sales. We present the result as a slightly offset column—properly scaled so we visually understand the share of the result in the revenue.

In addition, we place the return on sales as a line across the chart in order to compare its development independent of the absolute level. The return on equity, which is of particular interest for shareholders, is another line that we put above—scaled in the same way as return on sales.

Finally, we compare the two profitability figures with the industry average and highlight both the negative changes from the previous year and the positive differences from the industry average, FIGURE 3.3-4.

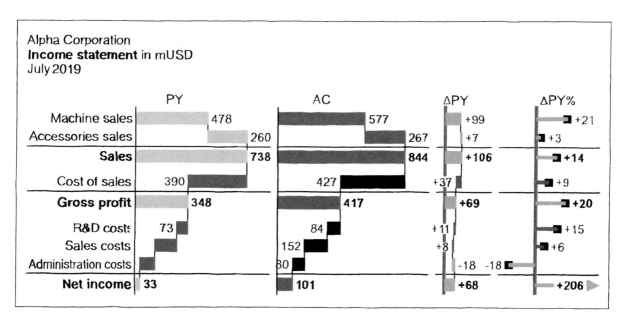

FIGURE 3.3-5 | SOLUTION EXERCISE #15

Income statement compared to previous year.
The calculation waterfalls on the left convey the contribution of the various measures to the net income. The colored variance waterfall shows how much these measures have contributed to the change in the net income. The pin chart with relative variances uses a triangle to show an outlier in the net income.

EXERCISE #15 **Determining the cause of the differences identified in Exercise #14 requires a more detailed analysis of the income statement in comparison with the previous year.**

To solve this task we can fall back on the standard analysis from Exercise #10. There we depicted the income statement and its reference as vertical calculation waterfalls and the corresponding absolute variances as a variance waterfall. We present the relative variances again as a pin chart, FIGURE 3.3-5.

The calculation waterfalls give a visual impression of the contribution of the individual measures to the result. For example, we can visually record the share of intermediate results, such as the gross profit on sales,

The variance waterfall, on the other hand, shows us how much the individual measures contribute to the change in earnings; for example, how higher manufacturing costs directly eat up parts of the sales growth.

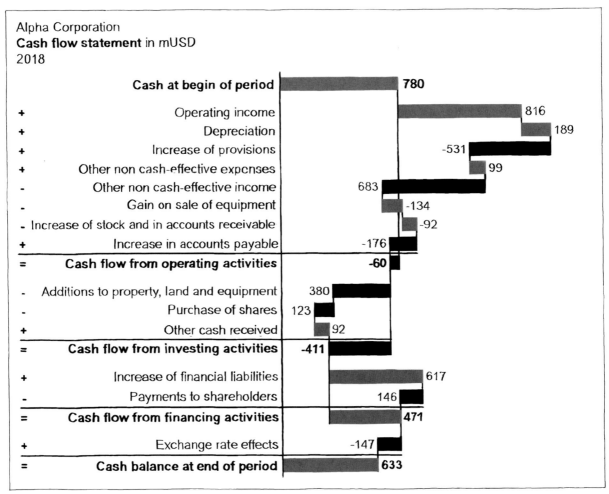

FIGURE 3.3-6 | SOLUTION EXERCISE #16

Cash flow statement. Calculation waterfalls are also the best choice to represent the origin and use of liquid funds. Subtotals show cash flows from operating, investing and financing activities.

CASH FLOW STATEMENT

EXERCISE #16 **In order to take a comprehensive look at the financial situation of the company, we are also interested in the source and use of liquid funds, using the traditional distinction between contributions from operating activities, investment activities and financing activities. We want to derive the cash flow from the balance sheet and income statement (indirect method).**

The object of this exercise is to present the cash flows that led to the change in cash and cash equivalents. This clearly implies the use of another vertical calculation waterfall: The first bar shows cash and cash equivalents at the beginning of 2018, the last one at the end of 2018. In between, we classify cash flows from operating, investing and financing activities. And that's the final part of our visual analysis of balance sheet, income and cash flow, FIGURE 3.3-6.

RECAP

Analysis of some business topics is largely the same for all companies, allowing for significant standardization. This applies especially to the analysis of the financial triad of a company's balance sheet, income statement and cash flow. By adapting the templates for time series and structural analyses developed in the previous section, we have developed five building blocks for the visual analysis of balance sheet, income statement and cash flow: Coverage of fixed assets, analysis of capital structure, development of sales and earnings, income statement and cash flow statement. But this is just an example. We expect that domain specialists and industry experts will develop a number of additional best practices for specific functional areas and industries over the coming years.

CHAPTER 4

NOTATION MANUAL AND REAL LIFE EXAMPLES

IMPLEMENTATION IN PRACTICE

After showing that the application of the proposed semantic notation to charts, tables, analyses and entire business topics works in principle, we now turn to implementation in practice. We are concerned here with the practical creation of reports in day-to-day business and the required tools: a company-specific notation manual, suitable templates and software support.

NOTATION MANUAL

The notation rules proposed in Chapter 2 are formulated in such a way that it is possible to discern meaning from the visual design. To leverage pattern recognition it was sufficient to stipulate, for example, that titles go at the top left and bad variances are marked in red. However, this is not sufficient for the concrete preparation of a report in a company: Where exactly is top left? And which red, i.e. which exact hue should we use? The internal standardization of such details is not only a question of aesthetics; it also brings calm to the reporting system and helps with pattern recognition. Therefore, the concrete form of these details should be defined and documented in a company-specific notation manual for reports, presentations and dashboards.

OPERATIONAL TEMPLATES

The templates presented in Chapter 3 already cover a large part of the requirements in practice. If a particularly important presentation in a given industry is missing, it will be supplemented. These sample templates become especially useful when already based upon the detailed specifications of the report notation manual and implemented within our company's reporting software. Why reinvent the wheel again and again? Using templates not only saves time but also guarantees good quality and provides the desired uniform look.

REAL-LIFE EXAMPLES SUPPORTED BY SOFTWARE

Many of our suggestions have long since ceased to be theory. They have been successfully put into practice in hundreds of companies and public administrations. At the end of this chapter, we will present real life examples from leading companies that have successfully designed their annual reports, management reports, presentations and dashboards according to our proposed rules of notation—in some cases for several years already. Most of the examples were created with software tools that significantly ease the application of notation standards.

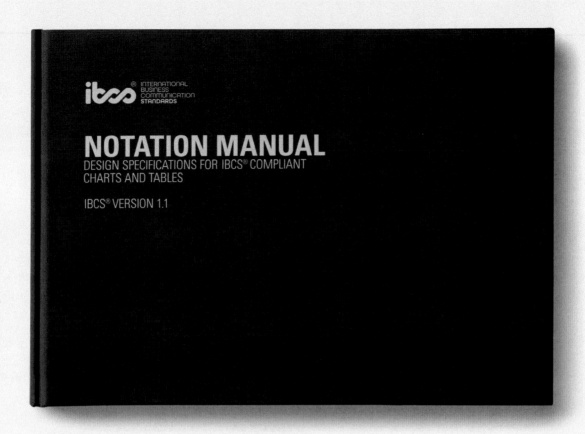

4.1
NOTATION MANUAL

HOW WE REGULATE THIS IN OUR COMPANY

Today it's not just the big companies that have corporate design manuals, regulating visual appearance in detail: How the logo is presented, which fonts are intended, which colors are used. In addition, they have specifications for page grids, the arrangement of design elements and the visual language. Everything is defined as concretely as possible and compliance is monitored. This is done in order to convey the identity of the company (corporate identity) through visual appearance. In other words: You should be able to recognize the company from its visual pattern and perceive it positively.

Our report notation manual has a similar objective. However, we are not concerned here with company recognition; rather, we want to record and understand the business contents and the associated statements as quickly and correctly as possible. But a corporate design manual and a report notation manual are crafted in very similar ways. We also need to define basic layout aspects like page grids, font and number formats, and the use of colors, patterns, and lines. This basic layout is supplemented with those aspects of the semantic notation presented in Chapter 2 that we want to apply in our company. Of course, the software in use plays an important role as limited functionality often demands compromises. The notation manual will also help in choosing the correct types of charts and tables as well as providing exact descriptions for their dimensions. This enables us to set parameters for the available software tools correctly and to design our reports perfectly.

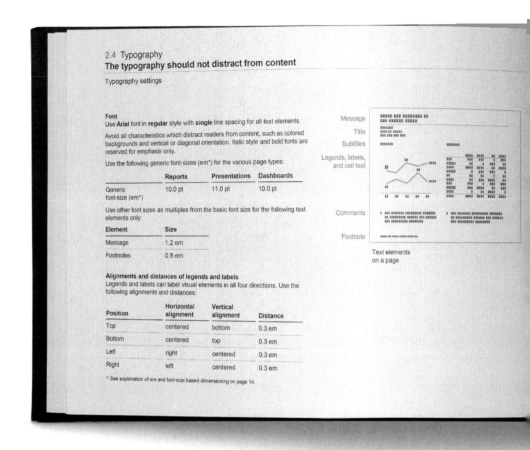

2.4 Typography
The typography should not distract from content

Typography settings

Font
Use **Arial** font in **regular** style with **single** line spacing for all text elements.

Avoid all characteristics which distract readers from content, such as colored backgrounds and vertical or diagonal orientation. Italic style and bold fonts are reserved for emphasis only.

Use the following generic font-sizes (em*) for the various page types:

	Reports	Presentations	Dashboards
Generic font-size (em*)	10.0 pt	11.0 pt	10.0 pt

Use other font sizes as multiples from the basic font size for the following text elements only:

Element	Size
Message	1.2 em
Footnotes	0.8 em

Alignments and distances of legends and labels
Legends and labels can label visual elements in all four directions. Use the following alignments and distances:

Position	Horizontal alignment	Vertical alignment	Distance
Top	centered	bottom	0.3 em
Bottom	centered	top	0.3 em
Left	right	centered	0.3 em
Right	left	centered	0.3 em

*) See explanation of em and font-size based dimensioning on page 14.

Text elements on a page

BASIC LAYOUT

Before defining the layout, we should survey the different reporting products in the company. Typically, these are different types of printed reports and presentation charts along with interactive analysis systems (often called dashboards) for PCs, tablets and mobile phones. For each of these reporting products, the notation manual determines their page layout. For static documents such as printed materials and presentation slides, a grid tailored to the respective page format helps arrange page elements such as messages, titles, charts, tables, comments and footnotes. With interactive analysis systems, it becomes much more difficult to determine how to display content that may vary greatly from analysis to analysis on the available space. This includes determining, in advance, the number of columns and bars to be displayed (e.g., 12 months of a year or the top ten of a structural analysis plus residuals), instead of simply distributing the result of a given data query over the available space[1]. Sometimes the complete representation, including font size, is scaled down to accommodate more content. Rules for business-responsive design also come into play, as indicated in the section on font size based layout.[2]

The notation manual then sets a standard font for each of these reporting products, referring to its size as "em" according to the font size based layout concept. This font is used for most inscriptions and as a reference for all other font sizes, e.g., for messages and footnotes (SECTION 2.4 in our notation manual above).

We continue with basic rules for the formatting of numbers like the choice of decimal and thousand

---

1   This is a decisive difference to the chart design commonly used today in Microsoft Excel and other reporting tools that for a given area draw the columns for a three-months chart significantly thicker than when there are twelve months. For our concept of a layout based on font size, see Section 2.7.

2   See page 109 and 164

Consistent usage of currency abbreviations and multipliers facilitates readability

Currency abbreviations and multipliers

Use the standard currency abbreviations based on ISO 4217 which provides a set of currency abbreviations using three-letter acronyms such as EUR, CHF, USD, and GBP.

Except when necessary, display monetary values without decimal places.

Use the following multipliers in combination with the currency units to keep the number of digits small:

	Multiplier	Basic value	Display
No multiplier	-	1 USD	1 USD
		10 USD	10 USD
		100 USD	100 USD
In thousands	k	1 000 USD	1 kUSD
		10 000 USD	10 kUSD
		100 000 USD	100 kUSD
In millions	m	1 000 000 USD	1 mUSD
		10 000 000 USD	10 mUSD
		100 000 000 USD	100 mUSD
In billions	b	1 000 000 000 USD	1 bUSD
		10 000 000 000 USD	10 bUSD
		100 000 000 000 USD	100 bUSD

separators as well as the number of digits in charts and tables.

Finally, we determine the definite appearance and use of colors, patterns, frames and lines in the basic layout.

SEMANTIC NOTATION
The second section of the notation manual specifies the uniform formatting and meaning of captions and labels, time periods, scenarios, variances and highlights. These are exactly the topics for which we developed notation concepts in Chapter 2.

CAPTIONS AND LABELS
In the section on the semantic notation of captions and labels[3], we addressed two topics: the uniform definition and spelling of terms and the recognition of the type of caption based on its appearance.

We suggest documenting the uniform definition and spelling of terms—in particular the designation, abbreviation and definition of measures, as well as product names, customer groups, subsidiaries and so on—in a separate glossary, as the scope of such topics quickly exceeds that of a notation manual. Such a glossary is also more subject to changes than the actual notation manual. It is worth noting that the creation and ongoing harmonization of a company-wide glossary can be a project in its own right.

Defining uniform abbreviations for currencies and their prefixes or suffixes for thousands, millions and billions is one of the simpler tasks, as can be seen in SECTION 2.5 of our notation manual (above). Units and multipliers of volume measures are documented in the same way (e.g., m² etc.). Standardized spelling of time aspects (e.g., Jun 2019), scenarios (e.g., PL) and their combination (e.g., ΔPL) round out this section.

3   See page 55.

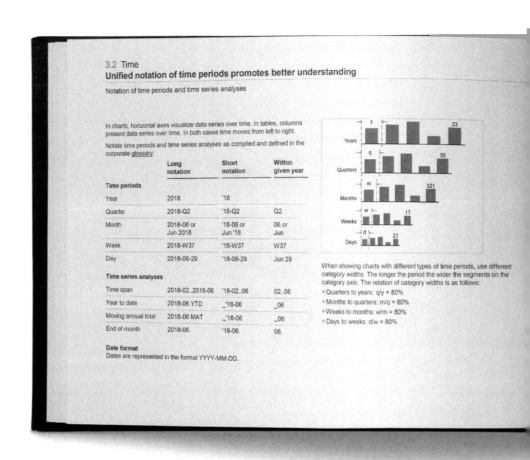

3.2 Time
Unified notation of time periods promotes better understanding

Notation of time periods and time series analyses

In charts, horizontal axes visualize data series over time. In tables, columns present data series over time. In both cases time moves from left to right.

Notate time periods and time series analyses as compiled and defined in the corporate glossary:

	Long notation	Short notation	Within given year
Time periods			
Year	2018	'18	
Quarter	2018-Q2	'18-Q2	Q2
Month	2018-06 or Jun 2018	'18-06 or Jun '18	06 or Jun
Week	2018-W37	'18-W37	W37
Day	2018-06-29	'18-06-29	Jun 29
Time series analyses			
Time span	2018-02..2018-06	'18-02..06	02..06
Year to date	2018-06 YTD	_'18-06	_06
Moving annual total	2018-06 MAT	_'18-06	_06
End of month	2018-06.	'18-06.	06.

Date format
Dates are represented in the format YYYY-MM-DD.

When showing charts with different types of time periods, use different *category widths*. The longer the period the wider the segments on the category axis. The relation of category widths is as follows:
+ Quarters to years: q/y = 80%
+ Months to quarters: m/q = 80%
+ Weeks to months: w/m = 80%
+ Days to weeks: d/w = 80%

The second aspect of captions and labels is their appearance. Ideally, the different types should be recognizable by their structure, position and format. The notation manual must therefore describe exactly how to structure titles, subtitles, legends, axis labels, value labels, footnotes, messages, comments and where to arrange them relative to the page margin or the object to be labelled. It should also determine how large the font is in relation to the standard font em and whether individual labels or parts thereof should be specially formatted (e.g., bold or italic).

TIME PERIODS
On to the visualization of time periods in reports. According to our suggestions in Section 2.2 on semantic notation of time aspects[1], the time axis in charts should stretch horizontally from left to right. In tables, time periods are preferably set in columns, likewise from left to right.

Following the proposal of adapting category widths to different period types (e.g., years and months) displayed on one page means making concrete specifications. For example, the category width of a period should always be 80% of the width of the next larger period, so if years are 4.0 em wide, then quarters are 3.2 em. SECTION 3.2 of our notation manual (above) summarizes the notation of time periods.

SCENARIOS
The next section of the notation manual describes the visualization of scenarios: black or an 80% gray for actual data? Which grayscale is used for comparisons to the previous year? The manual should also determine how thick the frame for planning data should be, what shade of gray it has and how the hatching should look when forecasting.

---

[1] See page 69.

Applying patterns helps identify the types of scenarios to be compared

Notation of scenario types

Use scenarios (also called data types or data categories) and abbreviations as compiled and defined in the corporate glossary.

Apply the following patterns to visualize the different scenario types when comparing them:

Type and scenario	Abbreviation	Pattern	
Measured data, e.g. Actual	AC		Solid dark
Previous year (comparison only)	PY		light
Expected data, e.g. Forecast	FC		Hatched
Fictitious data, e.g. Budget, Plan	BU, PL		Outlined

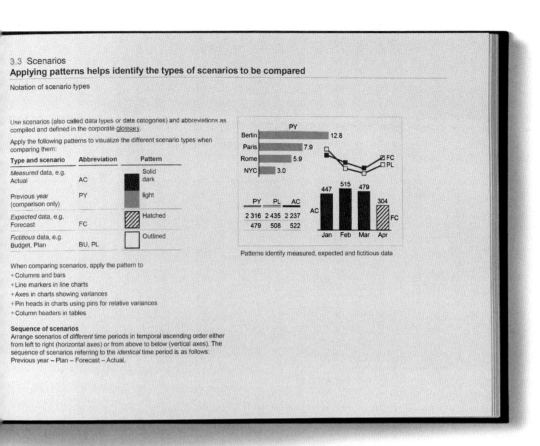

Patterns identify measured, expected and fictitious data

When comparing scenarios, apply the pattern to

+ Columns and bars
+ Line markers in line charts
+ Axes in charts showing variances
+ Pin heads in charts using pins for relative variances
+ Column headers in tables

Sequence of scenarios
Arrange scenarios of *different* time periods in temporal ascending order either from left to right (horizontal axes) or from above to below (vertical axes). The sequence of scenarios referring to the *identical* time period is as follows: Previous year – Plan – Forecast – Actual.

To differentiate between several actual, plan or forecast scenarios also requires a detailed description of their visualization. In Section 2.3 on the semantic notation of scenarios, we have made appropriate proposals for distinguishing between time scenarios (e.g., previous year and previous year) and update scenarios (e.g., budget and three-year plan)[2]. As mentioned in the same section, the notation manual should also include appropriate visualization suggestions for the comparison of variants of plans and benchmarks.

The notation manual then determines how the semantic notation of scenarios apply to different design elements: on columns, bars, markers in line charts, for example, or on pin heads for relative variances, axes for variance charts and column heads for tables. Even the application of scenario notation to stacked columns and bars must be described:

for instance, the lowest segment could remain in a simple column and bar chart's format, while the above segments take on different shades of gray, and become outlined and hatched, if necessary.

Finally we define the applicable order of scenarios with overlapping columns and bars, or in tables. The primary sorting—ascending by time—is clear: the previous year is to the left of the current year, the plan for next year to the right. This is no longer quite so clear for scenarios involving the same time period. Our proposal: plan before forecast before actual, mirroring the order in which the scenarios were created. The same order should apply to comparisons of scenarios in horizontal waterfalls: the reference scenario on the left, the scenario to be compared on the right. Otherwise the waterfall won't work. SECTION 3.3 of our notation manual (above) lists the most important rules for scenario notation.

2   See page 77.

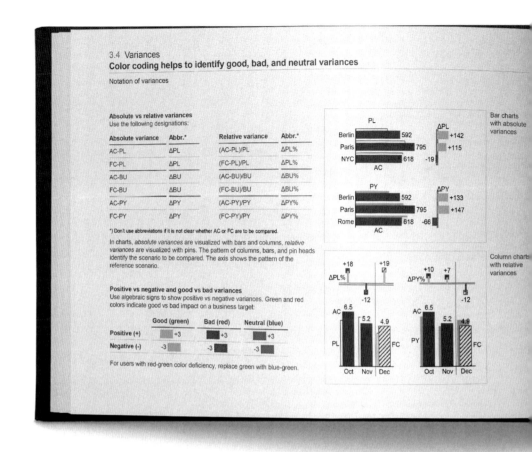

3.4 Variances
Color coding helps to identify good, bad, and neutral variances

Notation of variances

Absolute vs relative variances
Use the following designations:

Absolute variance	Abbr.*	Relative variance	Abbr.*
AC-PL	ΔPL	(AC-PL)/PL	ΔPL%
FC-PL	ΔPL	(FC-PL)/PL	ΔPL%
AC-BU	ΔBU	(AC-BU)/BU	ΔBU%
FC-BU	ΔBU	(FC-BU)/BU	ΔBU%
AC-PY	ΔPY	(AC-PY)/PY	ΔPY%
FC-PY	ΔPY	(FC-PY)/PY	ΔPY%

*) Don't use abbreviations if it is not clear whether AC or FC are to be compared.

In charts, *absolute* variances are visualized with bars and columns, *relative* variances are visualized with pins. The pattern of columns, bars, and pin heads identify the scenario to be compared. The axis shows the pattern of the reference scenario.

Positive vs negative and good vs bad variances
Use algebraic signs to show positive vs negative variances. Green and red colors indicate good vs bad impact on a business target:

	Good (green)	Bad (red)	Neutral (blue)
Positive (+)	+3	+3	+3
Negative (-)	-3	-3	-3

For users with red-green color deficiency, replace green with blue-green.

Bar charts with absolute variances

Column charts with relative variances

VARIANCES

Variances first need specific color tones that have semantic meaning but are clearly different from corporate design colors[1]. There is also the question of handling red-green deficiencies. This is not too big an issue, as most of those affected can still distinguish between red and green—just a little worse than others. Still, a bluish green can be chosen for a better contrast or the reporting software is configured with different color tones for users with and without red-green deficiency[2]. Either way, it must be written down. Likewise, the color for neutral variances: Blue or rather gray? And what color code exactly?

The notation manual also suggests adding a plus sign to positive variances in order to make the numbers immediately recognizable as variances.

If the available software permits, relative variances should be displayed as pins and oversized relative variances marked as outliers. SECTION 3.4 from our notation manual above has an excerpt on these topics.

In addition to further details, this section also decides whether calculation schemes are to be displayed using the addition method or the calculation method[3], i.e. whether the costs on an income statement have a negative or a positive sign. As we have described in Section 2.4 on the semantic notation of

---

1   In general, we encourage you *not to* use the colors specified in the Corporate Design Manual for the design of charts.

2   With some software programs, it is possible to define the most suitable color palette in the user profile.

3   See page 83.

Unified indicators help readers to find their way

Types and layout of indicators

Add *indicators* to highlight the message and to indicate outliers. Using indicators with the same design for the same purpose will help readers to find their way.

Highlighting indicators
Use the following three types of indicators for highlighting the message in a chart:

+ **Difference markers:** Highlight *differences* in charts by using two parallel assisting lines to project the respective lengths of two columns or bars to a *difference marker* highlighting the distance between the two assisting lines. Similar to variances, use green, red, and medium gray color to indicate a positive, negative, and neutral impact on a business target.

+ **Trend arrows:** Highlight *trends* in charts with a *trend arrow*. Similar to variances, use green, red, and medium gray color to indicate a positive, negative, and neutral impact on a business target.

+ **Ellipses:** Use blue *ellipses* to highlight single values that are linked to the message.

Outlier triangles
If a relative variance is (a) very big in comparison to the other relative variances, and this *outlier* is (b) not important for business, e.g. a big relative variance of a small value, then do not scale the whole chart to this outlier. Rather visualize unimportant outliers with *outlier triangles*. Omit the pin head and add *outlier triangles* pointing in the direction of growth.

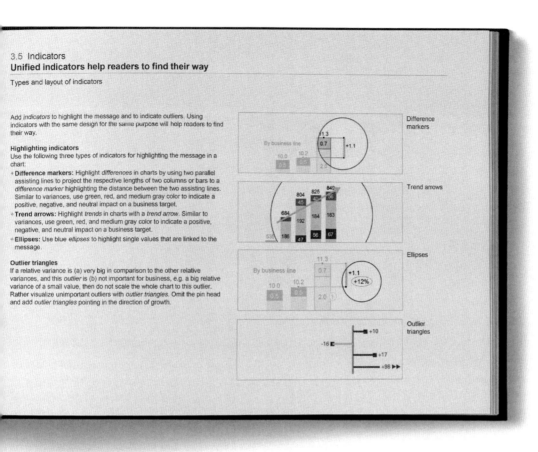

Difference markers

Trend arrows

Ellipses

Outlier triangles

---

variances, such a decision determines the direction of the bars in variance charts.

HIGHLIGHTING

We see the three most important types of highlighting as difference markers, trend arrows and highlighting of individual values[4]. The notation manual defines exactly how these should look: from line thickness to the size of the arrowheads to the question of whether connecting lines of difference markers should be dotted. These decisions depend heavily on the software used.

Highlighting individual values requires yet another distinct color tone as well as the decision to use either ellipses around the values or fluorescent marked backgrounds. Uniformity is key.

SECTION 3.5 from our notation manual (above) documents the indicators used for highlighting.

4   For semantic notation of highlights, see page 90.

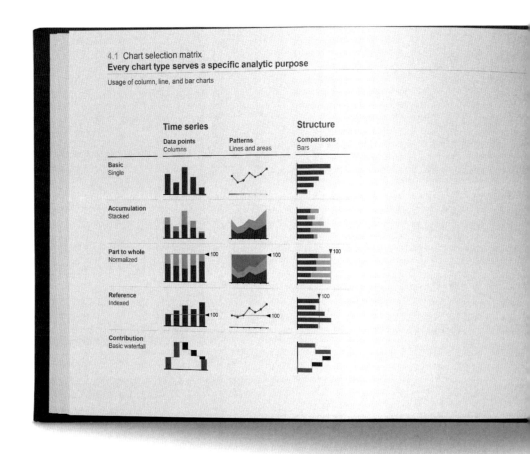

4.1 Chart selection matrix
Every chart type serves a specific analytic purpose

Usage of column, line, and bar charts

CHARTS AND TABLES

The notations manual helps choose suitable charts or tables by recommending appropriate types for specific application purposes. The appearance is then described in detail.

CHARTS

In Chapter 1 we stated our goal of getting by with as few chart types as possible[1]. We assume that the column, line and bar charts shown in SECTION 4.1 of our notation manual (above) in different variations (simple, stacked, normalized, indexed, overlapped or as a waterfall) will cover most practical applications.

Now it is a matter of describing the layout details of these chart types. For example, the column width in relation to the category width, the distances of the

legends, the thickness of the axis or the overlap ratio of reference columns and bars. This may sound exaggerated—and no report creator should have to deal with such details—but the graphic designers who have to design charts for an annual report and the IT colleagues who develop and set parameters for the reporting software or create style sheets need such specifications to ensure a uniform appearance. In this respect, it would be worth considering moving these details to an appendix to the notation manual.

SPREADSHEETS

A few basic types of tables also get the job done. The majority of business tables show time periods and scenarios, such as actual and plan, with variances in the columns but measures or structural elements, such as products or regions, in the rows. In rare cases, cross tables with two or more structural dimensions in both rows and columns might come into play, but all other table types are exceptions.

1   See Figure 1.3-2, page 30.

5.1 Table rows
Standardized layout of rows and columns reveals the table structure

Properties of table rows

In general, table rows show business measures or elements of a structure dimension. (Display time periods, scenarios, and variances in columns rather than in rows.)

Use the generic font-size (1.0 em*) and design the specific row types as follows:

+ **Header rows:** Use abbreviations for the column headers (e.g. AC, PL, ΔPL%). Add a dark gray line of 0.1 em to separate the column header row from the rows below. Semantic lines of 0.3 em replace the solid line when scenario columns are shown. Column header rows of more than one level are separated by a dark gray line of 0.1 em.

+ **Standard rows:** Use a row height of 1.5 em. Add light gray dotted lines of 0.03 em to separate the rows. Do not add these gray dotted lines above the top row of a row set.

+ **"Of which" rows:** Place "of which" rows below the corresponding mother rows. Use a font-size of 0.8 em and a row height of 1.0 em. Do not separate the "of which" row by a horizontal line.

+ **Totals rows:** Display totals of a set of rows or (intermediate) results of a calculation scheme in bold face below the rows of the corresponding set and separate them by dark gray lines of 0.1 em.
Add empty rows of 0.7 em height in order to support the perception of the table structure.

+ **Share rows:** Place share rows below the corresponding absolute row. Use a font-size of 0.8 em (italic face) and a row height of 1.0 em. Do not separate the share row by a horizontal line.

*) See explanation of em and font-size based dimensioning on page 14.

SoftCons International Inc.
P&L statement in mUSD
2018 PY, PL, AC

	PL	GER	of which Berlin	Others	Group	ΔPL
			AC			
+ Software	561	243	181	164	560	-1
+ Support	140	53	37	49	131	-9
+ Consulting	199	71	43	94	213	+14
of which Mgmt. Consulting	72	25	12	32	75	+3
= **Sales**	**900**	**367**	**261**	**307**	**904**	**+4**
- Cost of sales	221	91	45	119	267	+46
= **Gross profit**	**679**	**276**	**216**	**188**	**637**	**-42**
in % of sales	75%	75%	83%	61%	70%	-5%p
- R&D expenses	123	42	17	54	124	+1
- S&G expenses	44	15	10	15	43	-1
- Other op. expenses	9	3	1	3	8	-1
+ Other op. income	32	17	9	26	55	+23
= **EBIT**	**535**	**233**	**197**	**142**	**517**	**-18**
in % of sales	59%	63%	78%	46%	57%	-2%p

Within these few table types, recurring types of rows and columns should be recognizable by their formatting. However, the design proposals for these row and column types set forth in Section 2.6 on the semantic notation of tables[2] are not detailed enough for the implementation of a company-wide standard. Such details include: How high are the rows, and how wide are the columns for the respective row and column types? How wide are the gaps between two groups of rows and columns and what exactly do the different lines look like (see the notation of table rows in SECTION 5.1 above)? This section also includes the proper way to embed graphic elements such as variance bars.

2　See page 94.

At this point one or two may frown and wonder whether all this isn't too pedantic. Experience teaches: it's not. It brings a lot of calmness into reporting when tables are not only semantically correct but also no longer reveal the creator or the software product used. And it doesn't take more time. Templates provide the best way to implement the above formatting details without worry or hassle. For tables, such templates are often Excel templates. Five or six ready-made tables, perfectly formatted, which anyone can and should use. More about this in the next section.

RECAP

For the operational implementation of the design rules proposed in the second chapter, a company-specific manual for the notation of reports, presentation slides and dashboards—similar to a corporate design manual—is required. The details to be defined in this notation manual range from page grids, font sizes, line widths and color tones to the semantic notation of scenarios, variances and table rows. Suitable software solutions that support report writers in implementing the standards are crucial for success.

The structure of such notation manuals is inevitably similar; only the individual design varies from company to company. Therefore, it makes sense to use appropriate templates here as well[1].

1   Sample templates for notation manuals are available at www.ibcs.com/notation-manual.

4.2
OPERATIONAL TEMPLATES

DO NOT REINVENT THE WHEEL

Now there is a company-specific report notation manual that describes in detail how charts and tables should look. Surely this is a good foundation for dashboard developers accustomed to working with screen design and investing time in it? But let's be realistic: We can't expect our management accountants to pick up the notation manual every time they write a report and carefully check every font size, every distance and every hue. That won't work, especially when time is an issue.

It was not for nothing that we dealt with sample templates in Chapter 3 and found that we can cover many reporting requirements with a small number of repetitive representations. Not through simple charts and tables; rather through more complex analyses of time series and business structures like products or regions and their comparison with plan data, previous year data or other scenarios. We have even offered sample templates for complete business topics such as a balance sheet analysis.

Now it makes sense to create these sample templates using the technical tools at hand and following the report notation manual. Making the results available as copy templates throughout the company will kill, as it were, several birds with one stone:

1. SAME NOTATION   All reports are always notated in the same way, i.e. as written in the notation manual. This promotes pattern recognition and makes it easier for everyone.

2. SIMILAR ANALYSES   Similar analyses are always carried out using given templates. This promotes pattern recognition at the level of the entire analyses.

3. SOFTWARE USED   The sample templates have already been created with the available software tool(s). This ensures easy implementation.

4. FAST CREATION   Report writers finish faster because they don't think too much about visual design and technical realization. Rather they invest the time saved in content conception and analysis.

The following lays out the implementation of the conceptual templates already sketched in the previous chapter. We want to remain as neutral as possible in the choice of technology so we opt for PowerPoint. We could also have used Excel, but for that we would have had to dig a little deeper into our box of tricks. For instructions on Excel consult the book by Holger Gerths and Rolf Hichert[1] from 2013. Whether it makes sense to exhaust Excel in this way is another question. Perhaps it would be better to use Excel add-ins and other IBCS-certified software tools, as discussed with the real-life examples in the next section.

---

1   Gerths, Holger und Hichert, Rolf: Designing Business Charts with Excel based on the Standards of HICHERT®SUCCESS, Second Edition, Haufe, Freiburg 2013 The book based on Excel 2007/2010 is out of print, but the e-book is still available at www.ibcs.com.

The subsequent pages provide inspiration for creating company-specific sample templates. We focus on the most common chart and table types in management reports and dashboards.[2] We dedicate one double-page spread to similar templates and in each instance deal with a few selected details and special features.

TIME SERIES ANALYSES (COLUMNS)

The first template shows stacked columns with integrated difference markers, extended by columns that are stacked according to different criteria than the columns in the main chart. The second template overlays the column chart with lines.

TIME SERIES ANALYSES WITH VARIANCES (COLUMNS)

The two templates on the next double spread are very similar. The bar chart compares actual and forecast data with a reference scenario (for example, previous year or plan). Variances are visible on the two upper tiers. The difference between the two templates: In one the monthly figures are the focus; in the other, the years.

TIME SERIES ANALYSES (LINES)

On this double spread we show two templates for line charts that serve two entirely different purposes: Lines for displaying time series with many values and lines for displaying cumulative values as a Z-chart.

STRUCTURAL ANALYSES (BARS)

Here we show a simple template for stacked bars, sorted by size. We use the second template for the analysis of proportions with normalized bars. The weighting is expressed by the width of the bars (Marimekko chart).

STRUCTURAL ANALYSES WITH VARIANCES (BARS)

These two templates are the vertical counterpart to the time series analyses with variances (columns): comparison of actual data with a reference scenario (e.g., previous year or plan) supplemented by two tiers with variances.

ANALYSIS OF CALCULATION SCHEMES (BARS AND TABLES)

On this double spread we present three templates for the analysis of calculation schemes such as income statements. A pure waterfall chart, a table with integrated variance bars and a pure table. The smooth transition between bar charts and tables becomes clear.

VARIANCES ACROSS SEVERAL HIERARCHY LEVELS (TABLE)

On this double spread we present a template for the purely tabular presentation of variances across a multi-level regional sales organization. The particular challenge here lies in the visualization of the hierarchical structure.

MULTIPLE CHARTS

The two templates on the last double spread consist of several individual charts and are used to display higher information density: a ratio tree consisting of several charts for a calculated key figure and its arguments and a so-called small multiple chart in which several small charts of the same type are arranged on one page for a number of similar elements such as products, regions or branches.

---

[2] Suggestions for further sample templates based on other chart types, such as dot and bubble charts, can be found at www.ibcs.com.

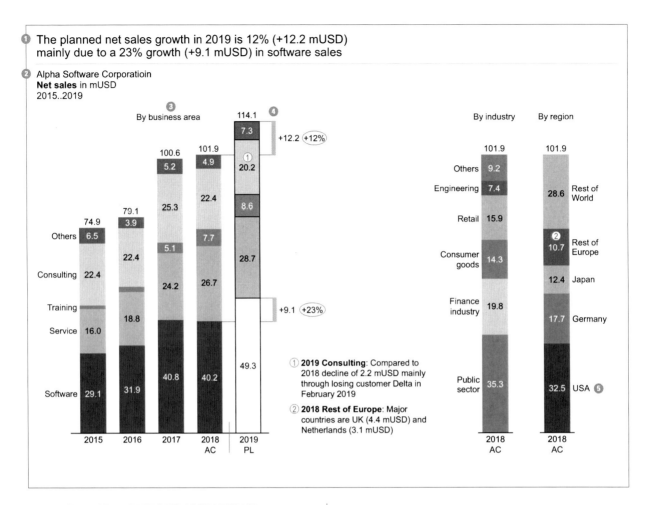

TIME SERIES ANALYSES (COLUMNS)

Column charts are a classic of time series analysis, but should only be stacked if the lowest data series is of primary interest or if there are only a few data series with small fluctuations.

STACKED COLUMNS ACCORDING TO SEVERAL CRITERIA

The extensions on the right side of the chart are well suited to display the same data in a different structure (here by industries and regions) or additional benchmarks (e.g., competitors). We would like to emphasize the following semantic details:

MESSAGE ❶   If the representation is a report conveying a message, we name the message first—either at the top of the screen, or to the right of the page title with a wider page format such as 16:9. SEE PAGE 65.

PAGE TITLE ❷   Usually three lines are sufficient for a unique page title: report entity (for example, organizational unit), business measure in bold followed by the unit and time reference. SEE PAGE 62.

SUBTITLE ❸   If there are several objects to distinguish on a page, we add subtitles. Here for the views according to business areas, industries and regions. SEE PAGE 62.

DIFFERENCE MARKERS ❹   To highlight the difference between two values use difference markers: positive effects with green (and a plus sign), bad differences red, and neutral differences blue. SEE PAGE 91.

INTEGRATED LABELS ❺   Data series labels integrated directly into the chart avoid colored links with external legends. Thus, the powerful stylistic device of color remains reserved for highlighting. SEE PAGE 63.

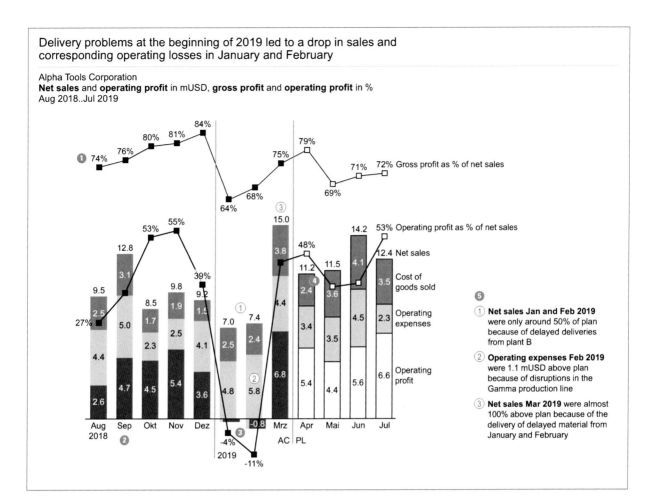

Delivery problems at the beginning of 2019 led to a drop in sales and corresponding operating losses in January and February

Alpha Tools Corporation
Net sales and **operating profit** in mUSD, **gross profit** and **operating profit** in %
Aug 2018..Jul 2019

COLUMNS WITH OVERLAYING LINES

We can easily overlay columns for absolute measures with lines for relative measures to compare their evolution over time.

INTEGRATED VALUE LABELS ❶ The direct labeling of values in the chart not only avoids value axes and grid lines, but also allows the figures to be apprehended more quickly. This works well even with two different value axes for absolute and relative figures. SEE PAGE 63.

COLUMN WIDTH ❷ The ratio of column width to category width indicates whether it is a basic measure or a ratio. Net sales are a basic measure and therefore the columns are twice as wide as the gaps between them. SEE PAGE 122.

OFFSET NEGATIVE COLUMNS ❸ The two dark column segments visualising the negative *operating profit* in January and February are slightly offset to the right. This way we can see that the *operating profit* in these two months is the difference between *sales* and *costs*.

OUTLINED PLAN ❹ We show plan figures outlined—as is the case with April 2019 on. Only the lowest column segment is outlined without a fill—as with column charts for one data series. The upper segments are outlined *and* filled. SEE PAGE 76.

COMMENTS ❺ If we add comments to written reports, each comment begins with a bold term that reflects the thematic structure of the comment. We number the comments consecutively and link them via connectors to the appropriate chart or table content. SEE PAGE 66.

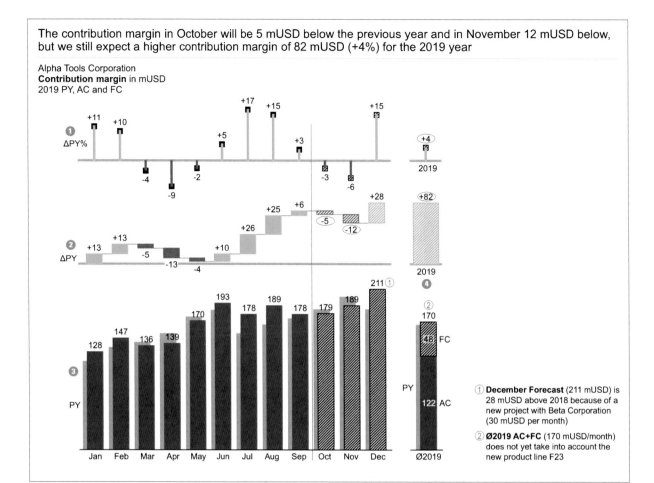

The contribution margin in October will be 5 mUSD below the previous year and in November 12 mUSD below, but we still expect a higher contribution margin of 82 mUSD (+4%) for the 2019 year

Alpha Tools Corporation
Contribution margin in mUSD
2019 PY, AC and FC

① December Forecast (211 mUSD) is 28 mUSD above 2018 because of a new project with Beta Corporation (30 mUSD per month)

② Ø2019 AC+FC (170 mUSD/month) does not yet take into account the new product line F23

TIME SERIES ANALYSES WITH VARIANCES (COLUMNS)

These two templates are suitable for comparing the development of scenarios over time in conjunction with the analysis of variances per period.

COLUMN COMPARISON FOR THE MONTHLY ANALYSIS

We compare the actual figures up to the current month and the forecast figures for the rest of the year with the previous year's values. The variance waterfall above explains the 82 mUSD higher *contribution margin,* supplemented by percentage variances displayed at the very top.

RELATIVE VARIANCES ❶   Unlike their absolute counterparts, we notate relative variances as pins. The pin head bears the semantic notation of the scenario to be compared; here solid for actual and hatched for forecast. The gray axis indicates that previous year is the reference scenario. SEE PAGE 87.

ABSOLUTE VARIANCES ❷   We select a waterfall for the representation of absolute variances in order to analyse the monthly contributions to the annual variance shown on the right. We put labels for the good contributions above the green columns and the bad ones below the red columns. SEE PAGE 81.

REFERENCE COLUMNS ❸   The columns for the previous year's values are to the left and behind the actual columns. Left, because the previous year is before the current year, and behind, because the actual values are more important.

MONTHLY COLUMNS VS. ANNUAL COLUMNS ❹   The absolute variance for 2019 represents an annual value and is therefore shown with a broader column width. The narrower absolute column is the monthly average of the year. This value can be compared with the individual months to the left of it. SEE PAGE 72.

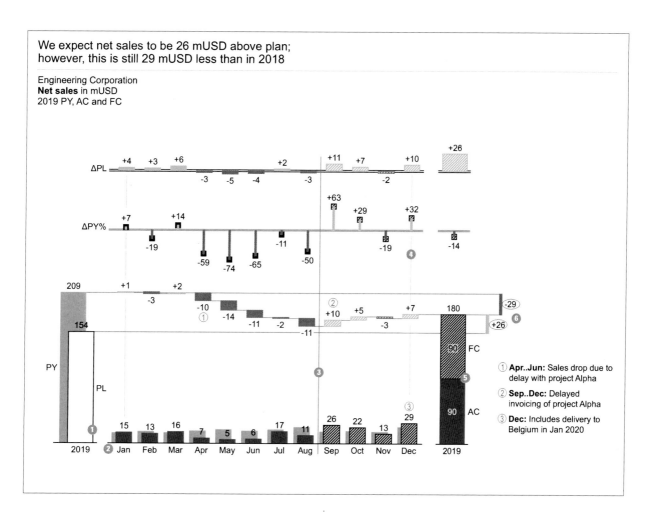

We expect net sales to be 26 mUSD above plan; however, this is still 29 mUSD less than in 2018

Engineering Corporation
Net sales in mUSD
2019 PY, AC and FC

① **Apr..Jun:** Sales drop due to delay with project Alpha

② **Sep..Dec:** Delayed invoicing of project Alpha

③ **Dec:** Includes delivery to Belgium in Jan 2020

COLUMN COMPARISON FOR THE ANNUAL ANALYSIS
In contrast to the chart on the left, the focus of the analysis here is on explaining the expected *annual* variances from previous year and plan.

SCALE FOR ANNUAL VALUES ❶ The scale now depends on the annual values. The columns for the monthly values are correspondingly small and should be understood as additional information.

LABELING OF THE TIME AXIS ❷ We do not label the periods—here years and months—in the middle of the categories, but in the middle of the actual columns. This prevents period labels from moving to the left when a reference column for the previous year or plan is added.

SEPARATOR LINE ❸ A separator line separates two time frames from each other. Here it marks the point up to which actual data is available. For charts that consist of several tiers, the separator line extends from the lowest to the highest chart to underline the coherence of the partial charts.

ASSISTING LINES ❹ The two vertical assisting lines in January and December also illustrate the relationship between the chart elements across all tiers.

STACKED FORECAST COLUMN ❺ The division of the annual column into actual and forecast gives a good visual impression of how much of the expected annual value has already been realized.

HIGHLIGHTING THE MESSAGE ❻ We use blue ellipses to highlight the sales variances from previous year and plan, as mentioned in the message so that the reader can find them easily. SEE PAGE 90.

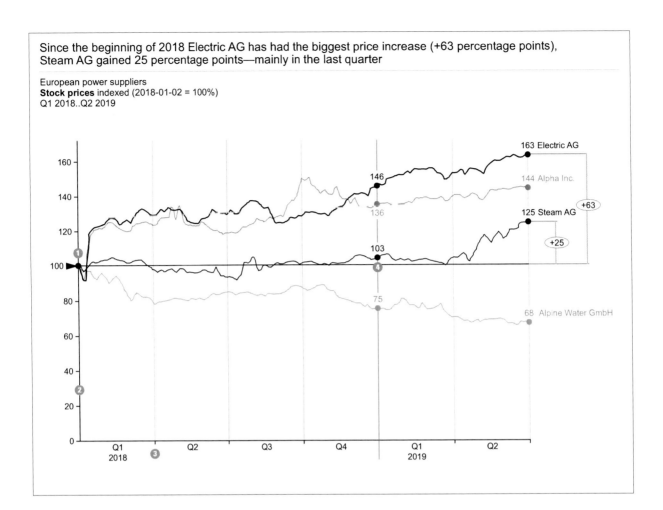

Since the beginning of 2018 Electric AG has had the biggest price increase (+63 percentage points), Steam AG gained 25 percentage points—mainly in the last quarter

European power suppliers
Stock prices indexed (2018-01-02 = 100%)
Q1 2018..Q2 2019

TIME SERIES ANALYSES (LINES)

We use line charts primarily to display a larger number of data points over time and to recognize temporal patterns such as trends or seasonal curves.

COMPARISON OF GROWTH BY INDEXING

If we want to compare the relative growth of several time series, we divide them by their initial values so that all lines start at 100%.

INDEX ARROWHEAD ❶   To make it clear that the values shown are not absolute figures, we mark the index point (2018-01-02 = 100%) with a black arrowhead.

VALUE AXIS ❷   Although we mostly do without a value axis, here it contributes to a better understanding as we have labeled only a few data points.

MARKERS ON THE TIME AXIS ❸   In contrast to column charts, it is not possible to label all categories in line charts with many data points. Therefore we choose small tick marks below the time axis to highlight certain points in time—here the beginning and end of the quarters. For better orientation, we can also extend these markers upwards with assisting lines.

LINE MARKERS ❹   Usually we mark measured values with points or small squares. If there are too many, we only mark important data points, like here the values at the beginning of 2019.

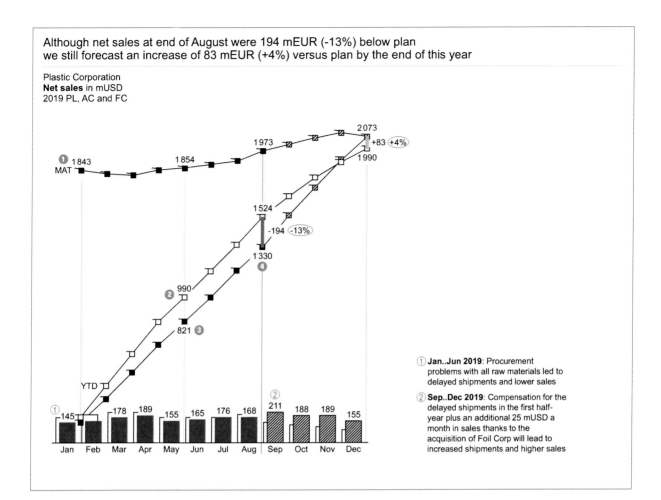

Although net sales at end of August were 194 mEUR (-13%) below plan
we still forecast an increase of 83 mEUR (+4%) versus plan by the end of this year

Plastic Corporation
Net sales in mUSD
2019 PL, AC and FC

① **Jan..Jun 2019**: Procurement problems with all raw materials led to delayed shipments and lower sales

② **Sep..Dec 2019**: Compensation for the delayed shipments in the first half-year plus an additional 25 mUSD a month in sales thanks to the acquisition of Foil Corp will lead to increased shipments and higher sales

ANALYSIS OF CUMULATIVE DEVELOPMENTS IN THE Z-CHART

Lines are also well suited for the representation of cumulative developments since the connecting lines between two measured points can be interpreted as a linear interpolation. In the Z-chart, such a cumulative line is supplemented by monthly values—shown here as columns—and Moving Annual Totals.

MOVING ANNUAL TOTALS ❶ A tilde on the left side of the square markers indicates the corresponding values as Moving Annual Total (MAT). Up to and including August, the previous 12 data points are actual figures. From september on forecast figures are added. SEE PAGE 61.

CUMULATIVE VALUES ❷ Analogous to the tilde for MAT, an underscore on the left side of the square markers indicates a value as Year To Date (YTD). SEE PAGE 61.

LABEL BELOW THE LINE ❸ With line charts, we can often support readability by labeling data points either above or below.

POSITIONING OF CUMULATIVE VALUES ❹ We do not position the line markers and the green and red difference markers in the middle of the monthly categories, but between two categories, i.e. at the end of the month. This underlines the cumulative character of these values.

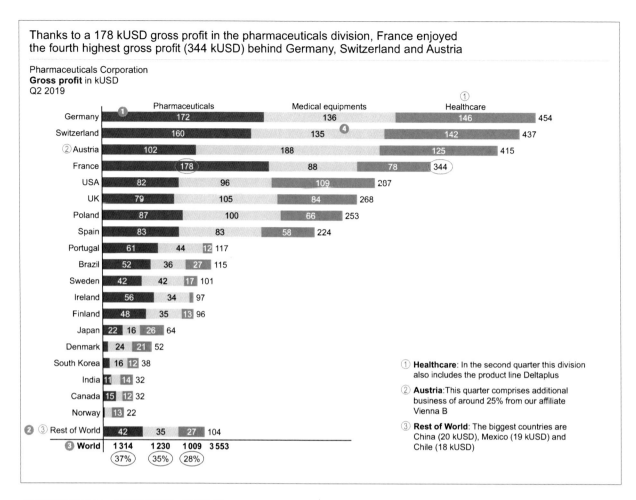

Thanks to a 178 kUSD gross profit in the pharmaceuticals division, France enjoyed the fourth highest gross profit (344 kUSD) behind Germany, Switzerland and Austria

Pharmaceuticals Corporation
Gross profit in kUSD
Q2 2019

STRUCTURAL ANALYSES (BARS)

Bar charts are the classic form of representation for structural analyses. As with stacked columns, the use of stacked bars is only useful when there are few data series without negative values and with low fluctuation.

ANALYSIS OF THE SEQUENCE BY SORTING

Descending sorted bars immediately give the impression of a ranked list and are therefore particularly suitable for the analysis of a sequence.

BAR WIDTH ❶   As with the columns, the ratio of bar width to category width indicates whether it is a basic measure or a ratio. Since *gross profit* is a basic measure the bars are twice as wide as the distance between them. SEE PAGE 122.

REMAINDER ROW ❷   A remainder bar is of decisive importance for the evaluation of the structural elements in any ranked list. Without the bar labeled *Rest of World,* we do not know how much of the world's gross profit is accounted for by the countries shown.

Since the remainder row is not included in the sorting, it is always at the bottom separated by a slightly larger gap.

TOTALS ROW ❸   The bold *World* total row comes below the black total line. Since the scale is too large to display the totals correctly as bars, they appear here as numerical values. SEE PAGE 96.

COLORING OF BAR SEGMENTS ❹   As we have reserved the stylistic device *color* for variances and other highlighting, the bar segments are gray scale. We alternate light and dark to achieve as good a contrast as possible with a few shades.

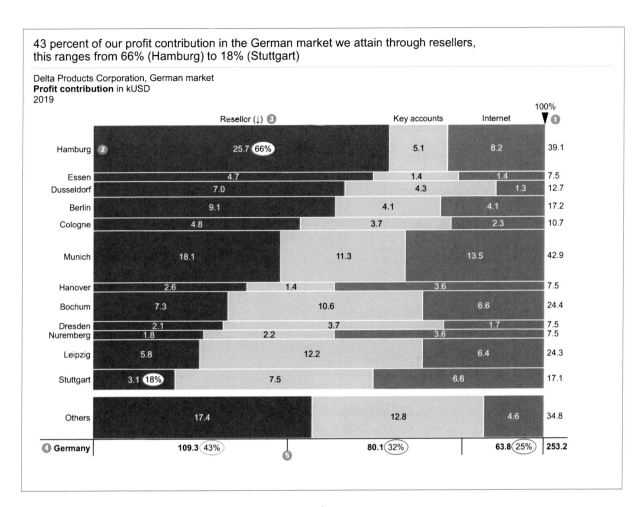

43 percent of our profit contribution in the German market we attain through resellers, this ranges from 66% (Hamburg) to 18% (Stuttgart)

Delta Products Corporation, German market
Profit contribution in kUSD
2019

	Reseller (↓) ❸	Key accounts	Internet	100% ❶
Hamburg ❷	25.7 (66%)	5.1	8.2	39.1
Essen	4.7	1.4	1.4	7.5
Dusseldorf	7.0	4.3	1.3	12.7
Berlin	9.1	4.1	4.1	17.2
Cologne	4.8	3.7	2.3	10.7
Munich	18.1	11.3	13.5	42.9
Hanover	2.6	1.4	3.6	7.5
Bochum	7.3	10.6	6.6	24.4
Dresden	2.1	3.7	1.7	7.5
Nuremberg	1.8	2.2	3.6	7.5
Leipzig	5.8	12.2	6.4	24.3
Stuttgart	3.1 (18%)	7.5	6.6	17.1
Others	17.4	12.8	4.6	34.8
❹ Germany	109.3 (43%) ❺	80.1 (32%)	63.8 (25%)	253.2

SHARE ANALYSIS IN THE MARIMEKKO CHART

With their bars of normalized length and variable width, Marimekko charts allow for the simultaneous analysis of absolute and relative shares.

NORMALIZED BAR LENGTH ❶   The small arrowhead at the end of the first bar indicates that we have normalized the length of all bars to 100%. The length of the bar segments thus represents the percentage of the profit contribution achieved with the respective sales channel.

VARIABLE BAR WIDTH ❷   The bar widths express the weight of the absolute profit contribution of the respective city. The resulting areas of the bar segments show the absolute profit contribution of the sales channel in the respective city. For example, it can be seen that Essen has a high percentage of resellers, but only a small volume behind it.

SORT ORDER ❸   The small sort arrow behind *reseller* indicates that the rows are sorted in descending order by *reseller profit contribution*. As with the classic bar chart, the remainder row is also excluded from this sorting and is separated at the bottom by a small gap.

TOTALS ROW ❹   We have entered the totals below a horizontal total line. With Marimekko charts, the sums of the areas of each gray tone correspond to the segment totals.

AVERAGE PERCENTAGE SHARE ❺   Vertical lines within the totals row separate the three segments from each other and correspond to the average percentage share.

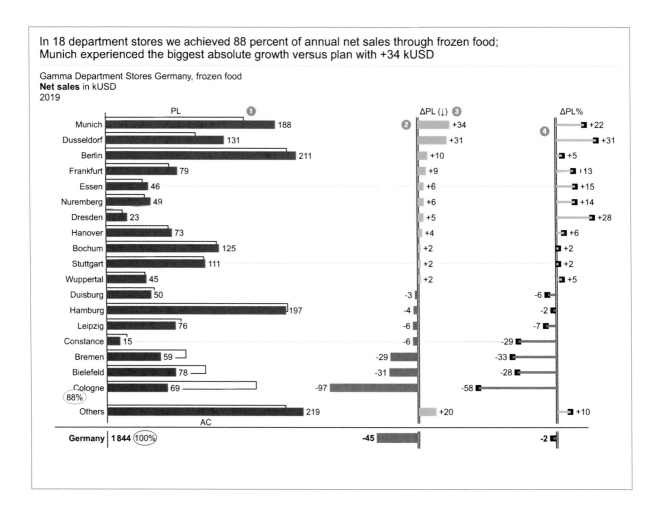

In 18 department stores we achieved 88 percent of annual net sales through frozen food; Munich experienced the biggest absolute growth versus plan with +34 kUSD

Gamma Department Stores Germany, frozen food
Net sales in kUSD
2019

STRUCTURAL ANALYSES WITH VARIANCES (BARS)

The two templates on this double-spread extend the simple bar chart for variance analysis: The actual data is compared with either previous year or plan as a reference. The two other tiers of the chart show variances.

COMPARISON OF VARIANCES

This structure comparison is a frequently used classic. The focus of the analysis is on comparing the plan variances of the individual cities to each other—either in absolute or relative terms.

GROUPED BARS ❶ The absolute bars for the actual numbers represent the weight of the respective city. The offset plan bars behind them are almost redundant in light of the absolute variances and could also be omitted.

ABSOLUTE VARIANCES ❷ The absolute variances immediately catch the eye with their green and red color scheme as well as with the descending order—as it should be in a chart for variance analysis. In addition, the visual impression is augmented by a plus sign for positive variances and the direction of the bars: good to the right, bad to the left. SEE PAGE 81.

SORT ARROW ❸ The small sort arrow behind (delta) L indicates that this analysis is sorted in descending order according to absolute plan variances. The position *others* is displayed at the bottom with a small gap because it's excluded from sorting.

SEMANTIC AXES ❹ The axes drawn with a double line in the middle and right chart tell us that the absolute and percentage variances refer to the respective plan values. SEE PAGE 86.

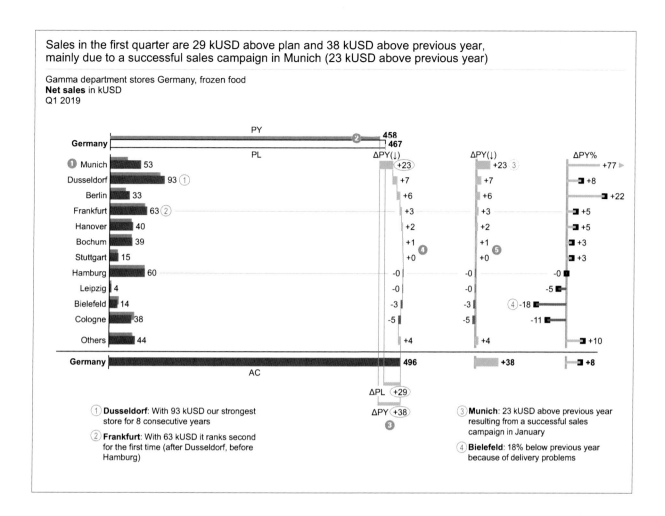

Sales in the first quarter are 29 kUSD above plan and 38 kUSD above previous year, mainly due to a successful sales campaign in Munich (23 kUSD above previous year)

Gamma department stores Germany, frozen food
Net sales in kUSD
Q1 2019

① **Dusseldorf**: With 93 kUSD our strongest store for 8 consecutive years

② **Frankfurt**: With 63 kUSD it ranks second for the first time (after Dusseldorf, before Hamburg)

③ **Munich**: 23 kUSD above previous year resulting from a successful sales campaign in January

④ **Bielefeld**: 18% below previous year because of delivery problems

ANALYSIS OF THE CONTRIBUTION TO THE TOTAL VARIANCE

In contrast to the chart on the left, the analysis here focuses on explaining the total variances from plan and previous year: Which cities contribute to the positive change and to what extent ?

LABELING OF CATEGORIES ❶   We do not label the individual categories—here cities—in the middle of the categories, but in the middle of the actual bars. This prevents the city labels from shifting upwards when a reference bar for previous year or plan is added.

SCALE FOR TOTAL ❷   Since the values for Germany are now also visualized with bars, we must adjust the scale. The bars for the individual cities are correspondingly small and understood more as additional information.

DIFFERENCE MARKERS ❸   The green markers indicate that Germany's net sales of frozen food are 38 kUSD higher than in the previous year and 29 kUSD higher than planned. SEE PAGE 91.

VARIANCE WATERFALL ❹   In the variance waterfall, the individual variances are added together to give the total variance shown in the difference marker. The variance bars are labeled in the direction of their contribution: green bars on the right, red bars on the left. SEE PAGE 85.

ABSOLUTE VARIANCES ❺   The chart to the right of the waterfall shows the same variances, but in an arrangement better suited to compare individual cities. Alternatively, we could also use this chart to display a plan variance. Then we would have to use an outlined semantic axis instead of the now gray one. SEE PAGE 86.

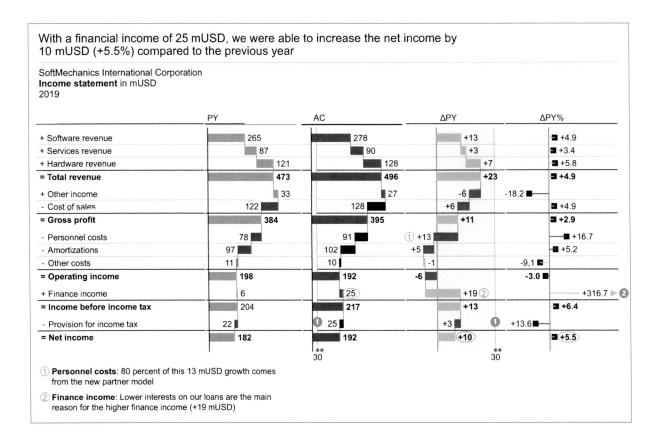

With a financial income of 25 mUSD, we were able to increase the net income by 10 mUSD (+5.5%) compared to the previous year

SoftMechanics International Corporation
Income statement in mUSD
2019

	PY	AC	ΔPY	ΔPY%
+ Software revenue	265	278	+13	+4.9
+ Services revenue	87	90	+3	+3.4
+ Hardware revenue	121	128	+7	+5.8
= Total revenue	473	496	+23	+4.9
+ Other income	33	27	-6	-18.2
- Cost of sales	122	128	+6	+4.9
= Gross profit	384	395	+11	+2.9
- Personnel costs	78	91	① +13	+16.7
- Amortizations	97	102	+5	+5.2
- Other costs	11	10	-1	-9.1
= Operating income	198	192	-6	-3.0
+ Finance income	6	25	+19 ②	+316.7 ②
= Income before income tax	204	217	+13	+6.4
- Provision for income tax	22	① 25	+3 ①	+13.6
= Net income	182	192	+10	+5.5

30   30

① **Personnel costs**: 80 percent of this 13 mUSD growth comes from the new partner model

② **Finance income**: Lower interests on our loans are the main reason for the higher finance income (+19 mUSD)

ANALYSES OF CALCULATION SCHEMES (BARS AND TABLES)

In comparing three versions of the same income statement, we want to illustrate the advantages and disadvantages of graphical and tabular analyses.

CALCULATION WATERFALL

The calculation waterfall makes it possible to visually determine which items contribute to the net income and to what extent. This, however, takes up a lot of space.

SCALING LINES ❶ The absolute variances are so small in relation to the base values that they would hardly be visible on the same scale. We have therefore scaled the two charts differently and linked them via scaling lines at a height of 30 mUSD (2 blue dots). SEE PAGE 137.

TABLE WITH INTEGRATED VARIANCE WATERFALL

If we omit the calculation waterfall, we not only avoid the above scaling problem, but we also create space for further information—like the breakdown of the operating income by quarter seen here.

OUTLIERS ❷ Large relative variances of small values are not important and lead to an unfavorable scale. This is why—as an exception—we cut them off and give them an appropriate indicator. SEE PAGE 88.

VARIANCE TABLE

If the variance charts are done away with completely, more information can be added—here planned figures and corresponding variance columns. But visual support for our analysis is sacrificed.

NO MESSAGE ❸ We usually use charts to convey a specific message. Because we don't have a message here, the table begins directly with the title. SEE PAGE 65.

SHARE COLUMN ❹ In this additional share column we express the figures of the income statement as a percentage of total revenue. For the different column types and their formatting SEE PAGE 97.

With a financial income of 25 mUSD, we were able to increase the net income by 10 mUSD (+5.5%) compared to the previous year

SoftMechanics International Corporation
Income statement in mUSD
2019

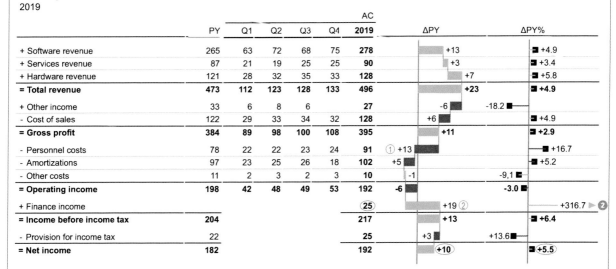

	PY	Q1	Q2	Q3	Q4	AC 2019	ΔPY	ΔPY%
+ Software revenue	265	63	72	68	75	**278**	+13	+4.9
+ Services revenue	87	21	19	25	25	**90**	+3	+3.4
+ Hardware revenue	121	28	32	35	33	**128**	+7	+5.8
= Total revenue	**473**	**112**	**123**	**128**	**133**	**496**	+23	+4.9
+ Other income	33	6	8	6		**27**	-6	-18.2
- Cost of sales	122	29	33	34	32	**128**	+6	+4.9
= Gross profit	**384**	**89**	**98**	**100**	**108**	**395**	+11	+2.9
- Personnel costs	78	22	22	23	24	**91**	① +13	+16.7
- Amortizations	97	23	25	26	18	**102**	+5	+5.2
- Other costs	11	2	3	2	3	**10**	-1	-9,1
= Operating income	**198**	**42**	**48**	**49**	**53**	**192**	-6	-3.0
+ Finance income						**(25)**	+19 ②	+316.7 ②
= Income before income tax	**204**					**217**	+13	+6.4
- Provision for income tax	22					**25**	+3	+13.6
= Net income	**182**					**192**	(+10)	+5.5

① **Personnel costs**: 80 percent of this 13 mUSD growth comes from the new partner model

② **Finance income**: Lower interests on our loans are the main reason for the higher finance income (+19 mUSD)

---

❸ SoftMechanics International Corporation
Income statement in mUSD
2019

	PY	PL	Q1	Q2	Q3	Q4	AC 2019 ❹		ΔPY		ΔPL	
+ Software revenue	265	266	63	72	68	75	**278**	*56%*	+13	+4,9%	+12	+4,5%
+ Services revenue	87	96	21	19	25	25	**90**	*18%*	+3	+3,4%	-6	-6,3%
+ Hardware revenue	121	122	28	32	35	33	**128**	*26%*	+7	+5,8%	+6	+4,9%
= Total revenue	**473**	**484**	**112**	**123**	**128**	**133**	**496**	*100%*	+23	+4,9%	+12	+2,5%
+ Other income	33	26	6	8	6		**27**	*5%*	-6	-18,2%	+1	+3,8%
- Cost of sales	122	134	29	33	34	32	**128**	*26%*	+6	+4,9%	-6	-4,5%
= Gross profit	**384**	**376**	**89**	**98**	**100**	**108**	**395**	*80%*	+11	+2,9%	+19	+5,1%
- Personnel costs	78	88	22	22	23	24	**91**	*18%*	① +13	+16,7%	+3	+3,4%
- Amortizations	97	120	23	25	26	18	**102**	*21%*	+5	+5,2%	-18	-15,0%
- Other costs	11	15	2	3	2	3	**10**	*2%*	-1	-9,1%	-5	-33,3%
= Operating income	**198**	**153**	**42**	**48**	**49**	**53**	**192**	*39%*	-6	-3,0%	+39	+25,5%
+ Finance income	6	29					**(25)**	*5%*	② +19	+316,7%	-4	-13,8%
= Income before income tax	**204**	**182**					**217**	*44%*	+13	+6,4%	+35	+19,2%
- Provision for income tax	22	14					**25**	*5%*	+3	+13,6%	+11	+78,6%
= Net income	**182**	**168**					**192**	*39%*	(+10)	(+5,5%)	+24	+14,3%

① **Personnel costs**: 80 percent of this 13 mUSD growth comes from the new partner model

② **Finance income**: Lower interests on our loans are the main reason for the higher finance income (+19 mUSD)

Cumulative net sales from January to November (32 489 mUSD) in Europe were almost the same compared both to last year and to plan

(1) Automobile Corporation
Net sales in mUSD
November 2019

① **Poland**: A strong month in the previous year explains the decline of 25%, however the _November plan was still met

② **Switzerland and France**: The variances of -9% in each country can be explained by high price discounts

③ **Others Central & Western Europe**: Belgium (-186) and the Czech Republic (-98) experienced the biggest negative variances

	November			ΔPY		ΔPL			January_November			ΔPY		ΔPL	
PY	PL	AC							PY	PL	AC				
560	590	559	-1	-0%	-31	-5%	Germany		5078	5611	5509	+431	+8%	-102	-2%
50	72	58	+2	+4%	-14	-19%	Switzerland		531	529	484	-47	-9%	-45	-9% ②
140	149	134	-6	-4%	-15	-10%	France		1290	1488	1354	+64	+5%	-134	-9% ②
345	279	260	-85	-25% ①	-19	-7%	Poland		3124	2815	2850	-274	-9%	+35	+1% ①
78	91	86	+8	+10%	-5	-5%	Austria		816	818	854	+38	+5%	+36	+4%
77	81	86	+9	+12%	+5	+6%	United Kingdom		809	722	764	-45	-6%	+42	+6%
61	70	66	+5	+8%	-4	-6%	Netherlands		604	582	678	+74	+12%	+96	+16%
502	498	545	+43	+9%	+47	+9%	Others		5602	6022	5441	-161	-3%	-581	-10% ③
1 819	**1 830**	**1 794**	**-25**	**-1%**	**-36**	**-2%**	**Central & Western Europe**		**17 854**	**18 587**	**17 934**	**+80**	**+0%**	**-653**	**-4%**
119	109	121	+2	+2%	+12	+11%	Italy		1205	1254	1314	+109	+9%	+60	+5%
65	71	59	-6	-9%	-12	-17%	Spain		629	656	718	+89	+14%	+62	+9%
346	326	311	-35	-10%	-15	-5%	Greece		3406	3124	3239	-167	-5%	+115	+4%
438	401	399	-39	-9%	-2	-0%	Others		4166	4219	4008	-158	-4%	-211	-5%
968	**907**	**890**	**-78**	**-8%**	**-17**	**-2%**	**Southern & Southeast Europe**		**9 406**	**9 253**	**9 279**	**-127**	**-1%**	**+26**	**+0%**
54	66	62	+8	+15%	-4	-6%	Sweden		517	609	588	+71	+14%	-21	-3%
266	204	231	-35	-13%	+27	+13%	Norway		2107	1925	2399	+292	+14%	+474	+25%
9	12	11	+2	+22%	-1	-8%	Denmark		67	87	144	+77	+115%	+57	+66%
234	311	255	+21	+9%	-56	-18%	Finland		2351	2099	2145	-206	-9%	+46	+2%
563	**593**	**559**	**- 4**	**-1%**	**-34**	**-6%**	**Northern Europe**		**5 042**	**4 720**	**5 276**	**+234**	**+5%**	**+556**	**+12%**
3 350	**3 330**	**3 243**	**-107**	**-3%**	**-87**	**-3%**	**EUROPE**		**32 302**	**32 560**	**32 489**	**+187**	**+1%**	**-71**	**-0%**

VARIANCES ACROSS SEVERAL HIERARCHY LEVELS (TABLE)

It's not just about charts. There is also a need for tabular presentations, especially as reference works. This makes it all the more important that they likewise have a uniform design facilitating quick understanding

VARIANCE TABLE

Table columns usually display periods, scenarios, and variances. The rows contain either a calculation scheme, as in the example on the previous page, or elements of a structure dimension such as a regional sales structure.

TITLE **(1)** At the top left we have the same title for tables as we have for charts: reporting entity, business measure and time reference. SEE PAGE 62.

SCENARIO NOTATION **(2)** For tables, semantic lines below the column headers indicate the scenarios for previous year, plan and actual figures. SEE PAGE 78.

SIGN FOR VARIANCES **(3)** Positive variances receive a plus sign in tables as well to immediately identify variance columns. SEE PAGE 81.

GAPS BETWEEN COLUMNS **(4)** We use narrow and wide gaps to give the impression of white vertical lines, allowing for a clear column layout. SEE PAGE 97.

RIGHT-JUSTIFIED NUMBER COLUMNS **(5)** Basically self-evident: Numbers are always right-justified. The corresponding column headers should be too. SEE PAGE 97.

ROW HEADERS IN THE MIDDLE **(6)** If the table consists of two parts—here a monthly view in addition to a cumulative view—we can also place the row headers

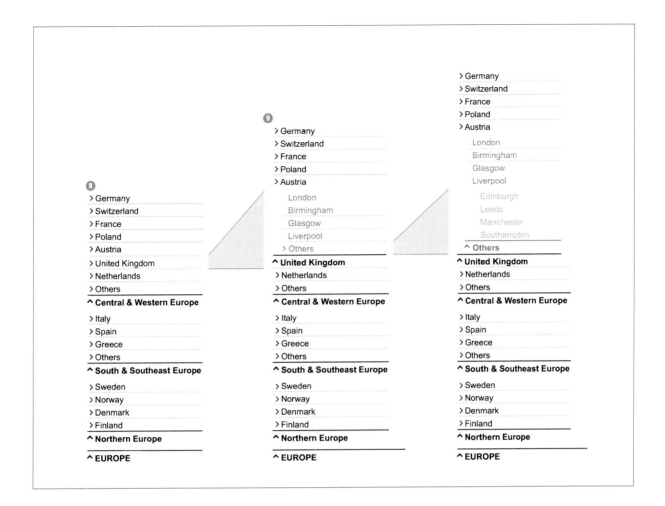

in the middle, reducing the distance between the headers and the columns further to the right.

TOTALS BELOW ❼ For good reasons, we in general opt to arrange calculation results, such as totals, below their arguments. SEE PAGE 98.

HIERARCHICAL ROW STRUCTURE
The design of multi-level hierarchical structures in tables is a challenge.

THREE LEVELS WITHOUT INDENTATION ❽ Because indentations display a hierarchical structure in the row headers only, and not in the subsequent number columns, we begin without them. We prefer vertical spacing which works quite well up to three levels. SEE PAGE 100.

INDENTATIONS FROM LEVEL FOUR ON ❾ Beginning with the fourth level—here the United Kingdom is further subdivided—we use indentations to visualize the structure. We can use an additional visual variable—here opacity—to depict the hierarchical structure in number columns as well. Here: the deeper the layer, the brighter the gray. Vertical spacing and indentations allow for the clear illustration of up to five levels. We fundamentally question any attempt to show more than five levels in a report. Omitting the top level(s) would be an option in these cases.

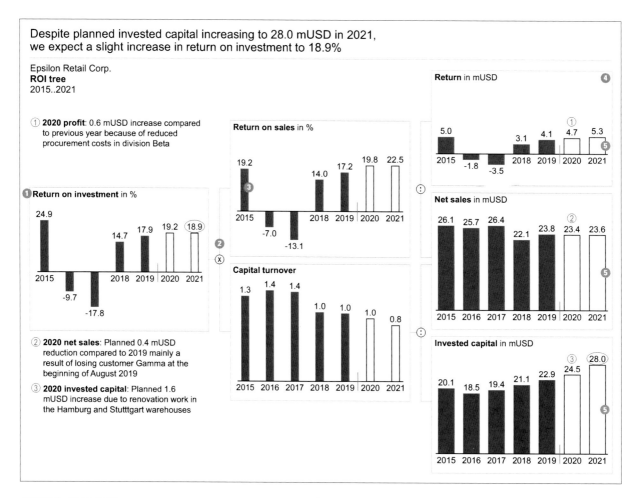

Despite planned invested capital increasing to 28.0 mUSD in 2021, we expect a slight increase in return on investment to 18.9%

Epsilon Retail Corp.
ROI tree
2015..2021

MULTI-CHARTS
We can increase information density by arranging several charts on one page. Such multi-charts have the most explanatory power when there is a comprehensible relationship between the individual charts.

RATIO TREE
In the case of calculated measures, such as the *return on investment* (ROI) shown here, the relationship between the charts follows the calculation logic.

SUBTITLES ❶ Chart-specific subtitles supplement the details mentioned in the page title—here by specifying the measure together with the unit. SEE PAGE 62.

ARITHMETIC OPERATORS ❷ Assisting lines with arithmetic operators help visualize the calculation logic.

RATIO NOTATION ❸ To distinguish ratios (quotients) from basic measures, we draw the former only half as wide as the latter. SEE PAGE 122.

SAME SCALE ❹ It is important for comprehension that comparable measures—here, for example, *return, net sales* and *invested capital* in mUSD—are scaled the same.

CHART HEIGHT ❺ The contents of an individual column chart in conjunction with its scale should determine its height and not vice versa. Here the *return* chart is somewhat smaller than the others, but this does not distract from the visual comparison with *net sales* and *invested capital.*

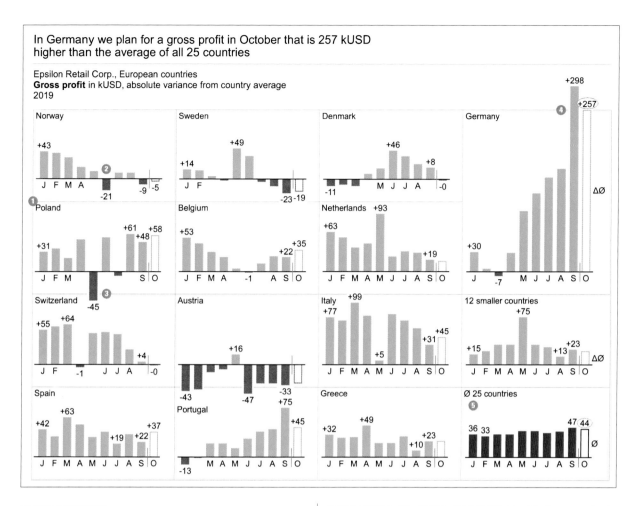

In Germany we plan for a gross profit in October that is 257 kUSD higher than the average of all 25 countries

Epsilon Retail Corp., European countries
Gross profit in kUSD, absolute variance from country average
2019

SMALL MULTIPLE

With a small multiple, we show similar charts—here the variance of the gross profits from the country average—for several elements of a structure dimension, in this case countries.

DISTANCE BETWEEN CHARTS ❶   In order to best use the available space, we collapse any distance between the individual charts of a small multiple.

ABBREVIATED AND SELECTIVE LABELLING ❷   Again for space reasons, we only label the months with J, F, M etc., here. In the months with negative gross profits— along with those on either side—we dispense with designations entirely. We don't label all monthly columns either, rather the current, first and last months, along with the maxima and minima.

OVERLAPPING OF CHART ELEMENTS ❸   If the result is unambiguous, we would allow individual chart elements to extend into neighbouring charts, as is the case here with Poland, Austria and Germany. With this trick, a slightly larger scale would be possible if the software in use supports it.

CHART HEIGHT ❹   Charts with significantly larger numerical values are challenging for small multiples. When using the same scale, the figures of other charts are rendered very small. We suggest giving charts with big numbers more space, as here with Germany, allowing for a much larger scale in all 15 charts.

BLACK BASE VALUES WITHOUT PLUS SIGNS ❺   Connoisseurs of our notation rules already know: The black columns labeled without a plus sign in the chart at the bottom right represent base values (the average gross profit).

RECAP

In addition to creating a report notation manual, we recommend readying company-specific templates using this manual and the software tools at hand. This is the only way to ensure that all dashboard designers and report writers deliver consistent results, even under time pressure.

Experience has shown that a company can get by with a manageable number of sample templates implemented across the technologies in use:

- Column charts stacked, overlapped and with variances or overlaying lines
- Line charts for time series with many values and for displaying cumulative values (Z-chart)
- Bar charts stacked, normalized (possibly also as Marimekko charts), overlapped and with variances
- Bars, tables and their combination for the analysis of calculation schemes
- Pure tables for the documentation of variances and temporal developments across several hierarchy levels
- Ratio trees and small multiples for the representation of larger correlations

As we will see in the next section, these and similar representations are actually frequently used in practice.

4.3
REAL LIFE EXAMPLES
SUPPORTED BY SOFTWARE

IT WORKS

Up to this point everything has been theory: the derivation of the necessity of semantic notation, the various concepts, their application to charts and tables as well as the creation of a notation manual and the respective templates. But does this also work in real life? Do companies recognize the benefits of standardized notation and change their reports, presentations and dashboards accordingly? And are the necessary technical means even available?

In the following section we provide the evidence. We show that companies of all sizes and industries have been relying on standardized notation for several years now. The desired pattern recognition effect is obvious: Despite minor differences in notation due to operational compromises with regard to corporate design, software restrictions or simply the use of older versions of the International Business Communication Standards (IBCS), one immediately feels at home with every example. Titles are in place, plans are outlined and forecasts are hatched, red and green are used only for variances, and so on and so forth. We think it's great—and we thank the many contributors for their support in creating these practical examples.

Onto the real reports and dashboards. For reasons of confidentiality, the figures are fake, and the designations are also partly falsified or made unrecognizable. We ask your indulgence in this. But that's not the point, it's the visual recognition of what is depicted. For this reason, we have decided on the following pages to largely dispense with explanatory text. The sample reports speak for themselves.

COCA-COLA İÇECEK A. Ş.

With around 10 000 employees, Coca-Cola İçecek is the fifth largest bottler in the Coca-Cola network. Reporting systems based on Zebra BI for Microsoft Excel are used both at the Turkish headquarters in Istanbul and in the subsidiaries in the Middle East and Central Asia. We show a dashboard the management team uses at monthly meetings.

SWISS POST AG

Management accounting at Swiss Post has successfully used our design rules for many years. Since 2009, they have also applied them in their external financial reports. The financial report presented here is probably one of the first in the world with a consistent implementation of uniform scaling. The sentence on the inside cover became famous: "True and fair view—20 mm is equivalent to 1 billion francs".

DAIMLER AG

Daimler AG's sales controlling has installed Longview Analytics to provide decision documents for the external organization, among other things. We show a dashboard that compiles important data on incoming orders, invoiced deliveries and inventory sizes.

GABOR SHOES AG

With over 3 000 employees, Gabor is one of the largest shoe manufacturers in Europe. A restrained layout—with the option for clear highlighting—is characteristic of the report examples shown here which were created by consultnetwork using Cubeware.

REGIONAL HOSPITAL OPERATING COMPANY (KABEG)

KABEG is the largest service company in the state of Carinthia, Austria and employs around 7 000 people. The dashboards shown here have been created with Chart-me, a product of Hi-Chart GmbH. All tables and charts are based on a uniform notation concept.

KONINKLIJKE PHILIPS N.V.

Royal Philips is one of the world's largest providers of healthcare technology. After an international project for the standardization of reports was successful in many functional areas, typical features of our standards were also adopted in the annual report shown here.

LSG LUFTHANSA SERVICE HOLDING AG

The catering subsidiary of Deutsche Lufthansa with over 30 000 employees is one of the world's leading providers of in-flight catering. The dashboards realized by HighCoordination using trueChart for Qlik Sense are closely oriented to our design suggestions.

MIGROLINO AG

migrolino is one of the leading providers in the Swiss convenience store market. This subsidiary of the Swiss Migros cooperative association has over 300 locations. We show dashboards for the provision of key figures for franchisees, which were developed with graphomate extensions for SAP Lumira Designer.

OPEN GRID EUROPE GMBH

Open Grid Europe operates the largest natural gas pipeline network in Germany. The dashboard presented here is an SAP Analytics Cloud energy data management application developed by Windhoff Software Services.

PROSIEBENSAT.1 MEDIA SE

The screen examples of the *mediaFACTS* application presented here bring important business figures of the entertainment company to the right decision makers. blueforte and mip have implemented this solution together with in-house specialists using Longview Analytics.

SAP SE

SAP has used the standards we propose in its internal reporting for many years. The examples presented here are based on the SAP products Analysis for Office and Crystal Reports. Due to the notation standards used, the solutions look very similar despite different reporting software.

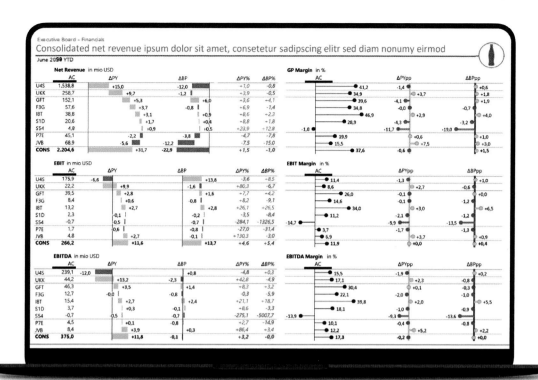

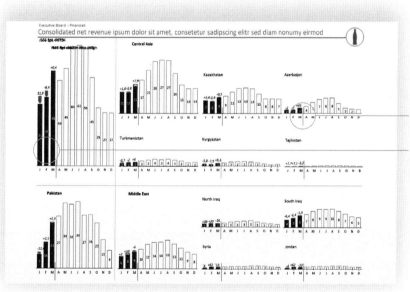

An additional line separates the outlined plan columns from the solid actual columns.

The charts have individual sizes that take into account the size of the figures to be shown, allowing for the largest possible scale when comparing the 13 countries.

Coca-Cola İçecek A. Ş.

CocaCola İçecek (CCI) is the fifth largest CocaCola bottler in the world. The financial team of CCI developed this dashboard (above) showing the contribution of CCI countries to CCI Group's sales and earnings.

Zebra BI

The dashboard (below) shows the monthly sales development of the CCI Group in Central Asia and the Middle East. Both dashboards are mainly used during the monthly meetings of the CCI management team and are based on the Zebra BI Excel Add-In.

Swiss Post AG

Source: Swiss Post Financial Report 2017,
pages 31, 34 and 35

Quote from the inside cover of this
report: "All charts are shown to scale
to present a true and fair view.
20 mm is equivalent to one billion
francs."

The *normalized operating result* of 630 mCHF
has exactly the same length in millimeters
in two different charts on pages 31 and 35.

The normalized operating result shown as a bar in this
waterfall chart is the same length as well: At a scale of 1 bCHF ≙ 20
mm, 630 mCHF results in exactly 12.6 mm.

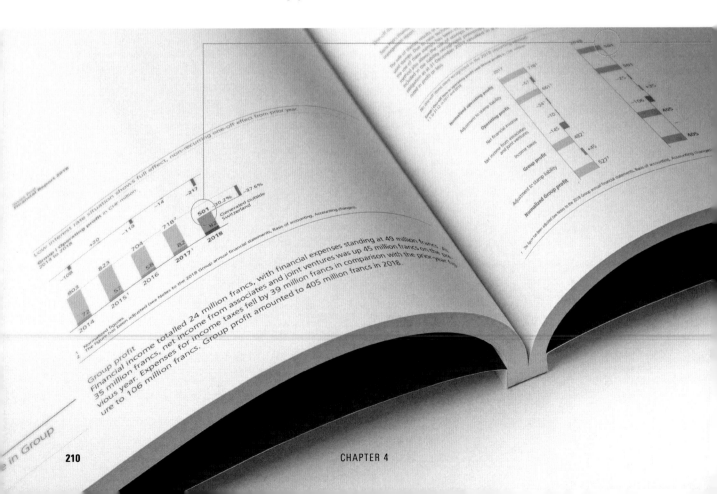

Another highlight of this financial report are the use of messages and uniform titles. All charts show short messages and the title concept consistently follows our proposals (see Section 2.1).

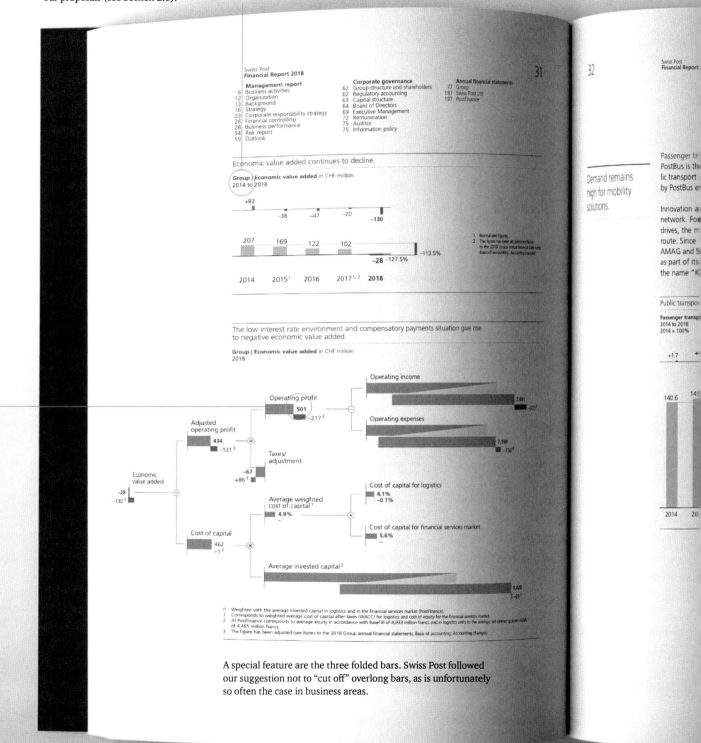

A special feature are the three folded bars. Swiss Post followed our suggestion not to "cut off" overlong bars, as is unfortunately so often the case in business areas.

The same scale applies to both vertical (upper chart) and horizontal directions (lower chart).

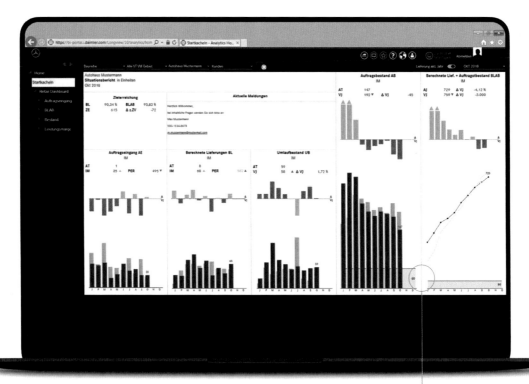

The scaling lines show that the cumulative values have a smaller scale.

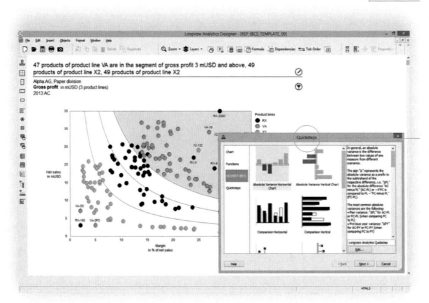

This menu is used to select the most important standard charts.

 Mercedes-Benz

Daimler AG

Screenshot above: Dealer situation report from Daimler AG sales controlling. The sales controlling department VAN has implemented the application with Longview Analytics powered by arcplan. Over 150 users have access to it via the web.

Longview Analytics

Screenshot below: The user interface of Longview Analytics when using a standard analysis.

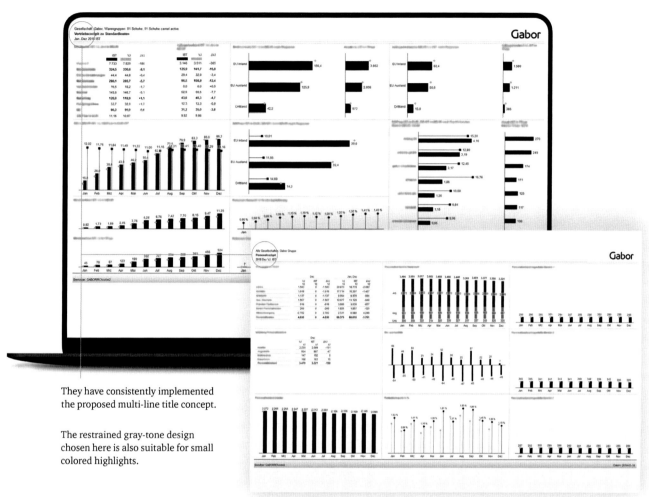

They have consistently implemented the proposed multi-line title concept.

The restrained gray-tone design chosen here is also suitable for small colored highlights.

Gabor®

Gabor Shoes AG

Screenshots of one-page reports
for the first management level of Gabor Shoes AG.

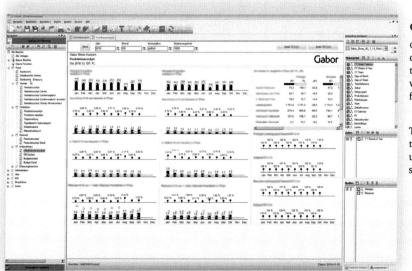

Cubeware

consultnetwork has created the application shown above with the C8 Cockpit from Cubeware.

The screenshot on the left shows the user interface of this software.

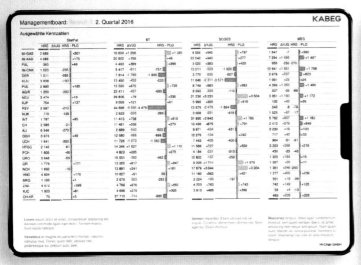

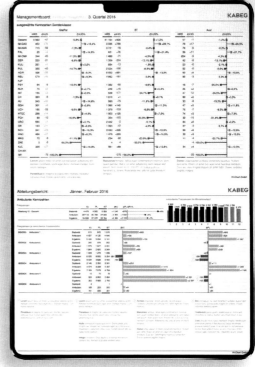

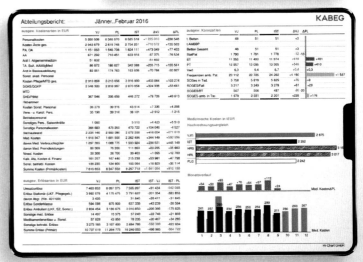

KABEG

Regional Hospital Operating Company—KABEG

These screenshots show the result of a group-wide implementation
of management reports at the Regional Hospital Operating Company
KABEG in Carinthia, Austria.

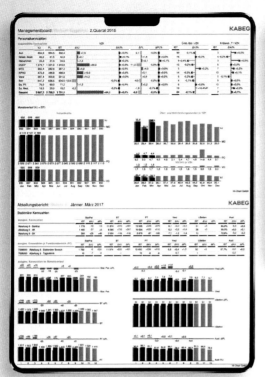

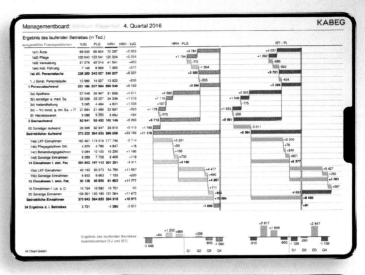

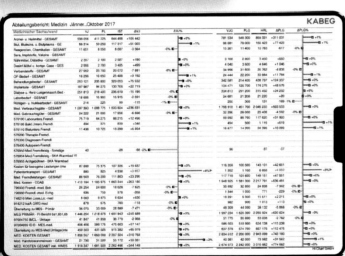

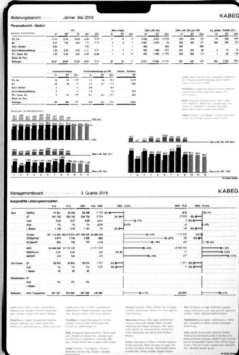

Chart-me

KABEG developed the solution on-site using Chart-me from
Hi-Chart GmbH. The compilation of tables and charts impressively
demonstrates the visual uniformity of the reports—despite the
diversity of content.

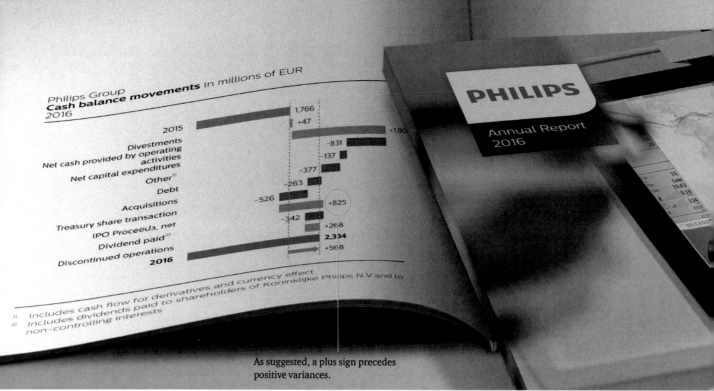

As suggested, a plus sign precedes
positive variances.

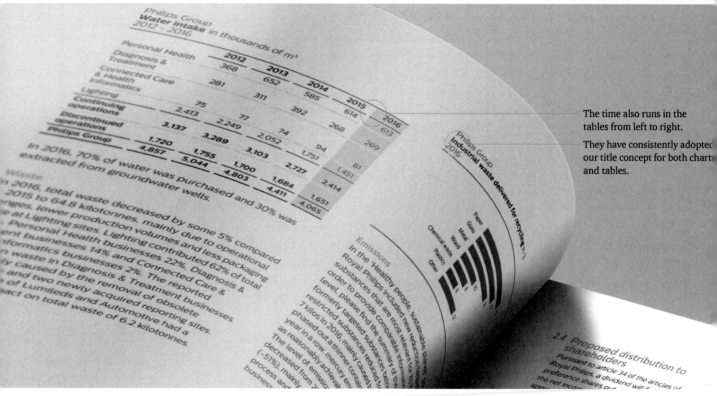

The time also runs in the
tables from left to right.

They have consistently adopted
our title concept for both charts
and tables.

Koninklijke Philips N.V.

Source: Philips Annual Report 2016, pages 16 and 28

Influenced by the successful standardization process in internal
reporting[1], some important elements of external reporting were also
adapted to our proposals.

1   Jürgen Faisst und Nina Michels-Kim: The Philips Journey toward
    IBCS, Montvale, NJ, USA: Strategic Finance October 1, 2016.

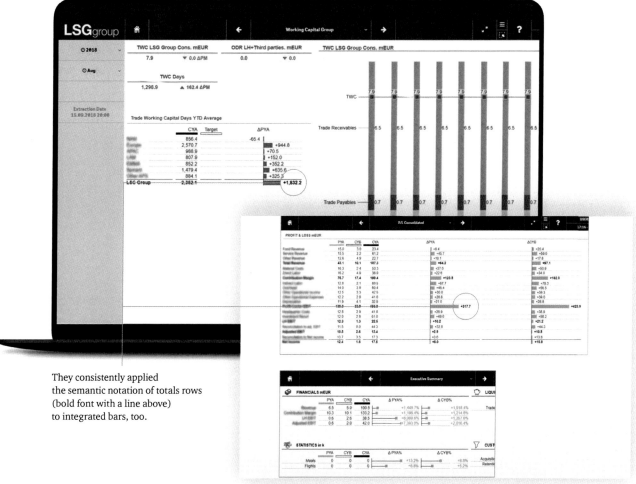

They consistently applied
the semantic notation of totals rows
(bold font with a line above)
to integrated bars, too.

LSG Group

The LSG Group was able to standardize its reporting according to the IBCS rules. **High**Coordination implemented the worldwide process for monthly settlement—including comments—using trueChart for Qlik Sense.

LSGgroup

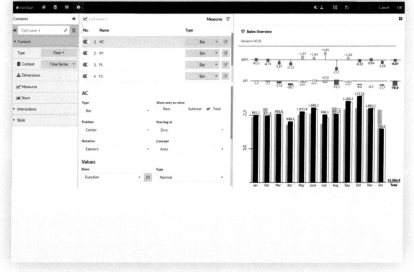

trueChart

Typical screenshot
of the user interface.
Here all necessary
settings can be defined
and then used as
company templates.

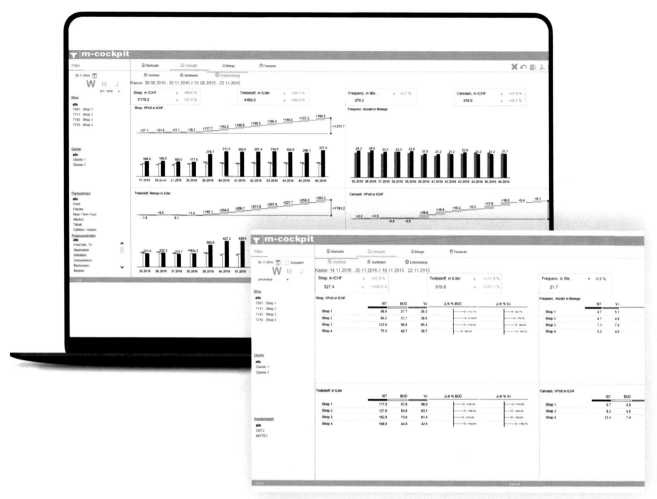

migrolino AG

Screenshots of a dashboard for management support of franchisees with key figures at migrolino, a subsidiary of the Migros Group.

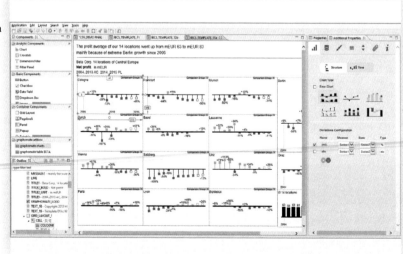

graphomate

The application shown above was implemented with graphomate extensions for SAP Lumira Designer.

The screenshot shows the user interface for graphomate charts.

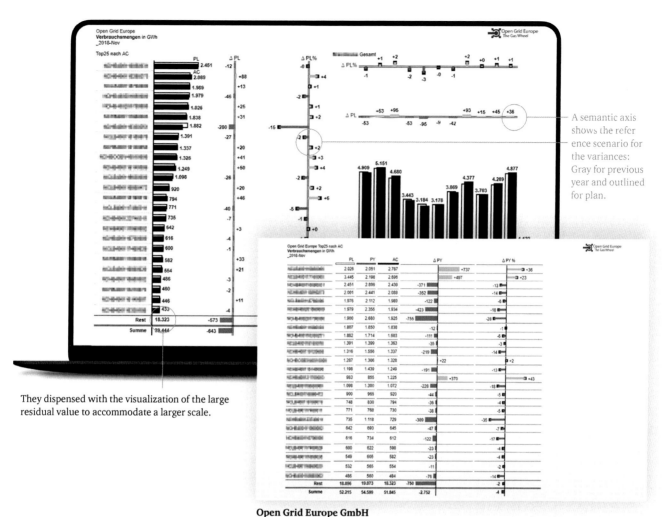

A semantic axis shows the reference scenario for the variances: Gray for previous year and outlined for plan.

They dispensed with the visualization of the large residual value to accommodate a larger scale.

Open Grid Europe GmbH

Two screenshots of an application in the energy data management of Open Grid. They show customer balancing groups with details of the transported quantities. Plan values and prior-year values serve as comparative figures.

Open Grid Europe
The Gas Wheel

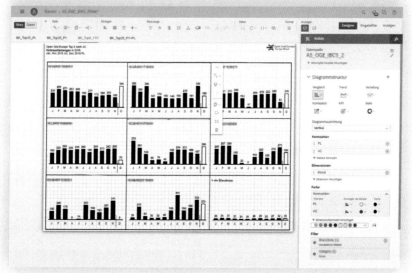

SAP Analytics Cloud

Windhoff Software Services has created the application shown above with SAP Analytics Cloud.

The screenshot on the left shows the user interface for this software.

The extended separator lines illustrate the relationship between the underlying values in the lower charts and the variances above them.

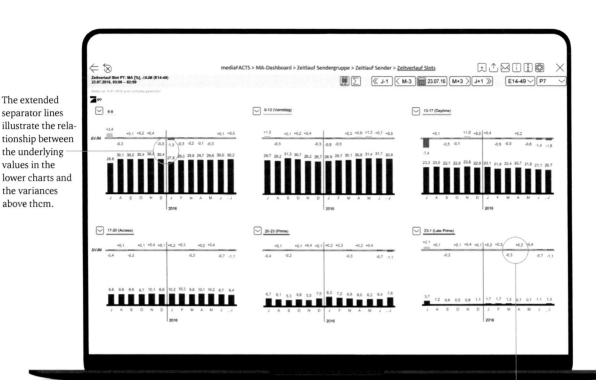

Consistent visualization of variances from the previous year: Above as a second tier atop the column chart, below as an integrated variance bar.

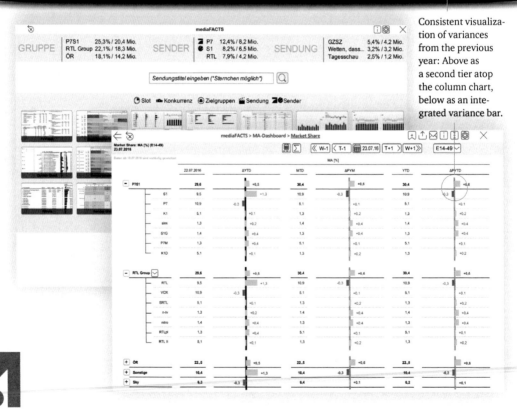

ProSiebenSat.1 Media SE

The interactive BI application *media*FACTS makes the analysis of strategically important key figures easily accessible and understandable for 1 120 users spread across 11 departments.

blueforte

blueforte GmbH implemented this project together with mip GmbH using Longview Analytics. To ensure that all 20 reports remain clear despite their high information density, they are based on the semantic rules presented in this book.

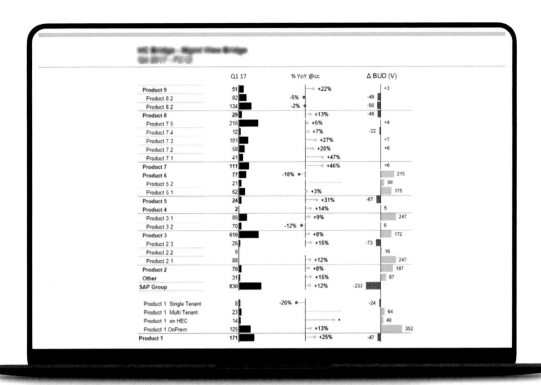

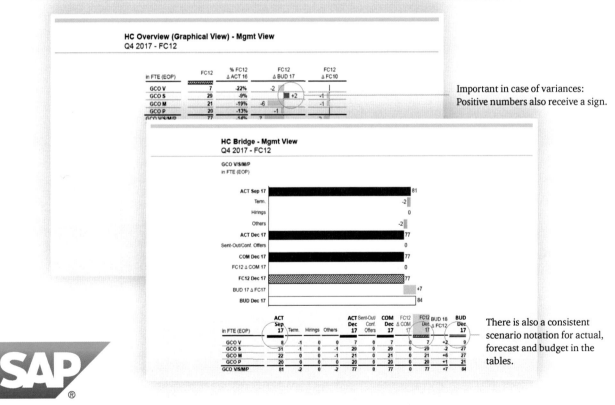

Important in case of variances:
Positive numbers also receive a sign.

There is also a consistent
scenario notation for actual,
forecast and budget in the
tables.

SAP SE

The above picture shows a standard analysis based
on the uniform notation concept. SAP has implemented it
with SAP Analysis for Office.

The two screenshots below show examples
from the SAP Group Management Journal
created with SAP Crystal Reports.

RECAP

The proof is in: it works. This applies both to the application of the rules to real life reports and to their technical implementation. We have looked at examples of different topics in different industries and have found that very similar representations are used again and again across diverse areas of application. And concerning the technical implementation: Some BI platforms already support IBCS natively, for others there are special IBCS plug-ins to extend functionality. However, the software shouldn't be a limiting factor. Even if 30% of the IBCS proposals presented in this book cannot be implement with the available software, there is no reason not to write the remaining 70% into the notation manual and implement it consistently. Both creators and consumers of reports, presentations and dashboards will benefit.

ACCEPTANCE AND DISSEMINATION

WHO FINDS THE RULES?

As in other areas of the company, we also have the feeling in business management that fewer and fewer personnel are available for more and more tasks. So concepts to increase efficiency are welcome and we immediately think of more computer use. With the *semantic notation* presented here, however, we have a concept that, on the face of it, has nothing to do with computers: quicker understanding through pattern recognition. Standardization increases both the productivity of report creation and the speed of its analysis along with understanding of the messages. All this with higher quality reports—in terms of both content and production. We make better decisions and potentially avoid wrong ones.

It is astonishing that we business professionals are only now coming up with the idea of using *pattern recognition* to increase efficiency in our communication. After all, many other professions have long set an example for us: musicians, engineers, architects and cartographers have all not only accepted notation standards, they actually demand it. It's just practical.

So we thought about what notation standards might look like for management reports and dashboards: We have regulated labelling as well as the presentation of time aspects, scenarios, variances and highlights—especially in charts, but also in tables. Since pattern recognition is more difficult when the proportions between report elements are not always the same, we have introduced font size based dimensioning.

We have also considered what is still missing for the complete visual identification of contents and presented concepts for the visualization of measures, structural dimensions and scales. In contrast to the notation proposals for captions and labels, time aspects, scenarios, variances and highlights, these concepts haven't yet been tested in practice and should rather be understood as a basis for further discussion.

Concepts alone don't provide any benefit. That's why we first applied them to charts and tables and then to the subsequent variance analyses. By doing this we showed that the concepts work well not only on their own but also together. Then we gave an outlook on future business templates for real management topics, visualizing a balance sheet analysis as an example.

For implementation in real life, we need to translate the concepts into practical guidelines and directly usable templates. To this end, we have explained the basic structure of a report notation manual, which, similar to a corporate design manual, regulates the fonts and sizes, color codes, spacing, row height and many more aspects specifically valid for a given company—especially the semantic formatting for time aspects, scenarios, variances and highlights. These specifications become really practical if they have already been applied to the sample templates for charts, tables and entire analyses with the reporting software in place. We have drawn examples of the most important sample templates without a special software tool to show what such in-house copy templates could look like in principle for report writers and dashboard designers.

Finally, we took a look at our concepts in practice and presented a few examples: reports and dashboards from companies of different industries and sizes designed according to our recommendations and created with different software solutions that already support our semantic notation rules. As we can see: The dissemination in practice has already begun. But do we already have such broad acceptance that we could speak of the establishment of a de facto standard? And are the new semantically noted reports really easier to understand than the old ones? What about dissemination in education? And is the concept already supported by software? In the following we compile a few facts about the current state of acceptance and dissemination.

IBCS ASSOCIATION

We have already introduced the IBCS Association, a non-profit organization whose mission is to further develop and disseminate the *International Business Communication Standards* (IBCS). The IBCS Association has already accepted most of the proposals made in Chapter 2. They are part of the published and adopted IBCS version 1.1.[1]

At the beginning of 2019, the IBCS Association had over 2 000 members from more than 50 countries. They have all dealt with the rules of notation and some of them have also participated in their discussion and further development. To date, no one has expressed significant criticism of the rules themselves or their usefulness. We therefore assume that the acceptance among the members of the IBCS Association is very high. Using this acceptance for the further dissemination of the standards is one of the most urgent tasks of the IBCS Association.

COMPANIES

As the IBCS standards are free of charge and available to everyone, we cannot reliably estimate their degree of dissemination in business practice. What we do know, however, is that by the beginning of 2019 around 7 500 participants had attended our IBCS seminars and lectures. Of these, around 100 project managers and consultants have successfully completed the IBCS certification program and now help companies introduce operational notation concepts based on IBCS. A further 8 000 participants took part in the ten-part online course "Semantic Notation—The Next Big Thing in BI?" and in some cases successfully passed the tests and examinations[2].

From this we conclude that at least in German-speaking countries hundreds if not several thousand companies and public organizations of all sizes are engaged with IBCS. These include vehicle manufacturers, television broadcasters, retailers and wholesalers, public administrations, banks, insurance companies, airports, hospitals and many other sectors. The degree of implementation ranges from prototypes in individual departments to the consistent conversion of thousands of reports and dashboards in large companies. In many cases, only a handful of people are familiar with IBCS, but there are also organizations where more than 10 000 employees have participated in internal IBCS information events. The interest in IBCS is also growing steadily outside the German-speaking countries. As we have seen in section 4.3, Royal Philips, for example, not only considers many IBCS recommendations in its global internal reporting, but more recently in its annual reports as well[3].

1   Hichert, Faisst et al.: International Business Communication Standards, Charleston, CreateSpace Independent Publishing Platform, IBCS® Version 1.1, 2017.

2   open.SAP.com, Walldorf 2016: Rolf Hichert and Jürgen Faisst: Semantic Notation — The Next Big Thing in BI?

3   Faisst, Jürgen and Michels-Kim, Nina: The PHILIPS Journey Toward IBCS, Strategic Finance Magazine, October 2016.

STUDIES

The first studies on the influence of notation standards on the perception of reports and dashboards are now available. The studies are structured in such a way that participants are asked to answer business questions using reports given them. A comparison of the share of correct answers and the time needed to produce them is made between conventional reports and those with standard notation. Studies by the Upper Austrian University of Applied Sciences show significantly lower error rates and shorter response times with standardized reports[4]. A study by the management consultancy blueforte and the Technical University of Munich, which specifically examined the effect of IBCS-compliant reports, came to the same conclusion[5]. Participants made 61% fewer errors with IBCS-compliant reports and were 46% faster.

EDUCATION

The recognition of patterns only works if you have learned them beforehand. You can only write and understand sheet music, technical drawings and construction plans if you have learned this during your education. This is no different with a standard notation for reports. Nobody can imagine an architecture student who doesn't learn how to draw building plans at university. The same with engineers and cartographers. Musicians already learn music notation in grade school.

So, it would only be logical to integrate the standardization of report notation according to IBCS into business education. Many universities with business administration courses have already started and the interest among students is high. IBCS is already presented in relevant textbooks such as the textbook "Einführung in das Controlling" by Jürgen Weber and Utz Schäffer[6]. Nevertheless, it has so far been left to the personal initiative of individual university teachers to deal with IBCS and to incorporate the learning of notation standards into their teaching. Supporting the further dissemination of standard notation at universities was an essential motivation for writing this book.

SOFTWARE SUPPORT

Let's not kid ourselves: As long as a visual language isn't supported by the relevant software products, it cannot establish itself as a standard. This is why it is so important that we can already implement IBCS with the main reporting platforms. Some vendors already ensure their product supports the IBCS standards natively, i.e. without additional products. For other reporting tools, third-party add-ins are available to create IBCS-compliant reports and dashboards. Some of these vendors have even had their software certified for its suitability[7]. We show some examples of reports and dashboards created with these tools in Chapter 4. The growing support of software solutions contributes considerably to the acceptance and further dissemination of the IBCS standards.

---

4 Losbichler, Heimo and Michels-Kim, Nina: Eye tracking for better reports, Strategic Finance Magazine, October 2017.

5 Freyer, J. et al.: More than just a standard — how IBCS facilitates the perception of business data. Creative Space Publishing, Charleston, USA, 2019.

6 Weber, Jürgen and Schäffer, Utz: Einführung in das Controlling, Schäffer Poeschel, 15th revised and updated edition, 2016.

7 See www.ibcs.com/software.

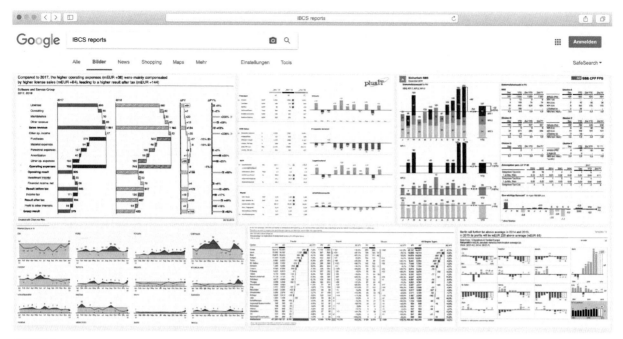

FIGURE 5-1

Visual language for reports and dashboards. Although the results of an Internet search for "IBCS reports" come from different software solutions, they all look similar. Source: Result of an image search on the Internet

INTERNET RESEARCH

In the introduction to this book, we highlighted the lack of a visual language for reports by doing two Internet searches and comparing the results: First we looked for sheet music and then for management dashboards. While all the sheet music looked similar, there was no commonality between the dashboards[1].

In closing, we would like to add another search to this list: this time not for management dashboards in general, but for IBCS reports in particular. FIGURE 5-1 shows the result: The reports found—just as in the dashboard search in the introduction—primarily originate from the product descriptions of software vendors. However, they all look very similar—as with the sheet music. And that's the way it's supposed to be. There are differences only in the design of the operating elements; but here, too, standards are gradually gaining ground—as in the operation of headlamps, power windows and windshield wipers in cars. And that took decades!

We want to be faster.

1 See page 12.

Convinced of the benefits of visual consistency in reports, presentations and dashboards? Then join the IBCS community and download extensive additional material free of charge.

www.SolidOutlinedHatched.com/register

INDEX

AUTHORS

DR. ROLF HICHERT has dedicated himself to the visualization of management information and the methods necessary to improve it. He has earned an international reputation as a critic of bad reports and hard-to-understand business charts. Known for not mincing his words and getting right to the point, Rolf Hichert is a sought-after speaker on information design.

DR. JÜRGEN FAISST is a business economist, musician, notation expert, experienced manager, passionate trainer and a sought-after speaker at international conferences. He instructs executives, management accountants, Business Intelligence employees and consultants on how to use the International Business Communication Standards (IBCS) to design successful reports, presentations and dashboards.

THANK

Our thanks go to Anne Hichert for the design, Helmut Stabe for the typesetting and Götz Wiedenroth for the drawings as well as Austin Diaz and Bernie Smith for helping us with the translation from the German original. We thank the IBCS Community for the many technical discussions.

IMPRINT

COVER DESIGN Anne Hichert
DESIGN AND SET Anne Hichert, Helmut Stabe

Wherever used in this book, a pronoun in the masculine gender shall be considered to include the feminine gender unless the context clearly indicates otherwise.

We have tried to quote in a scientifically correct manner. Unfortunately, it was not always possible to identify the owners of the image rights. We would therefore ask you to inform us if necessary. We are prepared to settle justified claims.

Originally published in German as "Gefüllt, gerahmt, schraffiert" by Rolf Hichert and Jürgen Faisst, © 2019 Verlag Franz Vahlen GmbH, Munich, Germany.

ISBN Soft Cover 978-3-9821414-0-4
2019-10-31

© 2019 IBCS Media
HICHERT+FAISST GmbH
Schürmannstr. 9
40723 Hilden, Germany

Made in the USA
Middletown, DE
04 February 2024

49052849R20131